CHRISTIAN ETHICS

A Case Method Approach

SECOND EDITION

Robert L. Stivers
Christine E. Gudorf
Alice Frazer Evans
Robert A. Evans

ORBIS BOOKS

Maryknoll, New York 10545

The Catholic Foreign Mission Society of America (Maryknoll) recruits and trains people for overseas missionary service. Through Orbis Books, Maryknoll aims to foster the international dialogue that is essential to mission. The books published, however, reflect the opinions of their authors and are not meant to represent the official position of the society.

Copyright © 1994 by Robert L. Stivers, Christine E. Gudorf, Alice Frazer Evans, and Robert A. Evans

This is a substantially revised edition of *Christian Ethics: A Case Method Approach*, edited by Robert Stivers, Christine Gudorf, Alice Frazer Evans, and Robert Evans, Maryknoll, N.Y.: Orbis Books, 1989.

Published by Orbis Books, Maryknoll, NY 10545

Manufactured in the United States of America

Library of Congress Cataloging-in-Publication Data

Christian ethics : a case method approach / Robert L. Stivers . . . [et al.].
    p.   cm.
    Includes bibliographical references.
    ISBN 0-88344-973-0
    1. Christian ethics—Case studies. I. Stivers, Robert L., 1940- .
BJ1251.C49   1994
241—dc20   94-15929
                                           CIP

Contents

Case: A Good Death for Gleason?   276

> *Gleason's son reflects on the events surrounding his father's death and wonders if family members, their doctor, and their pastor did all they could to help Gleason in his last days.*

Commentary   280

Appendix: Teaching Ethics by the Case Method   288

List of Authors and Contributors   297

Introduction

Christian Ethics and
the Case Method

The student pensively approached the case teacher after class and finally mustered some words: "That case really hit home. The characters were different, but they could just as well have been my family. Not long ago we went through exactly the same thing." Another student, laying back for the first to finish, finally edged up and joined in: "And the question that woman in the front row asked about euthanasia, that's the precise question I wanted to ask but couldn't find the right words."

These two statements, often encountered in one form or another by case teachers, reflect something enduring in human behavior: while every individual is unique, ethical problems and questions about what is right or good tend to recur. These recurrences and the dilemmas they represent can be recorded and replayed to help others learn to make better ethical choices. Case studies are one way to capture past occurrences, and case teaching is a method to enable individuals and groups to make better choices.

This book is about making ethical choices and forming Christian character. It contains sixteen cases arranged under eight part titles. Accompanying each case study is a commentary by one of the authors that is intended to aid understanding of the case from a Christian ethical perspective. The purpose of the book is to offer an approach to contemporary social issues and to underscore the importance of the Christian ethical dimension in these issues and in character formation. The authors are enthusiastic about the case approach as one way to aid in the process of making ethical decisions and forming character.

1

THE PAPER CHASE

Some readers may wonder whether the authors' enthusiasm for cases is warranted. Several years ago the movie and television series *The Paper Chase* stamped the case method with a popular but mistaken image. The setting in the Harvard Law School was establishment, hierarchical, and formal. The teacher was dour, crusty, and demanding. The students were over-worked, underrewarded, and overambitious.

The task of recommending such an abrasive approach to those who teach Christian ethics would be imposing. Few colleges, seminaries, or churches fit the mold of the Harvard Law School. By comparison most teachers of Christian ethics are soft touches. Few theological students are as ambitious or crafty as those in the drama. The title of the movie and series underscores that contrast. It conjures up the image of overburdened students questing after reams of detailed irrelevance disgorged by a paper-drunk photocopy machine.

But this book does not recommend the abrasive version of the case method employed in *The Paper Chase*. Rather it offers the method itself, and the potential of the method for teaching and learning about Christian ethics. The authors are confident this potential can be realized. Since the method was first developed at the Harvard Business School, it has moved far beyond Harvard, receiving wide acceptance nationally in business and law schools. In the past two decades it has also been successfully adapted to religious studies. This proven track record and personal experience with the case approach are the basis of the authors' enthusiasm.

MAKING ETHICAL DECISIONS

Ethical decisions are made on a number of levels. On one level decision making seems to flow easily. Individuals follow their gut-level intuitions and muddle through situations reactively. This approach can be effective if the individual is caring and the situation is uncomplicated and more or less personal. It is less effective in complex social situations and can be disas-trous when the individual is uncaring, ethically immature, or shut up in a small social world.

On another level making ethical choices is both difficult and complex. Logical and abstract reasoning comes hard to some. In certain situations the chooser is bombarded by a bewildering array of conflicting and com-plex facts. Finding relevant ethical norms from the tradition to apply to particular situations is difficult at best and can easily be shortcut or side-tracked with simplistic proof texting.

Once relevant norms are discovered, their application is tricky. The norms frequently offer conflicting counsel. Indeed, this is the primary reason that ethical decisions are problems. There is seldom a straight path from a single norm to an easy decision. If there were, no problem would exist. The decision maker is most often caught between equally attractive or unattractive alternatives. Worse, the path is usually made treacherous by intersecting problems and relationships which complicate situations and suggest "exceptions" to rules. Lastly, and hardly necessary to point out, relationships themselves are tricky. The chooser possesses a limited freedom and is quite capable of being arbitrary in its use.

The case method of instruction recounts past occurrences in order to assist individuals and groups through complexity to good or at least better choices. Cases help sort out the choices and give the student an opportunity to move down the path from the identification of norms through the maze of intersecting facts and exceptions to the selection of the best alternative.

CASES AND THE ELEMENTS OF AN ETHICAL DECISION

There are many types of case studies. They range from imagined dilemmas, to in-depth histories of organizations, to one-page "verbatims" which report a single incident. The cases in this volume are descriptions of actual situations as seen by a writer usually through the eyes of a participant. The situations normally entail a decision to be made which is left sufficiently open to allow students to enter the process of decision making.

Such a method is well-suited to the study of Christian ethics, for it drives the student to take the insights of tradition and theory, apply them to an actual situation, and then reconsider the adequacy of theory and tradition. Involved in this movement from theory to practice and back to theory are all the elements which go into an ethical decision.

The Normative Tradition

The first of these elements is the tradition, including insights from the Bible, historical and constructive theology, church positions, and one's own community of believers. The Christian tradition is the main source of norms in Christian ethics, although secular and other religious sources may inform those ethics.

The process of deriving norms from the tradition is complex and frequently abused. In actuality the tradition is many different traditions, each with its special nuances. Finding in these various historical traditions consistent ethical guidelines which also apply to the twentieth century is not as simple as it may first appear.

The appropriate way to go about finding out what the Bible or any other authoritative text has to offer is first to study the text prayerfully with consciously chosen interpretive schemes. Further, the text must be understood within its own context. Once these steps have been taken the text must be compared with similar texts in order to establish dominant themes, and those themes must be checked against more encompassing theological understandings of the community of faith. The themes then become guiding norms to be applied to present situations, which always exist in a time and culture alien to those in which the text was produced. None of these steps is either neat or clean.

Among abuses, especially with the Bible, proof texting is one of the most troublesome. Proof texting is understood here as using an unexamined text to support what is believed on other grounds. The method is simple and convenient: find an isolated verse or two which somehow relate to the decision, make a quick interpretive guess, and let those addressed assume you have authority for your point. Neat and clean, except that it often twists the texts and leads to poor decisions.

The teachings of the traditions on nonviolence are a good illustration of the complexity of deriving and applying norms. The many texts having to do with peacemaking in the life of Jesus, when studied carefully, establish a consistent picture of a man in whose life nonviolence was a dominant approach. Some texts suggest he might have been willing to make exceptions, but none is conclusive. Nonviolence is thus normative in the Gospels, and when that is coupled with the Old Testament understanding of shalom and the theological understanding of God's love, the result is sound authority for the pacifist who applies the norm without exception.

To some, however, the texts in Deuteronomy, Joshua, and Judges that picture God as demanding violence during the conquest of the land give authority for crusades to stamp out evil. Nonviolence is normative except when evil is obvious and threatening. To others, Jesus' equally consistent support for the poor and social justice means violence is permissible if certain strict criteria of justifiability are met. Thus, while all agree that nonviolence is normative, in fact the various traditions stress different elements in the Bible and apply the norm in quite different ways. The case "Vietnam's Children" is a good illustration of this.

All this attention to complexity is not to suggest that finding a normative basis and applying it consistently are impossible. Were this so, there would be no Christian ethics, and the Bible would be irrelevant for Christian life. Rather it is intended to help avoid oversimplification, to indicate that a range of positions have authority, and to counsel integrity and toleration in ethical debate.

Theory and Fact

A normative basis is not sufficient unto itself, since the tradition does not address all aspects of reality. Scientific theories which attempt to interpret empirical facts must be added. Both theories and facts are essential in ethics because they give understanding and empirical grounding to those in situations in which ethical decisions must be made. Without theories and facts, norms wander around in confusion, unable to inform the situation.

To illustrate the relation of norms, theories, and facts, consider poverty in the Third World. Approximately five hundred million people are seriously malnourished in a world with more than enough food to go around. This is a fact. The numbers, however, only indicate magnitude. Economic and political theories are necessary to give meaning to the numbers and suggest alternative courses of action. Norms, such as Christianity's concern for the poor, make these numbers a scandal and are the basis for selecting among competing economic theories and alternative courses of action.

Or consider the role of biological theory in the case "Snake in the Grass." Theories of evolution, genetic structure, and ecological balance give meaning to raw data about species extinction and alert communities to the consequences of reducing the gene pool and disturbing biotic communities. The norms of stewardship and care for the earth turn the realities of species extinction and biological equilibrium into moral problems.

In all this, cases provide a point of contact between empirical fact on the one hand and tradition and theory on the other. In addition, the insights of tradition and theory need actual cases to mark their limitations and test their validity. Actual cases, in turn, need tradition, theory, and empirically established facts to provide understanding and direction.

Cases encourage students to give moral principles, facts, and theories a work out, so to speak. Not quite the same as being in an ethical dilemma oneself, cases are a good substitute and as close as teachers and students can sometimes get to a particular problem. They also offer the critical distance which is often missing when a dilemma is one's own. Such critical distance keeps the dialogue between theory and practice alive.

Contexts and Relationships

The immediate situation of a case, the larger context, and the relationships found in it provide the setting for a particular ethical decision. The cases in this volume present actual moral dilemmas in the lives of real people. They are not fabricated.

A well-written case seldom presents a neat situation where decisions flow easily from norms. Theory does not always apply. Norms conflict. Individuals display a normal range of cantankerous behavior. In other words, there are no right answers, and students are faced with both the possibilities and the problems of being ethical as they are forced into the vortex between ideal and real in considering actual human problems.

Once in this vortex students and teachers discover the importance of additional factors found in situations. The individuals in a case often seem to have conflicting motives and goals. The means used to strive toward and attain goals sometimes seem questionable or not justified by the ends sought. The consequences of different courses of action must be weighed against each other and put into relation with motives, means, and ends. A choice between following principles and seeking effective compromises is often inherent in decisions.

Also in this vortex students and teachers encounter the vagaries of personal relationships and further problems with the exclusive use of norms to guide action. In recent years relationships and what is being called "embodied reason" have come into prominence in the study of ethics. Accompanying this newfound importance has been criticism of abstract dualisms, such as mind and matter or spirit and flesh, which tend in the tradition to devalue women and minorities. Also criticized has been the heavy stress on abstract norms and their deductive application in decisions to the exclusion of relationships.

While those who offer this criticism do not reject abstract distinctions and norms, they are urging decision makers also to consider the way many have traditionally made choices, that is, through reason linked to experience.

To make these distinctions clearer an illustration from the actual teaching of the case "Rigor and Responsibility" is useful. The teacher on one occasion used this case to demonstrate different modes of thinking. After some preliminaries, he asked the group what norms from the Christian tradition applied to the case. The teacher found the responses, mostly from men, to be predictable, logical, and concise. Stewardship of resources, care for the poor, and the seductive nature of possessions were each developed with precision.

The teacher then asked two women to sit in front of the class and discuss with each other the dilemma of building a vacation cabin which faces the couple in the case. No instructions were given except to say they were to reflect on the case. There was little if any mention of norms. What dominated was the relationship between husband and wife and how their decision would affect others in their lives.

The class did not immediately recognize the differences in the two approaches. When the teacher pointed out what he had intended and in fact had seen, there was general recognition and agreement that both deductively applied norms and inductively embodied reason are valid and contribute to making decisions.

But each has dangers as well. The exclusive use of deductively applied norms runs the danger of rigidity and legalism. Changed contexts and new relationships are ignored. Love between persons and the abnormal aspects of actual situations tend to get lost as traditional norms become the exclusive guide to decisions. The much used example of truth telling which leads to loss of innocent life is an obvious example.

The opposite is true of pursuing experience-based reason to the exclusion of larger contexts and norms. Students and teachers tend to lose themselves in relationships and the processes of everyday living. When they do, they lose sight of the larger context in which they exist and the wisdom of the ages embodied in traditional norms.

A vortex in nature, although more noticeable because of its swirling action, is always part of a larger air mass or body of liquid, as in a cyclone or a whirlpool. So also relationships have contexts, and the context is not always obvious. "Mary Gardner's Fourth Pregnancy" presents a woman faced with the decision of whether or not to terminate a pregnancy. The case does not, however, make reference to the heated national debate over elective abortion and its relevance for the freedom of women. In this instance students may be left to discover the larger context. In other cases the teacher may want to point it out. Whichever, both students and teachers should recognize that relationships always have larger contexts.

Much the same can be said for norms. As with cyclones in nature, the human conditions which produce ethical problems tend to recur. No ethical problem is entirely novel. And as meteorologists are able to forecast the paths of cyclones with a fair degree of accuracy, so traditional norms predict, so to speak, the ethical path in most situations and contexts.

Method

This leads to the fourth element in making an ethical decision. Method is the way the elements of making an ethical decision are pulled together to reach a conclusion. No single method of relating norms, facts, theories, contexts, and relationships to each other and to specific situations can be called Christian. There are a number of methods, each with advantages. The authors have not tried to impose a particular method in either their approach to the cases or the commentaries which follow them. They are convinced that method is important, however, and that an adequate method touches base with each of the elements.

The case approach is conducive to the teaching of method. A specific case can be used to focus on method. Over the course of a semester or study series the teacher can use and ask students to use a single method so that they will acquire skill in employing that particular methodology. Alternatively, the teacher can employ several methods and request that students experiment with and evaluate each. Or finally, consciousness of method may be left to emerge from the process of doing ethical reflection.

The commentaries which follow each case are organized around the elements of making an ethical decision. The commentaries do not spell out how these elements are to be put together to reach a decision. The authors would be remiss, however, if they did not indicate a few typical approaches. Students can, of course, start with any of the elements, but the usual approach is to begin with and emphasize either norms or situations.

The approach which starts with and stresses norms is called the deontological approach. The word "deontological" comes from the Greek word *deon*, which means "binding," and refers to the study of duty and moral obligation. For the sake of simplicity it will be referred to as the normative approach.

The tendency in this approach is to let norms, rules, principles, standards, and ideals be decisive or binding in making choices. The degree of

decisiveness that should be afforded to norms has been a matter of conten-
tion in Christian ethics. To call an approach normative means that it has a
fairly high degree of decisiveness. Most of those who take a normative
approach, however, are willing to admit some exceptions to norms occasioned by contextual and relational variations. Used in a flexible way, the
normative approach is appropriate. Indeed, the authors are of a common
mind that considerable attention should be given to norms in all situations.

The extreme, legalism, presents difficulties, however. Following rules to
the exclusion of contextual and relational factors is a problem for Christians
because of its rigidity, frequent heartlessness, and the obvious polemic
against it in the sayings of Jesus and the epistles of Paul.

If legalism is one extreme at the end of a spectrum, and the normative
approach is its valuable cousin, then making decisions solely on the basis
of one's own experience and desires lies at the other end, and the situational
approach is its cousin. The approach which starts with and emphasizes
situational factors and consequences of acts goes under the names "situational," "consequentialist," or, in extreme form, "antinomian," from the
Greek word *nomos*, which means "law." Antinomians are opposed to legal
approaches to ethics.

For simplicity the term "situational" will be used to describe this approach. In it the decision maker looks to goals and seeks the best possible
outcome. The contextual and relational elements which make situations
different are taken very seriously. The situationalist is much more willing
to admit exceptions and to grant greater weight to good results as opposed
to consistency with norms.

Again the extreme is a problem. An approach which excludes norms,
sees only the exceptions in situations, and relies on a "will it work" attitude
denies the Bible, theology, and historical norms as guides in the Christian
life. The extreme is hardly ever encountered and is bedeviled by sin. Its
effective use requires very good people with very well developed moral
habits, which is really to say people with ingrained norms.

That the extreme is a problem does not make a starting point in situations
and an emphasis on special circumstances and consequences invalid. The
authors are also in agreement that these elements must be factored into
decisions.

What this leaves is a mixed approach which includes attention to norms
and situations as well as the other elements of an ethical decision. Where
the student starts may produce a distinctive emphasis, but as long as the
other elements are factored in, ethical decision making can avoid the
problems associated with the extremes.

The authors offer no magical formula for plugging in the elements. It
would be helpful if they could. Unfortunately, differences in problems—
each requiring its special analysis and weighting of elements—the guidance of the Holy Spirit, human freedom, and the unpredictability of
situations rule out formulas. The authors can only urge that all of the

elements be consistently considered in situations. Students and teachers must finally develop their own methods and make their own decisions.

Character Formation

Character formation is distinct from the elements which go into ethical decisions, but is important nonetheless to the ethics of decision making. Character is formed in a complex interaction of self and society. Many elements contribute to this interaction: gender, social class, race, religion, ethnic background, family and institutional influences, specific experiences, worldviews, and loyalties. The interaction produces a distinct set of perceptions, habits, and intentions which dispose an individual or group to act in certain ways. The task of Christian character formation is to predispose individuals to act in situations in ways which are appropriate to Christian norms.

Central to any Christian understanding of character are the loving relationships between God and persons and among persons involved in faith. In ethical decisions no element is as important as faith. Rationality, the core of the preceding elements, keeps faith and love from wandering aimlessly down the path of good intentions. But reason easily degenerates into duplicity and hard heartedness without faith and love. As the saying goes, "Even the devil can quote scripture."

In doing ethics faith is the heart, reason the head, and Christian character the mature union of the two in love. Insofar as faith is a gift of grace, character cannot be taught. Insofar as character is a product of reason, it can be both taught and developed. Faith can change perceptions, habits, and intentions; good teaching and practice can develop them.

Few teachers have consciously used the case approach to form character. Case discussions are a good resource for character formation, however, and in the process of repeatedly making moral judgments, moral maturity does increase, or at least that has been the experience of case teachers. Character development may therefore be an unintended positive side-effect of the case method. Many teachers may prefer leaving it that way, but there is no reason why character development cannot be made more explicit.

The case approach is particularly conducive to what Paulo Freire calls education as liberation. For Freire a liberating education relies less on the transference of information than on the development of a critical consciousness which leads to the transformation of the learner's world. The transference of information is important to the communication of a collective memory; but if its goal and effect are only the "banking" of knowledge and the deposit of static, completed projects, character formation is seldom furthered.

Character formation in a Christian context is a process in which information becomes grist for liberation in Christ. Liberating education involves genuine dialogue between teacher and student. They are partners in education, teaching each other. The case approach promotes dialogue and in so doing encourages students and teachers to take what has been "banked" with other methods and appropriately "spend" it on critical consciousness.

FLEXIBILITY

Cases can be used to form character, to analyze problems, to teach method, to understand human relationships, to test theory, and so on. The case approach is flexible, and this flexibility makes the purpose of the teacher in using the method of great importance. Cases lend themselves to one or a multiplicity of purposes, and teachers need to be clear what they are trying to accomplish. Purpose should govern the selection of cases, how they are taught, and the outcome. This cannot be emphasized enough. Purpose governs use.

What the authors have not done and in fact cannot do is set the purpose for students and teachers. They can suggest a range of options, for example, introducing students to complex social issues, using cases as an entry into the tradition, the teaching of method, and the development of character; but selection must remain with the user. This also means that cases can be misused for the purpose of indoctrination and manipulation. Teachers and students should be aware of this, although misuse of method is not peculiar to the use of cases.

Flexibility has still another dimension. The case method is appropriate to a variety of learning situations from the classroom to church groups, to the small rump sessions found in coffee shops, dorms, and living rooms. Those who use the method regularly find that it stimulates discussion, breaks up the one-way flow of lectures, and eliminates the silence which often permeates abstract discussions. The method is dialogic and thus meets the needs of instructors and learners who prefer more dialogic approaches. But discussion is only the most frequent way cases are used, and discussion can be more or less structured by teachers depending on their purposes.

The method also has internal flexibility. Role plays, small groups, voting, and mini-lectures, a fuller description of which can be found in the Appendix, are only a few of the ways cases can be presented. Cases are not particularly good for presenting normative material and scientific theories. Experienced case teachers have found that lectures and outside reading are more appropriate for introducing this kind of material. Thus where significant background information is required for intelligent choices, the authors recommend using cases for the purposes of opening discussion of complex problems, of applying theory and the insights of tradition, of bringing closure and decision, and of encouraging the development of a critical consciousness.

ISSUES AND COMMENTARIES

The issues which the cases raise were given careful thought. The obvious issues are those designated by the part titles. A characteristic of a good case, however, is that it raises more than one issue. Some cases raise numerous issues. Thus besides the issues highlighted by the part titles there are what might be called connecting issues. There is no part that is explicitly about women and men, for example, yet at least six of the cases address problems associated with the changing relationships of contemporary women and men. No part is entitled "racism," but it is a central issue in at least three cases and a related one in several others.

The issues highlighted by the part titles were selected on the basis of current importance, lasting significance, availability of case material, and variety. Subjectivity, stemming from the authors' interests, no doubt also crept in.

The connecting issues are not so obvious and should be identified. In some instances these issues are as important as the highlighted issues. Women and men and racism are again examples. Other connecting issues are not as central and yet recur in a number of cases.

These connecting issues were selected on the basis of the same criteria as those highlighted in the part titles. A partial list includes: women and men; racism; land and resource use, including sustainability; national and global dimensions of poverty, wealth, consumption, and social justice; value consistency; the use of the Bible and the tradition in ethics; economic systems; corporate and government social responsibility; method; vocation; and character. Other issues could no doubt be identified and all of them could be developed with greater specificity. This list is merely to indicate that cases have multiple issues, and the rubric under which a case appears may not be the issue the teacher or student chooses to highlight.

There is still a third type of issue. Some of the commentaries speak, for example, of the coming reign of God. General criteria for decision making such as "the loving thing to do," "appropriateness," "the fitting," "following the way of the cross," or even the utilitarian theme "the greatest good for the greatest number" are common in ethical discussions. The commentaries are not organized around any such themes. To so organize the commentaries would in some cases have meant forcing a method on a case. There is no objection to organizing around such themes, and the authors occasionally use them, but teachers and students should make this choice.

The commentaries themselves are provided because past experience shows that interpretive summaries help students and teachers by providing leads into cases and avenues of analysis. These commentaries are not definitive interpretations. They are the observations of individuals trained in Christian theology, ethics, and the case method. They are not out of the same mold, although they do attempt to use the elements which go into an ethical decision as their starting point. There are stylistic differences and variations in emphasis resulting from their multiple authorship. They are intended as aids, not as substitutes for creative thinking, analysis, and decision making.

As mentioned before, the content of the interpretive summaries is not arbitrary. It is organized around the elements which go into making an ethical decision; however, for the sake of variety and flexibility it was decided that each commentary did not have to discuss elements in the same order. The commentaries are designed to touch base with these elements, although for a given case each element may not be covered with the same thoroughness and on occasion one may be omitted. Brevity has also governed design. In some of the cases analysis of one or more of the elements does not add significant insight. However, consistent consideration of the basic elements in ethical decision making is a commitment of the authors which has emerged from personal and teaching experience.

No doubt in these commentaries there are things omitted which teachers will want to add and points made which teachers will disagree with and want to comment upon critically.

THE NEW EMPHASIS ON ETHICS

This is the appropriate time for a vigorous new emphasis on ethics. Rapid social change and high mobility continue to tear people loose from their moorings in the extended family, settled communities, and traditional authority. The ethic of individualism, which in an effort to find new moorings in a sea of relativity made the self the center of moral deliberation and substituted feeling good for being good, has failed to deliver. This failure was predictable because the individual can neither feel good nor be moral apart from community, or at least that has been a key insight of Christianity from its beginnings.

There is no return to the simple past of extended families, settled communities, and traditional authority. This does not mean, however, that a new emphasis on ethics is doomed. New forms of community are emerging, and with the failure of individualism comes the need to find a center other than the self. For Christians that center is found in faith, the dynamic relationship to God and to others which is the foundation of both good feeling and good acts.

The case approach to teaching is dialogic and fosters interpersonal relationships. It is an approach which can be effectively used to teach the rudiments of ethical decision making, to form character, and to foster a philosophy of education as liberation. It is no panacea, just a very good tool to help invigorate a new and necessary emphasis upon ethics.

PART I

FAMILY

Case

Rigor and Responsibility

David Trapp hung up the phone and paused to reflect. He had just spoken with his good friend Al Messer. Al had offered to build the cabin. For several months David and his wife, Nancy, had considered building on the two acres of Clark Lake property left to them the year before by David's uncle. The nagging question returned to David. Now that the means were there, was it right to build?

David lived with his wife and two children on a quiet residential street on the outskirts of Toledo, Ohio. David was a lawyer with a downtown law firm which encouraged him to spend up to 15 percent of his time with clients who could not afford to pay. David always used the full allotment, considering it one way in which he could respond in faith to a pressing human need. David was also active in community affairs. He was vice-president of a statewide citizens' action lobby for more progressive taxation. Locally he was on the planning committee for the new community center and led adult education classes at his church. What troubled David the most was relating his sense of outrage at injustice to his enjoyment of good food, travel, and water sports.

Nancy Trapp was a buyer for an office furniture supplier. Her work involved increasing responsibility, and she found it difficult to leave unfinished business in the office. Recently she had been elected to a two-year term as president of the P.T.A. at the children's school. She had not foreseen the constant interruptions such a position would bring. The telephone never seemed to stop ringing, especially on the weekends when people knew they could find her at home.

Decision making was more or less a family affair with the Trapps. David and Nancy seldom disagreed on family matters and to David's recollection never on a major one. The children, Darcy and Ben, ages ten and eight, were consulted on major decisions and their voices taken into account.

Nathan Ferguson was the pastor of the local congregation in which the Trapps were active participants. Nathan had recently sold a piece of property he once had intended for recreational purposes. The proceeds from the sale had been donated to a church-sponsored halfway house for drug addicts in downtown Toledo. Shortly after Nathan had sold the property, he had begun to preach and teach in a low-key way on the subjects of possessions, overconsumption, and the materialism of American society. His eventual aim was to have his parishioners understand and consider forming a community based on the community in Jerusalem described in the opening chapters of the Book of Acts. He envisioned this community as one in which possessions would be held in common, consumption limited to basic necessities, and time and money given to programs among the poor that were based on a principle of self-reliance.

Clea Parks was David's colleague and an active participant in the church's adult education classes. What amazed David was how she could combine a concern for the poor with a way of living which allowed for occasional extravagances. Like David, Clea made full use of the firm's 15 percent allotment of time to work with poor clients. She was also on the board of the halfway house for drug addicts. In contrast she and her husband traveled to Bermuda for tennis and golf and to Sun Valley for skiing. This fall they were headed to the Holy Land for three weeks.

Shortly after the settlement of his uncle's will, which in addition to the two acres included enough cash to construct a modest cabin, David and Nancy discussed the matter of building. David expressed his ambivalence. He wondered about limits to self-indulgence. His desire for the cabin seemed to be locked in a struggle with his conscience. "How can we build a second place," he asked Nancy, "when so many people are living in houses without roofs or simply do not have a home at all? Can we in good conscience consume as heavily as we do while others are crying out for the very things we take for granted and consume almost at will?"

He also considered the matter of energy consumption. Again directing his reflections to Nancy, he said, "Think about the amount of energy used in construction and the going to and fro which will follow. Is this good stewardship of resources? Does it reflect our responsibility as American citizens to conserve fuel? And what sort of legacy are we leaving to our grandchildren, not to mention the lessons we are teaching our own children?"

He then rehearsed once again a pet theme: the excessive materialism of American society. "The Bible is quite explicit about possessions," he insisted. "Possessions can easily plug our ears to the hearing of God's word. A person cannot have two masters. The rich young ruler went away empty because he was unwilling to give up his possessions. The tax collector Zacchaeus is commended by Jesus for his willingness to give one-half of his possessions to the poor. And Jesus himself lived without possessions, commanding his disciples to do likewise."

He paused to think about this further. "Is it possible," he asked, "to avoid the spirit-numbing nature of possessions short of self-denial? And if I'm not going to opt for self-denial, then I at least have to ask in what way my consumption helps to perpetuate a system which is getting further and further away from the simplicity of Jesus." Again he paused, adding, "I guess it all boils down to the ethics of the Sermon on the Mount which Pastor Ferguson keeps talking about. Does the rigor of the sermon's ethic represent the only valid Christian option? Is it possible to live much in excess of basic needs if this ethic is taken seriously? And if we conclude that the sermon is not a new set of laws, what is its relevance anyway?"

Nancy's response was slow in coming both because she was sensitive to David's imaginative conscience, and because she wanted a place to separate herself from work and to teach the children the water sports she and David both enjoyed. "I can understand your commitment," she told him. "It's not a matter of guilt for you. But I just don't feel quite as strongly about those things as you do. The pressure has been getting worse lately, and I feel the need to share with you and the children in a more relaxed setting. The kids are getting older fast, and in a few years they'll be beyond the age where they'll be around to learn water sports."

"The materialism you are so concerned about," she went on to say, "has also made for creative new possibilities. It's not possessions themselves, but how we use them that makes a difference. It's the willingness to give, and we give enough what with 15 percent of your time and the giving of more than 10 percent of our incomes to church and charity. And think about what giving up our possessions will do. Without programs to transfer our abundance to the poor, giving things up will go for naught or perhaps contribute to the loss of someone's job. That is just the way things are. Think about Al Messer."

David had not been quite sure what to make of Nancy's comments. The old nagging questions kept coming back. His conscience just would not let him off easily.

Then Nathan Ferguson had begun his sermons and more recently had conducted a series of six sessions in the adult education class which David led. Nathan returned time and again to the teachings of Jesus: to the Sermon on the Mount, to the rich young ruler, to Zacchaeus, to the love communism of the early Christian community, and to the call of the prophets to justice and care for the poor. Nathan had not talked in a demanding or accusatory fashion, but neither had he let his parishioners off the hook. To David it seemed that Nathan's every thought had been directed straight at him.

At the office Clea hit him from the other side. At first she had merely commented on Nathan's sermons and classes. She thought Nathan was too much of a perfectionist. She appreciated his concern for the poor and his awareness of how possessions can close one's ears to the word of God. But she did not see how individual sacrifices produced the social change they all wanted. She also had a contrasting view of the Sermon on the Mount. "We cannot live the sermon," she explained. "It's impossible, and anyway wasn't intended for everyone. Ethical rigor is right for folks like Nathan, but what most of us are called to is responsibility: to the right use of possessions, to a willingness to give, and to advocacy of justice in word and deed. The choice is not between self-indulgence and self-denial. There is a third option which is living responsibly with concern for all those issues Nathan talks about and still appreciating the finer things in life."

When David told her about the lake property and Nancy's needs, she had begun to push him a bit harder. "Come on, David," she would say, "it's all right with Jesus if you build. Jesus enjoyed life and participated in it fully. The church tradition is quite ambiguous on possessions and wealth." Another time she put it bluntly: "What right do you have to force your values and views on Nancy and the children?" Lately she had been twitting him. Just the other day with a big grin on her face she had called him "the monk."

Al Messer's call had jolted David and increased his sense that something had to give. Al had told David he could build the cabin out of used lumber and had found a place where he could get insulation and thermopane window glass at reduced prices. Al had also indicated he needed the work because business had been a bit slow lately.

Nancy entered the room and guessed what was troubling David. "I know what's bothering you," she said. "If we build, those old questions about the poor, materialism, and limits to consumption will nag at you. You might not even stick to a decision to build. If we don't build, you'll feel you have let the kids and me down and you'll miss your favorite sports. How can we decide this thing?"

Commentary

Rigor and Responsibility

Taken at face value this case is about Nancy and David Trapp struggling to decide whether or not to build a vacation cabin. But at a deeper and more comprehensive level the case is addressed to all non-poor Christians, and the issue is how to live as Christians in a materialistic world where ostentatious luxury and grinding poverty exist side by side. That the focus is us should not be lost as this commentary threads its way through David and Nancy's dilemma.

THE ISSUES

The superficial problem of putting a considerable inheritance to use in a second home quickly gives way in this case to an underlying central issue and a number of important related issues. The central issue stated in very general terms is this: How is a family which calls itself Christian to live? This general question can be given greater specificity by considering the title of the case. Should an affluent family give up what it has and follow the rigorous "holy poverty" of Jesus or is there an alternative called "responsible consumption," which stresses right use and good stewardship of material resources? Realizing that a continuum of options is possible between the "either" of rigor and the "or" of responsibility, these two options may be contrasted for the purpose of analyzing the decision the Trapps must make.

Before getting into this contrast, however, note should be taken of the important related issues, since for some they may well be more significant. First are the issues raised by the context of the case. David and Nancy's decision does not sit in a vacuum. It stands tall in a world where over five hundred million people are seriously malnourished and live in miserable poverty, some without even a single roof over their heads.

It stands in a country where unemployment, symbolized in the case by Al Messer, has consistently run above 7 percent in recent years, and the distribution of income and wealth has shifted significantly in favor of the wealthy.

It stands within pockets of environmental awareness in which concern about the sustainability of natural resources and the capacity to absorb pollution is very real. Included in this is the problem of how to relate to the rest of nature given the injunction to subdue and have dominion in Genesis 1:26-28.

It stands finally in an historical situation where women and men are experiencing new freedoms, and the patriarchal domination of family decisions is fading.

A second set of issues arises from the family context. One is the problem of overwork represented by David and Nancy's need to "get away." Related too is the experience of their children, Ben and Darcy, who must now find their way in a family of overworked parents and the luxurious options presented by a considerable inheritance. What sort of character are David and Nancy trying to build in their children?

Still another contextual issue is that of individual action in a world with a human population over five billion. How do people like David and Nancy influence others to do justice and exercise Christianity's so-called preferential option for the poor? Will individual acts of self-sacrifice make a difference? Should they spend their time and money in church and political action groups as Clea and David now do? Should they stop consuming so much even though they know market economies need consumption to sustain high levels of employment?

Something also needs to be said about the guilt which is felt by Nancy and especially by David. What is the function of guilt in the Christian life? What resources are available to understand and come to terms with guilt?

Finally, there are a number of issues raised by the Christian tradition. What do the Bible and subsequently the tradition have to say about poverty, wealth, and consumption? What is the vocation of a Christian with regard to these matters?

THE MAIN QUESTION

So how are we to live? Over a recent six-year period this case was taught thirty-five times, and each time the participants were asked to indicate whether they thought David and Nancy should build the cabin. The sampling was not scientific, the question lacked nuance, and the teacher might have influenced the vote in subtle ways, but the results are interesting nonetheless. Of the 872 who indicated their preference, 629 or 72 percent said "yes." Undergraduate students were even more emphatic, weighing in at 80 percent.

What was more striking than the numbers was the tendency of those who voted "yes" to assume that consuming goods and services in quantity is the natural thing to do. This is not surprising given the daily barrage of commercial propaganda whose purpose is to sell a way of life which encourages heavy consumption. In spite of this assumption, the problems of poverty and materialism troubled many of them as indicated by their interest in the case, expressions of guilt, and apparent needs to dismiss Nathan Ferguson and to justify their own decision.

That North Americans consume more goods and services than any people in history is a fact. That they are more materialistic is a value judgment which would seem to be supported by the number and actions of those who voted "yes." In contrast it is instructive to probe biblical and historical Christian understandings.

The first thing to consider is the Bible's consistent call to justice. According to Christian tradition, justice is rooted in the very being of God. It is an essential part of God's community of love and calls followers of Jesus Christ to make fairness the touchstone of their social response to other persons and to the rest of creation. Included in the biblical understanding of justice is a special concern for the poor.

The biblical basis of justice and a special concern for the poor start with God's liberation of the poor and oppressed Hebrew slaves in Egypt and the establishment of a covenant. This theme continues in the prophetic reinterpretation of the covenant. Micah summarized the law: "to do justice, and to love kindness, and to walk humbly with your God." Amos was adamant that God's wrath would befall Israel for its injustice and failure to care for the poor. Isaiah and Jeremiah were equally adamant.

In the New Testament the emphasis on social justice is somewhat muted in comparison to the prophets, but the concern for the poor may be even stronger. Jesus himself was a poor man from a poor part of Israel. His mission was among the poor and his message was directed to them. He blessed the poor and spoke God's judgment on the rich. On the cross he made himself one of the dispossessed. In the early Jerusalem community, as recorded in Acts 1-5, the basic economic needs of all members were taken care of as the wealthier shared their possessions so none would be deprived.

There can be little doubt that justice, which involves a passion for fairness and a special concern for the poor, is one of the strongest and most consistent ethical themes of the Bible. The ethical aim of justice in the absence of other considerations should be to relieve the worst conditions of poverty, powerlessness, and exploitation, and to support programs which help the poor and malnourished to achieve productive, useful, and sharing lives.

With regard to wealth, poverty, and consumption, two general and not altogether compatible attitudes dominate biblical writings. On the one side there is a qualified appreciation of wealth, on the other a call to freedom from possessions which sometimes borders on deep suspicion of them.

The Hebrew scriptures take the former side, praising the rich man who is just and placing a high estimate on riches gained through honest work. Alongside this praise is the obligation to care for the weaker members of society. Nowhere do the Hebrew scriptures praise self-imposed poverty or beggars.

Both sides are found in the teachings of Jesus. His announcement of the coming community of God carries with it a call for unparalleled freedom from possessions, and complete trust in God. The service of God and the service of riches are incompatible. Jesus himself had no possessions and prodded his disciples into what has been called "holy poverty," which includes the renunciation of possessions.

Nevertheless, Jesus took for granted the owning of property. He was apparently supported by women of means and urged that possessions be used to help those in need. Jesus did not ask Zacchaeus to give up all his possessions. He dined with hated tax collectors and was fond of celebrations, especially meals of fellowship. These examples echo the Hebrew scriptures' stress upon the right use of wealth.

This mixed mind continued in the early church. On the one side was the Jerusalem community where goods were shared in common. This seems to follow Jesus' preachings about radical freedom from possessions. On the other side stands Paul, who did not address the problem of wealth, although he himself had few possessions and was self-supporting as a tentmaker. He did, however, stress right use, made clear his center in Jesus Christ, and called on his congregations to support the poor in Jerusalem.

The later tradition continued this mixed mind. One statement by Martin Luther recorded in the winter of 1542-43 during his "table talk" catches the mind which is suspicious of wealth.

> Riches are the most insignificant things on earth, the smallest gift that God can give a person. What are they in comparison with the word of God? In fact, what are they in comparison even with physical endowments and beauty? What are they in comparison with gifts of the mind? And yet we act as if this were not so! The matter, form, effect, and goal of riches are worthless. That is why our Lord God generally gives riches to crude asses to whom nothing else is given.

The biblical witness on consumption follows much the same twofold pattern. The basic issue in the New Testament and later in the early Christian community was that of self-denial versus contentment with a moderate level of consumption. On the one side were those who translated Jesus' radical teachings about wealth and possessions and his own way of living into a full-blown asceticism. This movement eventually evolved into monasticism. On the other side were those who took Jesus' fondness for celebrations and meals of fellowship as a reason to reject asceticism. Along this line Paul preached an inner freedom which stressed contentment with self-sufficiency.

The tradition thus has been of two minds, and if it has not finally been able to make these minds up, it is clear on at least one guiding norm. This norm is best called "sufficiency" and emerges when justice is added to the teachings on wealth and consumption.

Sufficiency is the timely supply to all persons of the basic material necessities, defined as the minimum amount of food, clothing, shelter, transportation, and health care needed to live some margin above subsistence. This norm does not resolve the divided mind of the tradition, but it does establish a floor below which a just community does not let its members fall.

Sufficiency alone, however, is not complete. Future generations need to be factored into present calculations of sufficiency. Sufficiency must be sustained, a task not as easy as well-stocked supermarkets and department stores would suggest.

The issue with sustainability is whether there are limits to some forms of economic growth, in particular those forms which use large amounts of finite mineral resources and cause pollution. The food to supply a world population growing at a rate of 1.7 percent is also a key factor in the issue of sustainability. Many are optimistic about the capacities of new technologies and the free-market price system to circumvent limits to growth. Others reject this optimism or are deeply concerned about the technological mindset which would result from "success." For David and Nancy this issue hits home when they stop to consider the resources they are using to build the cabin. The issue also surfaces in Al Messer's offer to used recycled materials and to make the cabin energy efficient.

One important biblical contribution to the discussion of sustainable sufficiency comes from the norm of stewardship. In the Bible stewardship is care for the earth and care for persons. The present generation takes in trust a gift from the past with the responsibility of passing it on in no worse condition.

The writers of Genesis introduced the concept in the very first chapter of the Bible when humans are given dominion and ordered to subdue the earth. In spite of the harshness of the words "dominion" and "subdue," their meaning in the larger view of the Hebrew scriptures is clear. Men and women are seen as God's viceroys. It is God who owns the earth as a monarch. The viceroys have complete authority as commissioned by the monarch, but their authority does not include despotism or despoliation. They are to pattern their rule on that of God. For the Hebrews this pattern was set by the God who delivered them from Egypt and entered into covenantal relationship with them. For Christians it is set by Jesus Christ. Neither of these patterns sanctions injustice toward people or misuse of nature.

To summarize, justice and sustainable sufficiency are guiding norms. What they do is give permission to people to put into practice the two minds of the tradition, which, for lack of commonly accepted names, have been called rigorous discipleship and responsible consumption. What they do not do is give people free reign to engage in heavy consumption, materialism, and selfish individualism. Nor do they come down on the side of either rigorous discipleship or responsible consumption, although proponents will argue for one or the other.

The option of rigorous discipleship counsels the Christian to live a life of simplicity, to satisfy only the most basic needs, and to give all that she or he has to the poor. It is a life of surrender to the community of God. And even if the ethics of Jesus as exemplified by holy poverty cannot be lived perfectly, at least the disciple of Jesus should aim in that direction. Living in the grace of God through faith, the Christian has resources to respond with total commitment.

The option of rigorous discipleship emphasizes the new age introduced by Jesus Christ almost to the exclusion of the old age of sin and death. Christians see the sin of the old age, and are freed from it through the power of God. Hence radical changes in ways of living are demanded, and followers make these changes with enthusiasm.

The option of rigorous discipleship is attractive. It does not bog down in the inevitable relativities of the old age. It is simple, direct, and often accompanied by communities approximating the sharing found in the early Christian community in Jerusalem recorded in Acts 1-5.

Unlike the option of rigorous discipleship, the option of responsible consumption does not take its main cues directly from the teachings of Jesus. This does not mean it is less biblical, but that it rests more heavily on the main themes of the Bible, in particular on the tension between the old and new ages and the persistence of sin. Like those taking the option of rigorous discipleship, Christians with this option are concerned for the poor and aware of the problem of being tied to possessions. They do not, however, take the asceticism of Jesus literally or urge the surrender of all possessions.

Reduced to basics, those who follow this option wrestle with what it means to live between the ages, taking both ages seriously. In contrast to a heavy stress on the new age, they point to the realities of the old age or to the ambiguity of life between the ages. The problem for them is not radical discipleship but how to act responsibly and to begin processes of change which will lead to sustainable consumption and greater justice. Their mood is sober, their program moderate and reformist in nature. They also have a greater appreciation of material consumption.

This option is attractive to less ascetic Christians. It avoids the temptation of appeals to feelings of guilt. It accounts for the complexities of living in the world as it is. It does not seek to achieve an impossible ideal and thus avoids illusion and fanaticism.

Rigorous discipleship and responsible consumption represent two options for Christian living. Stated in extreme form they offer a radical choice and are opposed to each other. While stating the options in this way highlights their distinctiveness, it also exaggerates their opposition and results in stereotyping.

In actual fact most North American Christians live beyond the option of responsible consumption. On them both options act as a moral brake. Of those who would call themselves rigorous disciples many live somewhere in between the two options. This gives room to find what the two options have in common.

They both put trust where trust belongs, that is, in God's community in Jesus Christ, not in material possessions or ways of life. Both seek to avoid a self-centered individualism and to be concerned with the affairs of the community. Both are sensitive to the plight of the poor. Both seek a greater approximation of justice in existing structures. Both are valid Christian options which should inform each other.

THE RELATIONSHIPS

While the task of finding guidance in the tradition is essential to making an ethical decision, once done conflicts still remain. In this instance the tradition offers two contrasting and persuasive options, and the Trapps are faced with trying to orient themselves in relation to these two options. Perhaps the relationships in David and Nancy's lives can help them decide how to act.

David and Nancy are like the hub of a six-spoke wheel with each spoke a link to persons on the rim of their lives. David and Nancy are the hub because they are the ones with the decision. The main burden rests with David since Nancy has already indicated that she wants to build and thinks building is a responsible use of their inheritance.

David's relationship to himself is important in this context. Some observers might characterize David as guilt-ridden. This may be true, and if so, David needs to consider further that his sense of guilt may be a warning signal to his own inner alienation.

Alternatively, what these observers characterize as David's guilt may be a projection of their own. It may be that when they see David wrestling with the two minds of the tradition, they become aware of their own avoidance of the issue. Further, this is not simply an interior matter for David. An important source of ethical guidance for David, as for anyone, is the counsel of close friends. David has been seeking their guidance and taking time to mull it over before he decides. This is healthy.

Ultimately he and Nancy must decide because not to decide is the decision not to build. David is drawn to both rigor and responsibility. He cannot have it both ways with the cabin, at least in his own mind. To see the cabin as a reward for David's considerable professional rigor and church work might be an out. Many will want to take this line and see David as deserving God's special favor for being such a good Christian. This out smacks of works righteousness, however. Worse, it assumes a god who plays with human freedom and acts arbitrarily with rewards and punishments. Since the holocaust, this god is dead.

So David and Nancy must decide and something will be lost in the process, either the joys of a cabin or the joys of living simply. Dealing with such losses is one reason that forgiveness is so crucial in Christianity.

Choices must be made, and sometimes bad choices are elected. The tradition says that with repentance, sin is forgiven.

David's relation to Nancy is not imperiled either way. She seems to understand his qualms and is willing to accept them as long as David does not impose them. The problem in the hub does not appear to be their relationship. Rather it seems to be their failure to recognize the sources of their felt needs for a cabin.

Is the real problem not one of overwork and an unwitting acceptance of materialism? And to think that a cabin will relieve work pressures is utopian in the extreme. Cabins are in fact a lot of work. Perhaps what David and Nancy ought to consider is slowing down. Self-sacrifice is not a virtue in itself, and when it becomes something which must be done, the saving power of the cross is lost.

Nancy may be trapped by many of the forces which enslave women today. Liberation for women produces the opportunity for satisfying jobs outside the home, yet at the same time the duties of homemaker, mother, and wife often remain as demanding as before. Life becomes a daily round of serving others, but without the joy and wholeness that comes with a freely given self. The self gets submerged in the processes of existence. Joy goes, and wholeness is lost. Before she adds a cabin to her list of things to do, perhaps she ought to sit down and find the self which she thinks she is giving, but in actuality may be losing in all her activity. The same thing probably applies to David.

The spoke to the children is particularly important. Children learn in myriad ways, consciously and unconsciously. While David and Nancy want Ben and Darcy to acquire skills in certain sports and to relate to their children more, building a cabin may have unintended side-effects, such as encouraging materialism and social apathy. Again, slowing down is probably the best antidote for insufficient time with children. Also, it is probably incorrect to assume the children will want to be at the cabin as they grow older and the action shifts to the high school scene in Toledo. A cabin can lead to less time with the children as their interests shift.

The spoke to their pastor is their bridge to rigorous discipleship. Nathan is the living example which has pricked David's conscience. Clea seems impervious to Nathan's soft sell. The rest of the congregation is probably divided and will become increasingly so the harder Nathan pushes. Given the great numbers for whom rigorous discipleship is foreign, Nathan will be ignored on this issue, however, unless he does push harder.

For Nathan to be ignored would be a shame because the satisfactions of simple living need articulation and modeling. David and Nancy's dilemma is intensified because Nathan offers an alternative and the occasion to be a light to others. To go in the opposite direction and build the cabin might even be a blow to Nathan. Whatever they decide, Nathan should be apprised early, and the lines of communication kept open. Too little is known about Nathan to gauge his reaction.

Much the same goes for the spoke to Clea. She obviously has not elected Nathan's option. In fact there are some indications she may even be exceeding the bounds of responsibility. In any case she represents a side of David and Nancy as well as the views of many in the church. What needs to be done is to avoid a division into factions. That could pull the community apart, which would be a tragedy given that both options are viable.

The relation to Al Messer is tricky. David and Nancy feel responsible to Al as a friend, but Al represents something far larger. Jobs are determined in a market economy by supply and demand. Al's services are not in demand, and David and Nancy have the opportunity to relieve his unemployment temporarily. The irony, even tragedy, of this situation is that the more materialistic North Americans become, the more people have jobs. And if they do not consume, good people are thrown into poverty. It is a "catch 22" for rigor, at least in the short run.

David and Nancy alone cannot make up for the shortcomings of an economic system. Thus their responsibility to Al is limited. If they do not give him the work, he should be in their prayers and conversations. His plight should be considered in their political action.

The fifth spoke runs to David and Nancy's larger family. It involves the inheritance. In some families close relatives would be horror struck if the inheritance were "given away." Family fortunes are heirlooms which the current possessors really do not own. The sole function of the inheriting generation is to steward for future generations. However much this family attitude reflects selfish attachment to material goods, and however much Jesus prepared his disciples for this in his warnings about divisions over the Gospel, the potential for family conflict is present.

The final spoke leads to the global village. David and Nancy do not live in a cocoon of only close relationships. They are citizens of the world, and this world has far too many malnourished and poor people who experience poverty as an unholy necessity. David and Nancy have the luxury of choosing or not choosing holy poverty. They also have a developed sense of responsibility to the larger world. These two things go hand-in-hand. What is given up may be transferred to others. This will not change the world overnight, but if wisely given, it may help improve a few lives.

DIRECTIONS

Since there are so many issues raised by this case, selection is necessary. The family decision with its normative bases in rigorous discipleship and responsible consumption is the most important of these issues. High levels of consumption are in tension with the norms of earlier Christians who never knew abundance and were suspicious of the pockets of overconsumption they saw. The other side of the coin, poverty, has always been rejected unless it is freely chosen as a vocation.

Ironically, many economists argue that the only way out of poverty is the increased consumption which is part of economic growth. In this view "holy poverty" and the virtues of simple living are in opposition with Christianity's preferential option for the poor. It is important to be cognizant of this view, but it is also likely that the view is propounded largely as a means of avoiding serious confrontation with the option of rigorous discipleship.

This case is located under family issues. This location was intentional and was meant to focus on the process of this man and this woman coming to a decision. Family decisions are fraught with snares. Little things are hidden away over the course of a marriage and sometimes trip up the partners. There is always the context of relationships, and today there is the added tension of changing male/female relationships. Steering the family between these snares and booby traps is no easy task.

ADDITIONAL RESOURCES

Birch, Bruce C., and Larry L. Rasmussen. *The Predicament of the Prosperous.* Philadelphia: The Westminster Press, 1978.

Cobb, John B., Jr. *Sustainability.* Maryknoll, NY: Orbis Books, 1992.

Hengel, Martin. *Property and Riches in the Early Church.* Trans. John Bowden. Philadelphia: Fortress, 1974.

Schrage, Wolfgang. Trans. David E. Green. *The Ethics of the New Testament.* Philadelphia: Fortress Press, 1988.

Scott, Kieran, and Michael Warren. *Perspectives on Marriage: A Reader.* New York: Oxford, 1993.

Stivers, Robert L. *The Sustainable Society.* Philadelphia: Westminster Press, 1976.

————. *Hunger, Technology, and Limits to Growth.* Minneapolis, MN: Augsburg, 1984.

Case

What God Has Joined?

Linda glanced through the large glass window of the restaurant and saw Beth and Jennifer already seated in a corner booth. She hesitated a moment at the door, then moved toward them, hugging and greeting each in turn. They had been good friends in college, but after graduation they had drifted apart. When the fourth member of their college quartet, Joanne, had died of breast cancer eight years after graduation, the remaining three had come together again to support her in her last months and share the pain of her passing. Over the next two years they had remained close. The lunch today was a kind of a celebration for Jennifer, who had concentrated on her career as an accountant after college, rather than marry and have children like the other three. Now, as the three survivors of the quartet approached thirty-five, Jennifer was engaged to be married to another partner in her account-ing firm. Next Saturday there was to be a big party, but this lunch was just for the three of them.

Twenty minutes later, having admired Jen's ring and listened to the couple's wedding plans, Linda was shifting uncomfortably in her seat. She realized both Beth and Jennifer were staring, waiting for her to volunteer information. Finally Jennifer, not the most patient or tactful of the trio, blurted out, "Tell us what's the matter, Lin. We both know that things haven't been great for awhile at home, but you seem desperately unhappy. We love you. What's going on?"

It was more than Linda could do to control the gulping sobs that rolled out of her. "I don't know what to do. It's all come back, and I can't go on. David's drinking, and he's hit me. I can't take it anymore."

When Linda had calmed down, Beth pulled the story from her a piece at a time. Beth and Jen knew that Linda's husband, David, had rarely used

This case was prepared by Christine E. Gudorf. Copyright © The Case Method Institute. All names have been disguised to protect the privacy of the individuals involved.

alcohol before he lost his job as manager of a bank branch, but both had seen him inebriated at least twice in the last six months. They knew David had not found another job. But both were shocked to hear that he had hit Linda. They immediately asked for details, for neither would have thought David capable of violence. Both remembered the extraordinary gentleness he had displayed in the hospital nursery holding and feeding Megan, their tiny premature firstborn.

Linda began by defending David, citing the pressures of unemployment on him, and the stress of seeing their unemployment insurance run out, and the prospect of their savings running out as well. With only the part-time secretarial work that Linda had found with the school board, they would not be able to keep up house payments. "He's drinking, but he's not really drinking that much. He has hit me two or three times, but always stops after the one slap. The real problem is me. It's all coming back. I love him, but I can't stand for him to get near me. And he thinks I'm rejecting him, that I don't love him anymore because he doesn't have a job."

Both Beth and Jennifer understood that Linda was referring to her memories of years of sexual abuse by her grandfather. From the time she was eight until his death when Linda was fourteen, her grandfather had used his position as her after-school baby-sitter to sexually molest her. Her family had more or less dismissed both attempts she made to tell about the abuse. She later suspected that her mother had been abused before her. When she arrived at college, Linda never dated. When the topic of child incest came up in a sociology class, Linda spoke to the professor, who referred her to individual therapy and to a support group for child victims of incest. After six months of therapy Linda had met David, declared herself cured, and quit the therapy. But both Beth and Jennifer remembered Linda's screaming nightmares and her fear and distrust of men. And they knew that though she kept in touch with her family, she never went back home after college and never left her children with any of her family.

"Are you and David talking, Linda?" Jennifer asked.

"What can I say? He doesn't believe me when I say that he's not the reason I don't want sex. He keeps telling me I was over the abuse years ago, that I have loved sex for all these years, that the only thing which could be turning me off is him. Maybe he's right, and the memories are just an excuse. Maybe I have invented them. That's what mother and Aunt Lucy told me when I was little. That I made them up. I don't really know how I feel, or whether I love him, or what I want to do. But I can't go on. Sometimes I just go and hide in a closet for hours at a time. I can't face anyone. I don't know how I got here—I haven't been outside the house in weeks."

Linda was calmer by the end of the lunch. Both Jennifer and Beth were disturbed by Linda's depression and her expressions of self-doubt and self-blame. They urged her to seek therapeutic help. Beth volunteered to make appointments for both David and Linda to separately see her neighbors, the Spencers, a husband and wife therapy team. Beth assured Linda that they worked on a sliding-scale fee schedule.

LONG-TERM RECOVERY ISSUES

Six weeks later, when the friends met after Jen's wedding, Linda reported that some things were better and some things were worse. David had liked Dr. Dan Spencer from the start. By the second session he had stopped drinking, and though there were no more incidents of either verbal or physical violence, David continued to work with Dan Spencer on issues around alcohol and violence. Linda reported that Alice Spencer was pushing her to face the violent episodes, to look at the effect they had had on her and on the marital relationship, and to think about how she might react to violence or the threat of violence from David in the future. David was continuing to look for work in surrounding communities. But he still had trouble accepting that Linda was not rejecting him when she declined sex.

Sitting in Beth's kitchen while Linda's and Beth's children played outside the backyard window, Linda confided, "Sometimes I really do want him to hold me, to give me affection. But the minute it turns sexual, I want to scream. For him, if I don't want sex, I don't love him. He tries sometimes to just be affectionate, but it really hurts him when I panic and push him away from me. Sometimes I can't even stand him being close; other times I want to be held, but then push him away later. He complains that he never knows what I want. And I *don't* know what I want. I don't know why it all came back. There was no clue for all those years. We have been really happy until after he lost his job. But it's been almost a year since we made love, and three months since I was last willing to try."

"What does Alice Spencer think of your situation?" asked Jennifer.

"She says that I need to concentrate not on David or the relationship but on my own feelings. She thinks that's why it all came back—I didn't stay in therapy long enough to heal from the abuse. I'm not good at explaining it, but what the years of abuse did was to teach me to respond to other people's needs and desires, and to lose sight of my own. She says now I need to respond to my own feelings, but first I have to learn what they are. And in some areas of my life, I don't have a clue as to which feelings are mine and which are David's, or my grandfather's, or even other people's—like yours. So many 'shoulds' in my life have come from outside me, without any conscious consideration or adoption on my part. She insists I can heal, that I can find my authentic self. But I don't know. In some things, yes, but I can't imagine ever having sex again and enjoying it without remembering the pain and hatred and ultimate emptiness inside. What does that mean for our marriage? Do I love David? Can I make him wait for what may never happen? Shouldn't I be working on accepting sex so I can stop hurting him? My rejection is hurting him much worse than his slaps ever hurt me. Can you have a marriage without sex? A real one with love and warmth, the kind we vowed to have?"

Jennifer responded, "That's a tough one. I remember that Christian churches used to forbid totally impotent men to marry, because sex was important to marriage, but I think so long as they had sex once, it didn't matter if they never did again. I don't know. I'm the newly married one here. Can there be a real marriage without sex? Won't that depend on what David wants and needs, too? Do *you* want to be married? Why don't you talk to somebody with some expertise? You like Pastor Link, and we've all known him for years. Why don't you and David talk to him?"

At that very moment David sat in Dan Spencer's office. "All right, all right. I am coming to see that she really is going back through all that past abuse. I don't understand why. I thought she was through it before we got married. She was never tense or nervous about sex, never afraid of being forced or hurt. She knew I would never hurt her. I just don't understand why it came back now, if not in response to me. But I can't do this much longer. I know that when I feel really threatened by her withdrawal that I can drink too much, and when I drink, the hurt and threat come out in anger. I don't know how I'd live with myself if I ever forced her to have sex. But not drinking is only a little part of the answer."

David continued thoughtfully, "I know I haven't slept the whole night through in over six months. Some nights I have to get up and get away from her, so I won't start making love to her while she's asleep. I have to go lie down on the couch. I love Linda. When I hold her or hug her, or just sit in the car with her driving the kids to Sunday school, I want to make love to her. And I want her to love me. It's not just selfish, or lust. I want to give her pleasure, to make her feel better, to show her that she can trust me with her body and her heart. Sometimes I think it would be easier to just stay away from her. But to avoid her, to get separate beds, or even separate rooms when we could afford them, would be like divorce. When will this be over? How long does it take? Will she ever get better? Is divorce the only option?"

When Linda picked up David at Dr. Spencer's, she asked if he were interested in seeing Pastor Link. David agreed and offered to make the appointment. When David called the church, he was told that Pastor Link was out of town for three weeks but that the associate pastor, Reverend Deerick, was available. David made an appointment with Reverend Deerick, explained the general situation to him, and mentioned that he and Linda were in therapy with the Spencers. Reverend Deerick asked for their authorization to speak with the Spencers. When David and Linda appeared the following week for their appointment, Reverend Deerick had briefly discussed the case with the Spencers. Linda and David began by describing their feelings about each other and their marriage, and ended with a flurry of questions about the nature of marriage. Was their marriage over? Could the wounded child in Linda ever really heal after all these years? If not, would remaining together be merely a hypocritical front, or would it be a heroic fidelity to the vows they had taken? Could there be a real Christian marriage without either shared genital pleasure or sharing of touch and affection? What did the church teach?

When they had finished, Reverend Deerick was still for a few moments, and then said, "I'm not sure that anyone can answer all your questions. I have never been married myself. And you probably know that our church, like most Christian churches, is in the midst of rethinking various aspects of our teachings regarding sexuality and marriage. I could tell you what Augustine or Luther would say to you, but I don't think that would do much good. From what you have told me, you didn't marry either to have children or to prevent fornication. You married because you loved each other in a deeply interpersonal way and because you found that the whole of the other person—body and soul—helped put you in touch with ultimate reality, with God. This contemporary understanding of the purpose and goal of marriage is radically different from Augustine's or Luther's, or any of the other classical Christian thinkers. So their likely advice in this situation—that you purify and consecrate your marriage by giving up sexual intimacy and rear your children as brother and sister—would probably strike you as effectively ending the marriage.

"Our theological tradition simply doesn't give us a lot of useful contemporary guidance about sexuality in marriage. But I do have some suggestions. The first one is personal prayer. I don't mean that you should pray that all this will mysteriously disappear. Prayer is communication with God. Sometimes it is spoken; more often it is silent. Sometimes we write our prayers. Think of prayer as a way of making a friend of God.

"David, I am very moved by your pain and your love of Linda. But you express a great deal of need for her, and that need clearly puts emotional pressure on her. Most men in our society are socialized to fulfill virtually all their intimacy needs in one sexual relationship. Developing an intimate relationship with God could not only take away some of your pain and need, but could also let you focus on Linda's needs more clearly. Linda, prayer for you could be a source of hope and strength for healing. Some victims of sexual abuse by males have a difficult time with prayer and with God, because of the traditional images of God as masculine. You may need to focus on the femininity of God, on God as Mother, to be able to pray. But regardless of what gender you attribute to God, the object is that you let yourself feel God's love for you and God's support for your healing. Feeling God's support for healing could help you feel more legitimate investing so much time and energy in the healing process. A prayerful relationship with God could help you reclaim feelings of trust, self-worth, and responsibility for your own life.

"You both have many questions about marriage and your future that I think only prayer can answer. Prayer can be a process of uncovering, one piece at a time, all our questions about who we are and what we should do.

If you like, I would be glad to meet with you periodically to discuss developments in your individual prayer life. Or I have some books or articles you could read, if you prefer."

As David and Linda drove home from the meeting, they wondered how valuable Reverend Deerick's advice had been. In some ways it evoked simplistic notions of passive religion in which prayer was the answer to everything. But Reverend Deerick had supported their therapeutic process with the Spencers as helpful, and seemed to want to coordinate this spiritual direction with that process. Perhaps prayer could help David find more patience with Linda's withdrawal and could help Linda feel stronger and more worthwhile. Halfway home Linda asked, "David, do you want to consider divorce as an option? I would understand if you did. I don't think it's right for me to ask you to continue with our marriage if that's not what you want, but for myself I prefer to work on our marriage. I'm just not sure *how* we work on rebuilding it, or what we can legitimately ask of each other. What do you want to do, David?"

Commentary

What God Has Joined?

Some of the social and moral issues requiring analysis in this case include alcoholism, domestic violence, and child sexual abuse (child incest). But as David's and Linda's questions indicate, the central question for them is whether or not they should remain together. This question raises the theological issues undergirding the nature of marriage. Let us begin with the more specific problems.

ALCOHOLISM

Linda and David both seem to treat David's drinking as if it were not a serious problem; Beth and Jennifer also seem to accept that judgment. However, Dan Spencer continues to ask about and treat alcohol as a possible ongoing problem, for he is not sure that alcohol is only temporarily a problem due to David's loss of work or Linda's withdrawal. While the use of alcohol has not been regarded as a moral problem within most of Christianity—certainly not within scripture—the abuse of alcohol has been consistently condemned from scriptural times to the present. It is not clear from the case that David's alcohol abuse is part of a larger pattern of alcoholism, but David's misuse of alcohol under the pressure of unemployment and his wife's withdrawal might well signal a pattern of relying on alcohol to cope with pressure.

Research has not determined whether persons who have had trouble with alcohol dependency in response to stress are permanently at risk. Alcoholics Anonymous says yes, and insists on lifelong abstinence. There are some people who seem to be able to return to moderate, even abstemious, use of alcohol after an episode of alcohol abuse and to maintain that lower use for years. But there are no reliable methods for separating those with such potential from those unable to use alcohol responsibly. If David does not decide to give up alcohol altogether, he needs careful monitoring and oversight of his consumption and response for some time.

DOMESTIC BATTERY

Linda's friends are perceptive to question her facile dismissal of David's violence against her. The Spencers need to elicit from both Linda and David their accounts of violence in the relationship. All too often domestic violence follows a pattern: psychological violence leads to verbal violence which leads to physical violence (including sexual violence) which may even lead to homicide. It is important to discover whether there has been a pattern of escalation in the violence within the relationship.

Between one in seven and one in four homes in the U.S. are scenes of domestic violence. Because male abusers often have a series of partners, one in every four U.S. women will be involved at some time during her life in a relationship of domestic violence. Christianity also bears some responsibility for high rates of domestic violence. Violence against women has been tolerated and sometimes actively supported in the churches. In Christianity before mandatory clerical celibacy was imposed at the end of the first millennium and among Protestants after the Reformation, for example, clergy were encouraged to be especially severe in beating their wives, since their wives were to be examples of wifely submission to other women. Scriptural verses that embody the household code of the Roman Empire, such as Ephesians 5 and Colossians 3, enjoin wives to obey their husbands and husbands to love their wives. These texts were interpreted to require beating as a form of loving discipline, ignoring the fact that the Colossians text reads: "Husbands, love your wives and never treat them harshly" (Col. 3:19).

The staggering level of domestic violence in modern society is supported by an attitude of social silence. Neighbors close the windows when they hear slaps, crashes, and shouting next door, rather than call the police. Family members ignore bruises and black eyes in silence, or whisper to each other that John and Mary "aren't getting along." Police sometimes treat domestic abuse as if it were another barroom brawl in which both parties were equally at fault, and merely need a short separation and cooling down. Too often the churches are totally silent about domestic violence and sexual abuse, assuming that things such as domestic violence and sexual abuse do not occur in the homes of church members, but only to the unchurched. Such an attitude discourages victims from turning to the church as a resource and fails to call the abuser to accountability.

Domestic violence is not accidental and is not typically about blowing off steam. Nor is the victim accidentally chosen. Domestic violence maintains control over the spouse. The batterer feels that he is losing control over the spouse and so "accidentally" loses control of himself in violence. Afterward, abusers frequently argue that they should be forgiven because they were not themselves; they were under the influence of alcohol, or temper, or fear, and did not mean the abuse. In fact, batterers' recourse to alcohol is itself usually deliberate, as is the attempt to find issues over which to explode (the quality of dinner, the size of a bill, the behavior of children, the length of a phone call, etc.). These are pretexts for recourse to violent acts that then terrorize the spouse into capitulating to the control of the abuser. When the violence is done and his control restored, the typical abuser apologizes for the damage, pledges his love, and woos the victim into both remaining in the relationship and forgiving him. Even during this expression of repentance, however, abusers typically refuse to accept responsibility. They insist that the victim was responsible for triggering violence brought on by alcohol, stress, or other factors not under his control.

Given this common pattern in domestic abuse, the Spencers need to ask both Linda and David questions about control in the marriage. Is there any evidence that David's use of violence in response to Linda's sexual withdrawal was part of a pattern of David's controlling Linda through violence or threat of violence? It is important to probe the issue of violent abuse because of Linda's past victimization. Her earlier sexual abuse has obscured her own feelings and interests so that she seems better able to focus on David's suffering and pain than on her own. Does Linda's tendency to brush off the violent episodes mask a low self-esteem which makes her see herself as an appropriate object for violence? Or is her easy dismissal of violence the result of over ten years of knowing David as a gentle, non-controlling partner demonstrating abiding love for her and the children?

Questions need to be asked about violence in either parents' interaction with the children as well, and about how the children have been affected by David's violence and alcohol abuse and by Linda's emotional condition. We have no indications that either parent has directed violence at the children, and we do not know the ages of these children. The children should be told as much about what is going on with their parents as is appropriate for their age. Linda and David should explain in simple terms why they are upset, that they are working on their problems, that the children have no responsibility for their parents' problems, and that no matter how they work out their particular problems, the parents will both continue to love the children. Having some idea of what is occurring may help the children feel secure enough to ask for additional reassurance when they need it.

CHILD SEXUAL ABUSE

In the U.S. one out of every four girls and one out of every nine boys is a victim of child sexual abuse, of which one type is child incest. One of every twenty young girls is the victim of step-father-daughter incest or father-daughter incest, which is generally considered the most traumatic type of incest, though specific incidents of other types of incest can cause as much or more trauma. In this case we have no mention of Linda's father; her grandfather may or may not have functioned as a father substitute.

The extent of trauma in child sexual abuse depends upon four factors: the intrusiveness of the abuse, the length of time the abuse continued, the degree of prior trust the victim had invested in the abuser, and the degree of pain, coercion, or threat used to obtain compliance from the victim. We have no information here about the intrusiveness of the abuse or the degree of coercion, pain, or threats in Linda's incestuous abuse as a child. But the abuse continued for several years, and it involved betrayal of trust. In Linda's case the abuser was not only a family member acting in a caretaker role, but the abuse was supported by her primary caretaker's refusal to believe her. Linda's experience is not unusual. Nor is she unusual in experiencing trauma from the incest many years after she thought she had put it behind her. It is often not clear what triggers such memories, but greater social awareness of incestuous abuse of children has supported many unhealed adult victims in getting help, rather than in remaining trapped in nightmarish fear, distrust, and self-loathing.

The U.S. is generally considered to have among the highest child sexual abuse rates in the world. But data is not readily available for most parts of the world, and even U.S. data is incomplete. In general, researchers are coming to believe that large proportions of the children of the world are at risk for sexual abuse. Both religious and secular culture here and elsewhere include strong supports for child sexual abuse, including socialization of children to universal respect and unquestioning obedience to parents and other adults; failing to recognize children's rights over their own bodies; and a silence about sex that prevents both information flow and ease of communication around sex, even between intimates. Both church and society, which hold up the family as a protector of children, have been largely blind to familial abuse of children.

Healing from sexual victimization is almost always a long and painful process. When victimization is endured as a child and is unaddressed for decades, the internalization of the abuse, which usually does the most damage, is often unobstructed, even reinforced. In Linda's case, however, it is extremely positive that she did not suppress all memories of the abuse and that she seems to have a history of both sexual satisfaction and intimacy with David. Whatever deficiencies existed within that intimacy (and there are always greater depths of intimacy to achieve), the fact that both partners experienced the relationship as intimate for over a decade testifies to the advantage Linda has over incest victims in general. Many victims find themselves unable to trust others enough for intimacy and unable to feel that they have an authentic self worthy of being disclosed to another. While Linda may always carry some degree of damage from her childhood experience, she may well develop moral strengths from her battle that help her resist and heal from her family's sinful abuse.

It is important for Christians to insist that Linda can heal, both because there is objective evidence of the healing of other victims and because Christians believe in the Resurrection, the ground of Christian hope. What

Christians mean when they speak of Jesus Christ's Resurrection as victory over sin is not that sin ceases to exist. Victims of child sexual abuse are victims of sin. Rather, Christians mean that sin is not final and decisive; because of Jesus Christ's Resurrection, others can overcome and recover from the effects of sin. It is through healing from sin that we participate in the Resurrection of Jesus. In this case, there is a very real possibility that dealing with the present problems in the relationship—both the memories that plague Linda and David's recourse to alcohol and violence—may allow them to reestablish and strengthen their earlier intimacy.

In order for that to happen, David needs to move beyond his present step of acknowledging that Linda is not yet healed from the earlier abuse. He needs to become truly supportive of that healing. Perhaps Reverend Deerick's suggestion that prayerful intimacy with God could alleviate some of David's intimacy needs could support David's becoming more supportive of Linda's healing. Only support from David himself can remove the sense of demand Linda now feels about David's desire for sexual intimacy. Her feelings of guilt about not being able to give him what he wants echo lessons learned in the abuse and interfere with her ability to concentrate on her own healing process. If David could learn to rely less on sexual intimacy as symbolic of the overall intimacy of the relationship and be more open to emotional intimacy and non-genital physical intimacy with Linda, he could assist Linda's healing and satisfy physically some of his own need to be reassured of Linda's love for him.

At the same time, it would be wrong to demand that David immediately accept a marriage without genitality or even physical touch. Human beings are integrated persons, and their relationships and growth and development should be integrated. While David seems to be extremely focused on physical and even genital activity for expressing his feelings for Linda and meeting his own intimacy needs, other avenues of interpersonal interaction should be developed in addition to, and not in place of, sexual activity. Genital activity in marriage is an important foundation for other forms of intimacy because of its symbolic power. The vulnerability symbolized both by nakedness and by the letting go of consciousness and control in orgasm are powerful images of trust and self-giving. Shared pleasure in sex both rewards lovers for their willingness to offer themselves to the other and bonds lovers together.

Linda should be encouraged to assume that she can heal and that the healing process will include her ability to reclaim her sexual feelings and activity. Healing will mean ending the power of the abuse to dictate her feelings, her actions, and her life. To assume from the beginning that she will never be able to resume a full marital relationship is victimism, accepting that the effects of victimization are permanent.

SPIRITUAL COUNSELING

Reverend Deerick's offer of support for guiding Linda's and David's prayer life seems to include spiritual counseling around the specifics of their situations. Spiritual counseling when coordinated with psychological counseling frequently complements it, and is often the most effective therapy for dealing with lingering feelings of guilt and sinfulness in victims of sexual abuse. Spiritual counseling for Linda might also include encouragement to approach her family as a mature adult who needs to have her suffering and the family's responsibility acknowledged in ways that allow her to get on with her life. We do not know whether she faced her mother (or her aunt) with the fact of her abuse after it ended, whether they feel estranged from her, and if so, if they know the reason for the estrangement. Even though her grandfather is dead and Linda is not close to her family, she may need for her own sake to confront them with her abuse. Spiritual counseling could also help protect Linda from family pressure for premature forgiveness and reconciliation.

MARRIAGE AND DIVORCE

There is little doubt that both David and Linda are experiencing great pain and suffering and asking serious questions about the permanency of marriage. Even though some denominations recognize divorce, Christian understandings of marriage have always taught that marriage should be undertaken as a permanent commitment. Some variety of the "for richer or poorer, in sickness and health, until death do us part" vow has been a part of the Christian wedding service for centuries. The degree of suffering involved is not, in itself, an indication of the appropriateness of divorce. A physician would not help a patient with appendicitis to die merely because her immediate pain is severe. Far more important is the prognosis for restoring health and alleviating the suffering.

For many readers, the question as to whether David and Linda should remain married is moot, because they are both clear that they love each other. Until the twentieth century there would have been no theological support for the understanding that marriage endures only when love endures, even though it was increasingly common after the sixteenth century to understand that love was a motive for marriage. Because women were not economically franchised, and because of the association of marriage with the bearing and rearing of children, it was assumed that women and children required the presence of the husband/father for their well-being.

Today Christian churches are divided as to how to understand marriage and divorce. The Roman Catholic church does not recognize divorce and therefore forbids remarriage. However, if Linda were a Catholic, she might be able to obtain an annulment, a declaration that no true marriage ever existed with David, on the grounds that she was not fully free to consent to marriage because of the unresolved trauma of child sexual abuse. Most other Christian churches do not exclude the divorced and remarried, though their preference for permanency is clear. Across denominational lines, the criteria which divide marriages in crisis into viable and non-viable categories are disputed among pastors and pastoral counselors. The most common question is whether contractual obligations in marriage endure after feelings of love have been lost. A related question is whether fidelity to the contractual obligations can, over time, rekindle lost feelings of love. Is love more than a feeling? If yes, does this mean that feelings of love are not important for marriage? There are no clear answers to these questions, which is one probable reason for Reverend Deerick's focus on personal prayer in response to David's and Linda's questions about the future of their marriage.

A second reason for Reverend Deerick's shift of focus from church teaching on marriage to prayer is that the positive and useful insights on marriage in scripture are embedded within and often distorted by patriarchal depictions of women as men's property: Women achieve virtue through fruitful wombs, sexual fidelity, and homemaking skills. The Mosaic law and the scriptural authors allow little scope for the personhood of women; while a few women are singled out in the text, only an exceptional handful of women are recognized for their own initiatives, rather than for their submission or for the fruit of their wombs. For this reason it is difficult to apply any of the scriptural stories or teachings to the crisis in David's and Linda's marriage. From the perspective of many of the communities from which scripture emerged, Linda would have no right to deny David the sexual use of her body, and David would be expected to exercise his rights regardless of her wishes. Linda might not even feel sexual aversion from her childhood memories, for she would have been raised to understand women's bodies as the property of men and might well regard her abuse by her grandfather as a universal hazard of being female. At the same time, the expectations of David and Linda of their marriage would have been significantly different had they lived in scriptural communities. They would have understood the marital bond as characterized much less by interpersonal intimacy and more by contract, especially contract between clans or families.

Theological treatment of marriage as a covenant modeled on the covenant between Yahweh and Israel is a contemporary reversal of the biblical attempt to personalize the covenant relationship. Ancient Israelites came to see their relationship with Yahweh as more personal and intimate than the feudal covenant between lords and vassals which gave the covenant its form and name. The Israelites came to image the covenant as a marriage, the most personal and intimate relationship they knew. In a society in which women were chattel that husbands bought from fathers, the inequalities of power, status, and worth in the divine/human relationship were not barriers to the effectiveness of the analogy. St. Paul later extended the marital analogy to Christ and the church. But when the contemporary church uses the relationships of Christ/church and Yahweh/Israel relationships to understand and explain marriage, it imports into the marital relationship assumptions about inequalities of power, worth, and initiative between the partners that are alienating, making the analogies less than effective.

Until the modern age, theological treatment of marriage focused almost exclusively on procreation as the purpose and chief blessing of marriage, rather than on the quality of the relationship, which has become the central theological concern over the last few centuries. Few helpful historical resources on the role of sexuality in Christian marriage exist. Between the early medieval era and the Reformation, Christianity taught total impotence as an absolute bar to marriage and sexual consummation of marital vows as necessary to finalize marriage. Before the Reformation, and in Roman Catholicism even afterward, couples were often encouraged to consider Josephite (celibate) marriages; clergy regularly cautioned couples to abstain from sex on Sundays, holy days, and during Lent, as sex was understood as an obstacle to prayer and contemplation. Procreation was regarded as a sufficient good to justify sexual activity and consequent pleasure. But sexual pleasure was morally suspect and forbidden as motive for marital sex. The difficulty of resisting sexual pleasure in marriage caused pre-Reformation Christianity and post-Reformation Roman Catholicism to understand celibate religious life as a holier vocation than marriage.

The Reformers raised the status of marriage compared with vowed celibacy and gradually abandoned some of the more negative traditional attitudes toward sex. For the most part, however, the churches of the Reformation continued to understand procreation as the primary purpose of marriage and sex. For limited numbers of Protestant Christians, sexual activity came to be seen as an important way to cherish the spouse and as a source for generating warmth and intimacy which could influence children and the wider community. Among the Puritans and Quakers, for example, new understandings of marriage as primarily a personal bond, within which children were an additional but not the central blessing, gave rise to an appreciation of sex in marriage.

Within American Christianity a positive understanding of sex in marriage has been in tension with a more traditional and more widespread understanding of sex as morally dangerous and sexual desire as something to be resisted by the virtuous. Contemporary Christian theologians are attempting to recover and develop the few examples of positive treatment of body, sexuality, and sex found in Christian theological traditions. Since Christian faith is grounded in the Incarnation—the doctrine that the second person in the Godhead became fully and humanly embodied in flesh—there should be no room for hatred or suspicion of the human body, its appetites or actions *per se*.

Some Catholics point out that though the traditions of Catholic moral theology were decidedly anti-sexual, the sacramental tradition regarding marriage incorporated a number of positive elements, including the understanding that sexual intercourse (especially orgasm itself) operates as a primary sacramental sign. Marital sex does not merely represent the spousal love that it signifies but actually contributes to the creation and development of that love. It has even been suggested by a Catholic clergy/lay team commissioned and funded by the U.S. Conference of Catholic Bishops (*Embodied in Love*, 1986) that mutually pleasurable marital sex is perhaps the most accessible human experience of the love that characterizes the persons of the Trinity.

CONCLUSION

What should David and Linda do about their marriage? Despite all their problems and pain, they both state their concern for each other and act as if they care very much about the other. For that reason they may not want to abandon the marriage now but may prefer to continue work with the Spencers and perhaps to begin seeing Reverend Deerick to work on personal prayer as a means of clarifying what they should do. The teachings of Christian churches on the issues of permanency in marriage and sex in marriage have begun to shift away from fear and suspicion of sex in marriage and from insistence on marital permanence regardless of the costs to those involved. Christian churches have come to see that marital sex can be an integral part of both interpersonal intimacy and communion with the divine, and that the costs of preserving marriage in some circumstances can include physical and emotional violence and the erosion of self-hood. Ultimately only Linda and David can decide what level of cost is acceptable to them and to their children in the attempt to rebuild their marriage.

ADDITIONAL RESOURCES

Angelica, Jade. *A Moral Emergency: Breaking the Cycle of Child Abuse.* Kansas City: Sheed and Ward, 1993.

Black, Claudia. *It Can't Happen To Me: Children of Alcoholics.* Denver: MAC Publications, 1979.

Gallagher, Charles A., George A. Malony, Mary F. Rousseau, and Paul F. Wilczak. *Embodied in Love: Sacramental Spirituality and Sexual Intimacy.* New York: Crossroads, 1984.

Miller, Alice. *Breaking Down the Walls of Silence: The Liberating Experience of Facing Painful Truth.* New York: Meridian Books, 1993.

Poling, James Newton. *The Abuse of Power: A Theological Problem.* Nashville: Abingdon, 1991.

Quebec Assembly of Bishops. *A Heritage of Violence: A Pastoral Reflection on Conjugal Violence.* Montreal: 1989.

Russell, Diana E. H. *The Secret Trauma: Incest in the Lives of Girls and Women.* New York: Basic Books, 1986.

Scott, Kieran, and Michael Warren. *Perspectives on Marriage: A Reader.* New York: Oxford, 1993.

PART II

LIBERATION

Case

Prophets from Brazil

Alan Johnson's chain of thought was momentarily interrupted as the Boeing 747 began its approach to John F. Kennedy Airport, New York. Alan was returning from a three-week business trip to Brazil, and he had been mulling over the meetings with business and church leaders in São Paulo, one of the largest cities in the southern hemisphere. A company conference awaited his report on Monday, and, perhaps equally troubling, the Social Concerns Committee of the Catholic parish he belonged to in Stamford, Connecticut, expected his recommendations.

Questions raised during his trip raced through his mind. Should Brazil be the parish's mission focus for the next year? If so, how should their influence and resources be brought to bear? Should they focus upon the social, political, economic, and religious structures that work to oppress the poor? To do so would mean working with the poor and in opposition to those who hold power in Brazil. Or would it be more responsible to work with those in the hierarchy of the government and church, funneling money into their hands and agencies so that they could then dispense it in the form of food, medical supplies, educational supplies, and resources to help further evangelism. In short, Alan would have to recommend whether his church should work within or against the established structures in Brazil.

But that was not Alan's only dilemma. There was also the tension between his two roles. Could he recommend that his company expand its business investments in Brazil and at the same time argue that the church should oppose structures that seemed to be at the root of the oppression of the poor and the violation of human rights in Brazil? Those suggestions would seem to be at cross-purposes. Alan's recommendations had seemed

This case study was prepared by Robert A. Evans. Copyright © The Case Study Institute. The original case appears in *Human Rights: A Dialogue between the First and Third Worlds* (Maryknoll, N.Y.: Orbis Books, 1983). Case revised in 1987, Alice F. Evans.

clearer before he had begun serious preparation for the visit. Now after that preparation and the visit itself, he was flying back into New York confused by the wealth of conflicting information and insights he had encountered.

SOCIAL CONCERNS

On Tuesday evening Alan was scheduled to share his findings during his trip to Brazil with the other members of the Social Concerns Committee of his 1,500-member church. The parish was composed largely of the families of business executives and professionals, many of whom commuted each day to New York. The committee in recent years had been involved in promoting charitable causes on a local level, such as a children's home, family counseling services, meals-on-wheels, and some mission interpretation for the national church. The year before, a new chairperson, John Andrews, had urged the committee to take an active position on national and international issues of justice, drawing on the expertise and knowledge of several members of the congregation. John declared that the committee's mandate was set by Jesus himself at the beginning of his public ministry. John had read from the prophet Isaiah:

> The spirit of the Lord is upon me, because he has anointed me to preach good news to the poor. He has sent me to proclaim release to the captives and recovering of sight to the blind, to set at liberty those who are oppressed, to proclaim the acceptable year of the Lord [Luke 4:18-19].

Andrews personally recruited Alan for the committee, knowing that he was committed to issues of civil rights and that he traveled widely for International Electric as a vice-president of the international division. Although initially reluctant to serve because of a heavy work schedule, Alan found the committee work exciting. It was, in his judgment, however, too scattered; there were reports to the congregation on everything from drug abuse to world hunger. Alan urged the committee to make an impact upon the congregation through the identification of a specific mission priority for the new year. Given the concerns of several committee members for human rights and for the poor of the world and the growing significance of South America for both U.S. government and business interests, this area was selected by the committee.

BACKGROUND PREPARATION

In preparation for his trip, Alan read briefing documents prepared by the International Electric research department, several reports on Brazil by Amnesty International, the human rights organization, and the U.N. report on Human Development. Alan had also consulted with a friend, Tom

Perkins, who taught in a nearby university and had access to U.S. State Department reports. Alan was struck by the startling contrasts in the largest country in South America. One document indicated that in terms of gross national product, Brazil ranked eighth in the world, placing it in the company of countries such as Japan, West Germany, and the U.S. Brazil had become the world's second largest exporter of food (following the United States). However, in terms of infant mortality, poverty, and malnutrition, Brazil ranked near the bottom, in the company of nations such as Haiti, Nepal, and Bangladesh. According to Tom's analysis, a primary factor was that control of the great natural and industrial wealth of the country was in the hands of a small minority. In addition, several years of drought in northeast Brazil had brought extreme hardship to the area. Hundreds of thousands of landless peasants had migrated south toward the urban centers of Rio de Janeiro and São Paulo in order to survive. At one point a number of years earlier there had been reports that as much as one-third of the total population was in migration. Although many had now returned to the north, countless thousands of homeless remained in and around the urban centers.

By earlier government estimates, 45 percent of the nation's 400 million acres of arable land was in the hands of 1 percent of the nation's landowners. Tom Perkins traced these figures historically to colonial policies introduced by Portugal in the sixteenth century. Eager for the new colony to be explored, settled, and defended, the Portuguese monarchy granted vast estates to vassals of the crown. These vassals were given total power in return for a percent of the taxes and revenues collected. Portugal later moved to appoint a governor general for the whole of Brazil, but the pattern of single-family ownership of hundreds of thousands of acres remained. Specific land reform laws were introduced in the early 1960s and in 1985, but the government did not actively pursue enforcement of the laws.

Ninety percent of those who owned these large tracts farmed a small percentage of their land. Alan learned that significant portions of the land that was cultivated were used to grow export crops of sugar, coffee, and soybeans. Beef and leather were also major exports. Alan noted that extensive burning and development of large tracts in the Amazon Basin were proceeding on a massive scale, much of it intended to provide grazing land for cattle and access to mineral and oil deposits. He also read about "irreversible ecological damage" to the rain forests in northern Brazil.

The mid-1980s was a period of great hope that many of these situations would change. From 1964 to 1985, Brazil had been ruled by a series of military dictators. During those years federal and state legislatures had been disbanded, the constitution suspended, and strict censorship imposed. There had been severe repression, including secret arrests, torture, and murder by the military and police. Following elections, a civilian president, Tancredo Neves, was elected by the Congress that had approved a constitutional amendment to restore direct elections but was unable to convince the military to accept it at that time. Neves' platform opposed state economic intervention and authoritarian control; he personally vowed to give priority to dealing with the annual inflation rate, then at 230 percent. Unfortunately, before his installation Neves was hospitalized for abdominal surgery. Many questions raised by the national and international press about his subsequent death were left unanswered. José Sarney Costa, who had been elected vice-president, assumed the presidency. Until the previous June, he had led a party that supported five consecutive military governments.

This change from military to civilian rule had inspired considerable hope, and many in the United States assumed that civilian rule would bring about significant changes in life in Brazil. Many people at International Electric and at Alan's church had made that assumption. But, as Alan read the various reports and talked with Tom Perkins, he learned that there were many signs that fundamental changes had not occurred. Wealthy landowners were violently opposed to two land reform bills approved in 1985 and little was done by the government to implement the mandated reforms. One of Amnesty International's reports expressed concern for "an increase in the politically motivated killings of rural trade union leaders, peasants, and others during land disputes." The organization "welcomed official inquiries into some of the worst abuses."

Before he left on his trip, Alan learned that in November, 1985, the Roman Catholic church in Brazil released a list of four hundred people charged with torturing political prisoners during the 21 years of military rule. The list included several high-ranking officers who were on active duty when the report was released. There was no official response to the report.

Studying current statistics, Alan learned that despite the fact that Brazil is counted among the world's ten largest economies, with a GNP of $420 billion, it has the greatest income concentration on earth. The last U.N. economic report revealed that in Brazil the poorest 10 percent of the population earned less than 1 percent of the nation's total income. At the same time, the richest 10 percent earned more than 50 percent of the nation's wealth. Alan learned that almost 12 percent of the working population consisted of children and teenagers. He also read that "social exclusion" was the appropriate name for the present Brazilian economic model as well as for the period of rapid economic growth in the 1960s and 1970s.

One of Alan's sources provided evidence to show that in the 1980s the economic situation was made worse by the adoption of structural adjustment policies decided and imposed on Brazil by the International Monetary Fund and the World Bank, both of which are heavily influenced by the U.S. The policies devalued the Brazilian currency, repealed protectionist legislation, and privatized state-owned companies. While the policies did begin to slow the inflation rate, they cost more than one million jobs and dramatically affected the lives of the poorest people. Sixty-five percent of Brazil's inhabitants now suffered from malnutrition. While Brazil's economy had grown remarkably, functional illiteracy (24 percent of the population) also continued to grow at a significant rate. Figures from the industries indicated that as many as 58 percent of the workers were functionally illiterate. Rural teachers, whose salaries were often only ten dollars per month, had little or no training. Alan read that teachers of the poor had said that "the children of the poor often drop out of school to work or are too restless and hungry to concentrate." He also read that the "country is reaching the limits of peaceful coexistence between the rich and the poor."

Alan reached Brazil trying to sort out this conflicting and complicated mass of data and the contrasting signs of hope and despair. He hoped that by meeting with business and church leaders he would be able to reach conclusions about how International Electric and his church's Social Concerns Committee could proceed in relation to the social, economic, and political forces at work in Brazil.

THE MISSIONARY

Alan spent the first week of his trip immersed in conferences and formal dinners with Brazilian business executives. The first Sunday afternoon he had free, Alan called on Doug Williams, a friend of a minister who had worked with Alan's pastor in Stamford. Doug had served as a missionary in Brazil for twenty years. Deeply concerned about the reports he had read of human rights violations and the desperate poverty of the people, Alan asked Doug what position his mission had taken.

Doug Williams was emphatic in his response: "Missionaries are the guests of the country and the Brazilian church. It is presumptuous of outsiders to speak out as natives. The task of the church is set by Jesus himself in the Great Commission. We are to go into all the world and preach the Gospel. This is a mission of conversion. When people are liberated from sin, they are liberated to change their own situation. Jesus also calls us to minister to the needs of the poor and those who suffer. This is the basis of our mission health clinic which serves thousands in the *favelas* (slum areas) and of the mission school. If we spend our time fighting the government or the rich, we will drain our energies and resources and will neglect the power of the Gospel to change lives.

"I may not always agree with the government's course of action," Williams continued. "However, as foreign nationals we have to understand the position of a government trying to survive in a nation with an enormous gap between the rich and poor and with political controversy always being stirred up from the outside. The communists are seen by those in power as a threat to the survival of Brazilian life. It is like going into the *favela* and being challenged to a fight. You and I have been taught in our protected society to fight fair. But if the boy who challenges you has sand to throw in your eyes and a broken bottle to cut your throat, to fight fair would be to die. The government sometimes takes extreme measures, which may seem oppressive to outsiders, to survive these foes.

"There are those Christians who have directly challenged the government. However, you must realize that some strategies of confrontation hurt the mission of the church and even the cause of human rights. A number of years ago the U.S. administration took a strong stand on human rights issues. There was broad U.S. media exposure of human rights violations and direct criticism of the Brazilian government's policies.

"And what was the result," Doug asked, "of all this intervention? A greater pressure put on those advocating change and the recognition of human rights. Also a change in policy: for a time no missionaries or church personnel were granted resident visas.

"As Christians, we must continually remind ourselves of our mission. Paul was clear when he warned: 'Let every person be subject to the governing authorities' (Rom. 13:1). Remember that Paul was speaking of the Roman government, which was both cruel and unjust to early Christians. The church is not called to be a political agent. The church is called to conversion."

CALL FOR LIBERATION

Following the conclusion of Alan's business consultations, his company had suggested he spend an additional weekend in Brazil "for personal relaxation." Alan decided to spend some of this time in conversations with members of the Inter-Faith Task Force for Liberation. Tom Perkins and members of the Social Concerns Committee had suggested this group.

It was difficult for Alan to believe that those he met at the headquarters of the Inter-Faith Task Force were describing the same country as were his business associates. "Identification of the church with the poor, not the powerful," the Reverend Paulo de Souza declared, "is the only hope for the Catholic or Protestant churches in Brazil." A dedicated group of churchpersons, including priests and lay people, Protestants and Roman Catholics, men and women, had formed the task force to demonstrate the need to "labor together across ecumenical and geographical lines in the name of the universal church of Jesus Christ." They were often criticized by members of their own church bodies, and under the military government in particular they had been harassed, arrested, and imprisoned when they sought to "denounce and expose the violation of human rights and dignity of all God's children."

Father Antonio Cardosa, a Dominican priest and teacher, reminded Alan that over 60 percent of Brazilians were hungry, living far below the poverty line as defined in the U.S. "There is enormous wealth in Brazil, concentrated in a tiny portion of the population that exerts power to maintain the status quo. In these circumstances, what does it mean to follow Jesus' command to preach good news to the poor? The critical issue is: How can a people be free? How can the church as church be free? Conscientization of the church would mean moving from focusing on purely spiritual matters to engagement with the community in Christ's name."

Paulo de Souza was clear about the major issues that face the church in Brazil and what was required of those seeking to be faithful. He summarized those issues and requirements while speaking with Alan. He told Alan: "First the church must become a true companion in favor of justice—an advocate of justice, not in principle only but in concrete situations. Problems of poverty and violence can no longer be ignored by the church. Second, the church must identify with the populace. In the past the church has always been linked with the powerful. The church can no longer simply react; it must take its place in the struggle and initiate action. Third, identification with the poor—the special concern of God in the Old and New Testaments—involves ceasing to spiritualize the problems of the poor. Poverty in Brazil has a social structure that is a direct result of the capitalist system. This system—nurtured by the United States and protected by the rich, which includes the present church—breeds injustice. Fourth, there is a built-in relationship between creative pastoralization and politicization. The church is involved in the problems and must work at the issues. Politics is a form of faith for an institution seeking to be a church of the poor. Three elements required are: (a) a practical alliance with the poor; (b) a methodology for the scientific interpretation of social reality; and (c) biblical and theological reflection resulting in the stress on action with the poor excluding any compromises with power. Fifth, local congregations are inadequate. There is need for a new form of church where believers are not domesticated, but take part in the decisions that affect their lives. Our hope is in the base communities [*comunidades de base*] in the Roman Catholic church that are attempting to change the structure of an unjust society. The question is not so much individual rights as it is the social rights of a whole community. Although they may seem threatening to some priests, these lay groups provide new structures of hope for the church."

Father Antonio agreed that the new hope of the church was in those same base communities now numbering two million persons, with fifteen thousand new groups in one year alone. "They have no sacrament and no priest, but they are studying the Bible and politics in order to discover a way to liberate themselves and the world. The need is for an honest, aggressive, and compassionate world church that will be willing to suffer with the people. Galatians says we are 'to bear one another's burdens.' Let us then do this for one another."

During these conversations Alan was struck with the parallels to one of the church-related human rights reports he had read which stated that to confess belief in the communion of saints meant to share the suffering of brothers and sisters in Christ in every section of the earth. To do anything less would be to avoid Christ's call to set at liberty those who are oppressed. As he returned to his hotel, Alan was seriously considering that those who demanded a new position from the U.S. government and a new life-style from Christians in the U.S. church may be on the right track.

THE MEDIATORS

Some church bodies, Alan found, represented neither the drive toward structural change of the Inter-Faith Task Force nor the personal, spiritual focus represented by conservative evangelical Christians such as Doug Williams. "The mediators," as the Reverend Benjamin Villaca described them, "are the practical moderates present among Roman Catholics, Presbyterians, and some other Protestants. They call for gradual transformation of our Brazilian society. This nation, which occupies over half the land mass of the South American continent, has been characterized by evolution, not revolution. We Brazilians are a relatively gentle and tolerant people who have had such a stable development that even our coups have been relatively bloodless. Realistically, social change will be slow, and the church must be present and faithful. The answer lies in the responsible use of the God-given talents of individual Christians in the public service of their people.

"Education and evangelism are at the heart of the matter," Villaca continued. "Religious and secular education of the people provides the foundation for a renewed church and a developed society. Christians must devote their talents to providing better schools, more adequate housing, and medical facilities at every level of society. Evangelism programs will allow Brazilians to see that the church has the key to a better life. The Christian message will take different forms in the *favelas* and on Copacabana Beach in Rio. The Christian is called to be responsible to God, neighbor, and self. Catholics constitute over 90 percent of the overall population in this 'most Catholic nation of our times.' If only 5 percent of them and the 5 percent of the population who are Protestants are active, then the opportunities for evangelism are enormous.

"Ecumenical radicals are as much Marxist as Christian. They cannot really affect government or the privileged class despite their claim that 'only a revolution in the structure of society and the church will bring liberation.' Christians are entitled to the fruits of their labor if the gains are responsibly shared with others. The World Council of Churches has been ignored ever since it began to support terrorists and guerrillas who only bring violence and loss of life by preaching liberation, not reconciliation.

"The conservatives and Pentecostals are individualistic escapists, unwilling to face their societal responsibilities. Their refusal to dance, smoke, drink, gamble, or in general participate in society evades the reality of an evolving society. A few hours of ecstasy each week through baptism of the Holy Spirit is little different from our spiritualist cults. Moral rigidity that judges and condemns all practices except one's own builds enthusiasm for a righteous minority, but will not attract those who need the Christian Gospel of forgiveness.

"We need," Villaca concluded, "the support of the North American churches as we have usually experienced it, only to a fuller measure. We need more money and trained personnel for schools, hospitals, housing projects, and Christian education projects. Send us aid without strings attached. Help establish better relations with our president. He has promised progress in several areas of life, from land reform to a more active anti-poverty program. This is a religiously oriented nation. The church could help us by private and government gifts. Let your church and companies know we need their continued support."

DOUBLE DILEMMA

After circling for thirty minutes, the captain announced he was entering the final approach to New York. Alan's thoughts spun from his confusion on the church recommendation to the business advice he must provide. With over 500,000 color television sets sold in Brazil in one year, and with the promise of the U.S. government to guarantee the investment, it seemed good business sense to recommend expansion. There was substantial evidence that the profits for International Electric would be high. However, the 230 percent inflation rate in Brazil and the standard practice of private lending companies to finance television sets and refrigerators at an 8 percent monthly interest rate made Alan hesitate. He was disturbed by the loan policies with which newly arrived immigrants in Rio and São Paulo were unfamiliar. They made little more than the fifty dollars a month national minimum wage—if they had a job at all. The buy low, sell high attitude of retailers, coupled with aggressive debt collections, spelled tragedy for low-income consumers, though a boon to the appliance business. The members of the Inter-Faith Task Force had pressed Alan to understand and communicate to North Americans that multinational corporations such as International Electric expected twice as much return on investments in countries such as Brazil as on the same investments in the United States; those corporations helped to maintain the often oppressive regimes and political and social structures that fostered the profits at the expense of the poor. Alan seriously considered that analysis, but then reminded himself that stockholders at home wanted a return on their money, not a speech about corporate social responsibility.

The church report was equally a problem. Should he recommend Brazil as a mission priority? If so, which request by Brazilians should he honor? What is the most faithful and effective: political and economic intervention; lobbying at home combined with a new awareness of the world church; a campaign for major mission funds for education and evangelism; or not recommending Brazil as a mission project because the issues are unclear and involvement from outside is not wanted?

As the clouds parted over Long Island, the face of Carlos de Carvalho—Alan's host, old friend, and an active Christian layman in Brazil—came to Alan's mind. After a lively discussion of the options on the last evening, Carlos had said, "It's a tough decision for you to make, and I am not sure what you ought to do. I am convinced the world church must learn to make decisions in light of needs everywhere in the world. To make no decision is cowardice. A sustained strategy is needed. When will the church in America have the courage to be a prophet and not just a provocateur?"

"Fasten your seatbelt, please, Mr. Johnson," the flight attendant said. "The landing in this wind may be a little rough."

Commentary

Prophets from Brazil

Alan Johnson's problem seems simple enough. He has reports to make to the two different worlds he lives in: the world of his suburban parish and the world of International Electric, a large transnational corporation (TNC). Alan's visit to Brazil, however, has added several new worlds, making his problem far more complex. He must now consider the rich and poor worlds of Brazil as well as the world of U.S. foreign policy.

Whose world should he stand in to view the reality of Brazil and the mission of the church? He has the briefing documents of International Electric, no doubt with their eye for profitable opportunities; U.S. State Department reports, which regularly view the rich/poor division in terms of the East/West conflict; a report from Amnesty International and another written for Brazil's president; the outlook of Brazilian business associates, probably urging his company to expand the production of big-ticket consumer goods; the charity-based perspective of his own congregation; Doug Williams's individualistic Christianity; the view of those in the Inter-Faith Task Force who work within the reality of Brazil's poverty; and Benjamin Villaca's reformist approach. With these conflicting worldviews before him, the storm over Kennedy Airport is also in Alan's soul.

The immediate task is the reports. Since Alan is in a quandary, perhaps the frequently used technique of delay in such situations is appropriate. Alan could make preliminary reports and then undertake a more thorough study involving members of his church and business associates. Both research and experiential learning would be part of this study.

Alan would have to decide what his study would entail. Certainly it would have to include something on the history of Brazilian social structures, and how the Brazilian experience relates to other Latin American situations. Alan needs to understand the dynamism of the Brazilian economy and the 40 to 60 percent of the people in poverty who do not participate in it. He needs to know how his company contributes to both the economic growth and the persisting poverty. Finally, further reflection on his encounter with Brazilian Christians, perhaps even returning to dialogue further, would help him to identify his options. With this Alan could make more comprehensive reports with recommendations for action. By bringing others along in his study he would increase the possibility for successful learning and implementation. This delay and further study would no doubt ultimately produce a better report, and yet Alan is still faced with the need to reach some conclusions for the reports he must soon give.

BRAZIL: UNIQUE YET REPRESENTATIVE

Alan undoubtedly knows that among countries in Latin America Brazil is unique because of its Portuguese colonial rule and its rate of economic development since 1930. It is the latter which really sets it apart, however, since Portuguese colonial administration and the religious imposition which accompanied it were not substantially different from that of the Spanish. Since 1930 Brazil has industrialized at a rate that proponents of development call "phenomenal" or "miraculous." It is now the richest country in Latin America. Still the same development process has occurred to a lesser degree but with many of the same elements throughout Latin America, so that even with its more rapid economic growth, Brazil can be considered representative of the region. In particular, the division of Brazilian society into a well-off minority and an impoverished majority is characteristic of countries in Latin America.

In addition, the same general historical forces pushing Latin American economic and social development also pushed Brazil, only much harder after 1930. From the sixteenth century until the latter part of the nineteenth century the economic life of Brazil was dominated by gold mining and the production for export of sugar, coffee, cocoa, rubber, and hides. Brazil, as was the case in almost all colonial countries, supplied the raw materials for the industrial production of the more developed countries and in turn imported finished products.

While a few Brazilians in the colonial period became very wealthy on this relationship, they made little effort to invest this wealth productively. Much of it was consumed in maintaining a high standard of living. The revolution of 1821, which brought formal independence, did not alter this pattern.

The social system which supported this pattern was based in agriculture, unequal, and dominated by a feudal aristocracy. The Roman Catholic church mirrored the pattern. It was hierarchical, state-supported, and aloof from the vast majority of Brazilians whose popular religion saw them through life's passages and taught them not to raise questions about inequities. State and church were two well-integrated parts of one system which benefited the ruling oligarchy and left the rest to subsist as they could on a limited range of basic necessities.

As the nineteenth century unfolded, some parts of Latin America began to attract foreign capital. In many countries there emerged a new elite based in expanding commerce; they were called "liberals," in contrast to the landed aristocracy who were known as "conservatives." The political history of the late nineteenth and early twentieth centuries in Latin America was dominated by conflict between liberals and conservatives as now one, now the other, gained control. The two elites had one thing in common, however—disdain for the Indians, mixed-bloods, peasants, and Afro-Americans who did their bidding.

During the early part of the twentieth century almost everywhere in the region liberals gained the upper hand and then joined forces with conservatives to form a fairly tight oligarchy. In Brazil liberal ascendancy is usually dated from 1930 when the export market for agricultural commodities collapsed in the Great Depression. Thereafter Brazil embarked on a period of industrialization marked by the substitution of domestically produced consumer goods for foreign imports.

Industrialization picked up steam in the late 1940s and 1950s fueled by deliberate government policies to restrict imports, to stimulate demand, and to encourage domestic production of consumer durables such as automobiles and electrical equipment.

Important in this strategy were TNCs such as International Electric and executives such as Alan who were called on to provide the needed capital-intensive technologies to advance the domestic production of consumer durables. Attracted by government policies and the prospect of substantial profits, TNCs answered the call. They thrived. What resulted was the cozy relationship, which Alan has inherited, between the TNCs and the small class of Brazilians who benefited from rapid growth and held political power.

Whether the eventual dominance of the TNCs had more to do with their ability to penetrate markets or the conscious choice of a few Brazilians to let them take over is a matter for economic debate. Whichever, today's reality is fairly clear. TNCs own about 50 percent of Brazil's total assets. Forty percent of its largest firms are TNC subsidiaries. TNCs dominate the most profitable sectors, such as automobiles, pharmaceuticals, and electrical equipment, leaving the production of less profitable, nondurable consumer goods to private Brazilian firms. Their domination has given them power over prices, which they have translated into what is known as monopoly profits.

In charging higher prices than would be normal in a more competitive situation and in turn realizing higher profits, TNCs help to redistribute income to the rich inside Brazil who own subsidiaries and to owners in the industrialized countries through repatriated profits. The skewed distribution of income and wealth characteristic of the colonial period has become a seemingly permanent inheritance, even though a few poor people have entered the ranks of the new elite.

During the 1960s Brazil's industrialization slowed down. The Brazilian military, always an important source of stability, stepped in and governed with severe repression, justifying civil rights abuses in the name of national security and the fight against communism. That pattern of military take-over and its justification were widespread in Latin America. As Alan has learned from reading a number of recent documents, in 1985 civilian rule, or at least the veneer thereof, returned to Brazil. Human rights violations were greatly reduced and a measure of democracy was instituted. Effective power, however, still rested with a coalition of military men, bureaucrats, industrial leaders, and wealthy landowners. Little structural change occurred except for the adoption of a new constitution by the Congress. What little energy there was for substantive change was siphoned-off as the new civilian leadership became emboiled in accusations of corruption with one president, Fernando Collor de Mello, being impeached in 1992.

In the early and middle 1970s the generals and their economic advisers did manage to set Brazil on another growth spurt. But this spurt ended in the late 1970s with rising oil prices and world recession. In the 1980s the problem became the massive debt which Brazil had run up in the 1970s. The debt problem plagues many poorer countries today, but Brazil's is the biggest of all, $122 billion in 1990, up from $64 billion in 1980.

During the 1980s Brazilian economic policies shifted to adjust the economic life of the country to pay the debt. By devaluing the currency and restraining consumption, policies mandated by the International Monetary Fund that the U.S. government controls, exports increased and imports decreased. The crisis subsided for the time being, but the effects of these policies on the poor, who gained little if anything from incurring the debt, were tragic. They were in effect made to foot a large part of the bill through lower wages, higher prices, increased unemployment, and more emphasis on cash crops and exports.

The U.S. government has had an important role in all this. The United States has supported the Brazilian government through a succession of military and civilian regimes. It has furthered the penetration of the Brazilian economy by U.S.-based TNCs. It has trained Brazilian and other Latin American army leaders and provided them with military equipment. Finally, it has ensured "stability" in the region through direct intervention, as in the overthrow of Jacabo Arbenz in Guatemala in 1954 and Salvador Allende in Chile in 1973, and through "low intensity warfare." The latter is a strategy to destabilize potentially hostile regimes, for example, the Sandinistas in Nicaragua during the 1980s. Combined with military support of friendly regimes, for instance, El Salvador, Guatemala, and to a degree even Brazil, "stability" is assured. Until recently, the U.S. government had been doing all this in the name of the East/West conflict and national security, maintaining that friendly governments were democratic and capitalist and that popular movements keyed to the interests of the poor were totalitarian and communist. With the apparent end of the cold war, Alan must weigh these claims carefully and ask himself if this strategy really ensures long-range stability.

THE REALITY OF POVERTY

Statistics offer some indication of Brazil's two worlds. As Alan learned from the report prepared for Brazil's president, the richest 1 percent of Brazilians receive about 17 percent of the national income, while the poorest 50 percent receive 11 percent. Inflation rates during the 1980s ranged from a low of 11 percent in 1980 to 1,795 percent in 1989. During the same period the real minimum salary fell 40 percent, and the number of Brazilians living under the poverty line grew from 24 percent to 39 percent.

But abstract statistics do not reveal the misery and suffering that Alan Johnson could not have avoided on his business trips. Occasionally such things as mud slides in Rio de Janeiro kill enough shanty dwellers to attract media attention. For the most part, however, the poor are invisible and silent, eking out a subsistence on marginal land or muddling through in urban slums. The truth is that one-third of Brazil's families exist in wretched and miserable poverty with little hope for improvement.

One element in this tragic picture is directly relevant to Alan. In small part the misery of Brazil's urban poor is attributable to the demand which TNCs such as International Electric stimulate through advertising. The poor no less than their better-off cousins develop a "need" for television sets. Food is traded off for a television set in the family budget, and hunger increases. Although the effect is seldom linked to the cause, for Alan's company to increase its sales is to decrease nutritional standards further.

Alan encounters and will continue to encounter conflicting interpretations of this poverty. For supporters of Brazil's "economic miracle" it is temporary. It is the inevitable state of affairs which always accompanies rapid economic growth. These people argue that the need to depress consumption and to increase savings in order to generate capital creates great inequality for a limited time period, as it did in the United States and Western Europe during their industrial revolutions. This short-term side-effect will eventually be overcome as the wealth and income generated by growth trickle down to the poor. When that happens the distribution of income and wealth will improve of its own accord. Thus the antidote for poverty is more rapid growth. This is best achieved by social stability, TNC and World Bank investment, rewards sufficient to persuade entrepreneurs to take risks, and government policies which stimulate demand for consumer durables and protect Brazilian industries.

Alan may wonder why this trickle-down process has been so slow to take effect. Yes, it is true that a few have become fantastically wealthy, and a few more have shifted from the land and found work. Still the reality for the overwhelming majority of poor is the same grinding existence.

In contrast to the official explanations of economic theory, Alan hears from those who hold that the bottom 40 to 60 percent of Brazilian society will remain poor so long as power is wielded by a narrow oligarchy and

TNCs buttressed by U.S. military might. There are indeed gains from economic growth, but poverty will persist if these gains are siphoned off by a few, taken out of the country in TNC profits and in deposits to Swiss bank accounts, spent on luxury consumption, and invested in inappropriate technology.

To make matters worse, worsening terms of trade for primary agricultural and mining exports relative to manufactured imports continue to funnel the gains of international trade to the industrialized countries. This brute fact and the need to repay staggering debts keep most poor countries on a treadmill of dependency. They must export more and more to import the same or less, and the anomaly of prime land being used to produce speciality agricultural commodities for export while poor people go landless and without staples will continue.

Perhaps Alan will come to think of Brazil's economy in terms of a closed circle. During the colonial period the circle was tiny. Using slave labor, wealthy landowners exported raw materials and agricultural commodities and imported luxury goods. The circle of the well off increased somewhat with the addition of the new urban commercial class and their military allies, but the post-1930 policies kept the circle closed by concentrating the gains of growth in the hands of a few.

Executives, such as Alan, were invited into the circle because they provided access to financial capital and the technical expertise to produce and market the consumer durables those inside the circle wanted and could afford. These executives also fortified the circle. The gains they brought were appropriated by the few. Their capital-intensive technologies created relatively few jobs so the circle did not appreciably expand. The military preserved the status quo. In simple fact the TNCs served themselves and a few in Brazil, all the time reinforcing the circular pattern.

Moreover, Alan will have to confront what should be for him a very disturbing conclusion. There is no particular reason to expect TNCs to change practices honed to perfection in developed economies just because those practices do not fit the needs of the poor. To change would mean huge new costs developing less capital-intensive technologies and basic products, both of which would be inappropriate to their primary markets. Risk would increase because TNCs are not adept at labor-intensive technologies and the mass production of basics.

In fact it is easier for TNCs to manage economies such as Brazil's so that these economies consume what TNCs already produce well. TNCs control modern technology. They have the capacity to set prices to gain monopoly profits. They can create demand through superior marketing skills and advertising. They are large enough to realize the reduced costs of large-scale operations. Finally, they have superior access to financing, the capability to bail out subsidiaries, and the resources to acquire local firms.

TNCs simply are not geared to the needs of poor people. They never have been and never will be as long as capital-intensive markets are their main arenas and profits their major preoccupation. Poor people in countries like Brazil need labor-intensive technologies. They do not have sufficient purchasing power to meet the profit and growth needs of the TNCs. To secure a change in policy and to gain purchasing power they will have to be admitted to the closed circle or force their way into it. For them to be admitted means a redistribution of income and wealth which is of little interest to TNCs, not to mention local elites. Redistribution would in the short run only mean a reduction in consumption and a loss of TNC business as more basics were consumed. Forcing their way in means revolution with its instabilities and threats to growth and profits. It is thus in the immediate interest of TNCs both to promote the status quo and to sell consumer durables to the wealthy.

THE POOR AS THE POINT OF DEPARTURE

Assuming for the sake of discussion that Alan had the power to embark on development plans which did not depend on trickle-down economics but took the poor as their point of departure, what are a few things he could do?

In rural areas, a three-pronged strategy called "integrated rural development" has gained strong support. The first prong of this strategy is concentration on smaller-scale, more labor-intensive and appropriate production which generates more employment and productivity than larger-scale, more capital-intensive production for export. Agrarian reform is crucial. It includes land redistribution and the provision of financial, legal, and technical services to ensure that newly acquired land is used productively and does not revert to former owners.

The second prong involves the integrated improvement of the various dimensions of community life. Nutrition, health, sanitation, education, and family planning are simultaneously addressed along with the promotion of cooperative endeavors and the encouragement of a new sense of self-worth. Some of the more creative plans focus on women as the primary agents of social change.

The third prong is the building of a framework for development by concentrating on the institutions and skills necessary for sustained growth. Individuals must learn the techniques of productive agriculture, sanitation, nutrition, and family planning. They must master the organization of regional structures, local cooperatives, and volunteer associations.

In urban areas, concentrating on labor-intensive production with massive subsidies to develop intermediate technologies would be one way to create more jobs. Combined with some form of income and wealth redistribution to broaden the base of consumers, enough demand could be stimulated to soak up the output of labor-intensive production.

Alan might have to conclude for obvious reasons that prospects for development plans which take the poor as their point of departure are not bright. Still, experiments with integrated rural development and the recent movement away from repressive military dictatorships are at least a few steps in the right direction. The electoral process which brings new administrations to Washington at least every eight years also leaves hopes for a changed U.S. role.

The possibility of a new era in Brazil, Latin America, and the poor world generally could even mean opportunities for Alan and International Electric. Perhaps Alan's task within his firm is not the expansion of the market for more television sets but research into ways that a TNC could provide appropriate technologies and financial services to the poor yet still make a profit. He probably will not have an easy time persuading his associates at International Electric, however. That is one reason why their education is so crucial.

THE MISSION OF THE CHURCH

Using his free time well, Alan Johnson managed to touch base with a remarkable cross section of Brazilian Christians. In Doug Williams he encounters Protestant evangelical Christianity with its individualistic bent. The Reverend Paulo de Souza and Father Antonio Cardosa represent the liberation movements in Latin America. Finally, in the Reverend Benjamin Villaca, Alan sees an evolutionary, middle-of-the-road approach stressing political moderation and education. By taking time to experience these perspectives firsthand, Alan immeasurably enhances his understanding. Indeed he represents a model of dialogue which he can encourage members of his congregation and business colleagues to follow.

Protestant Evangelical Christianity

This form of Christianity has enjoyed remarkable growth in Latin America spurred by missionaries from the United States such as Doug. The reasons for its growth are not hard to find. The traditional aloofness of its clergy and its alliance with the landed aristocracy had for centuries put the Roman Catholic church out of touch with much of Latin American society. Moral values supportive of market capitalism and the tendency to stay out of economics and politics give the evangelicals a natural affinity with the new commercial class. The evangelical approach with its message of individual salvation, its warm fellowship, and its otherworldly concerns appeals to poor people in an unstable and repressive political atmosphere.

For Doug Williams the mission of the church is set in Jesus' Great Commission to his disciples (Matt. 10:35ff.): To preach the Gospel of the kingdom of God. The Gospel Doug preaches is one which appears to divide human reality into personal and social realms, the former the province of the church with its message of individual salvation, the latter the province of civil authorities with their obligation to maintain order. While he is critical of Brazilian inequality and preaches to the poor the Gospel of liberation from sin, he is even more critical of Christians who take direct action to end social abuses and liberate the poor politically. In the final analysis, Christians are to be subject to the governing authorities (Rom. 13:1ff.), and the church's task is to bind the wounds of society's victims and help them to find salvation.

For Doug the way to change society is to change people. Convert individuals to Jesus Christ and the "born again" life, and they will in turn change society from within. To superimpose social change on sinful people is fruitless, for sin will inevitably reassert itself.

Although he does not say it explicitly and is even critical at points, Doug seems generally supportive of the social status quo. The closed circle does not bother him, probably because he considers it outside of his purview and irrelevant to his task. "Life in Christ," he might say, "can be lived inside or outside the circle, it makes no difference."

Much of what Doug preaches is very traditional. Alan needs to ask him further, however, about his tendency to separate individual and social realms and his neglect of social justice questions. Alan might want to say that Jesus Christ is Lord of both realms and works to bring liberation from political oppression as well as from sin. He might question Doug on the mission of the church and whether it is so exclusively tied to individual conversion. And will saved souls in fact be agents of social change or supporters of both the status quo and the closed circle? Finally, Alan may wonder if the Gospel Doug preaches does not act as a drug salving only the wounds of injustice and ignoring their causes.

Liberation Theology

Liberation theology is a movement that began in Latin America. It is represented in the case by the Reverend Paulo Souza and Father Antonio Cardosa of the Inter-Faith Task Force. This movement arose in Roman Catholic circles, but its rapid growth and popular appeal have carried it to Protestants. As a result, ecumenical groups, such as the Inter-Faith Task Force, have developed. Today liberation theology stands in tension with both traditional Latin American Catholicism, with its hierarchical structure and popular piety, and with evangelical Protestantism, which arose out of the North American experience and its concentration on individual salvation.

In Brazil liberation theologians Leonardo and Clodovis Boff have been especially prominent. Several Brazilian cardinals, for example Aloisio Lorscheider and Paulo Evaristo Arns, have also lent the movement support. The case itself offers a good summary of liberation themes, and a further discussion of liberation theology can be found in this volume in the commentary on "Vietnam's Children."

Liberation theology is an interpretation of Christian faith which emerges from the experience of the poor. It seeks to empower poor people to develop a new consciousness about reality and their faith for the purpose of changing the conditions which oppress them. By liberation three things are meant, according to Peruvian Gustavo Gutiérrez: (1) liberation from social, economic, and political injustice; (2) liberation from false consciousness— an example of false consciousness might be the religious and economic ideologies which support the closed circle of Brazilian inequality and oppression; and (3) liberation from sin. God works on all three levels of liberation.

Central to these understandings of liberation is a critique of existing social institutions and the ideologies which sustain them; this critique is carried out from the perspective of the poor. The thought of Karl Marx is at times used selectively for this social criticism because it can be a helpful tool for understanding the economic and political injustice which the poor experience. Following Marx, liberationists frequently take an historical approach, tracing the path of oppression from the colonial period to the so-called national security state of the present day.

Liberation theology is a "bottom-up" perspective and may as a result seem foreign to Alan, the members of his church, and his business associates. Not only is existing reality viewed from the angle of the poor, but the poor are also to be the agents of their own liberation. Liberated from social repression, false consciousness, and incompletely from sin, the poor will take charge of their own futures. This process begins in small groups called *comunidades de base* (base communities) stressing prayer, worship, Bible study, and community. First instituted in Brazil, base communities are a platform for broader liberation, although they face tough opposition from a conservative government and church hierarchy.

While violence is not ruled out, most liberationists envision liberation as proceeding nonviolently. The overthrow of ruling oligarchies and the shape of liberated societies are both left purposely vague. Liberationists refuse to be "top-down" social engineers. The shape of the new society, they insist, must emerge in the process of liberation from the old and be tailored to the many different situations of Latin America. Social ownership is frequently mentioned although a full-blown socialism is usually rejected in favor of mixed public/private ownership.

The biblical basis for the liberation project is God's preferential option for the poor. God, according to liberation theologians, has taken the side of the poor. God has made this option clear in freeing the Hebrew slaves from bondage in Egypt, in the teachings of the prophets, and preeminently in Jesus Christ. Jesus reading from the Book of Isaiah in Luke 4:18-19 (cited in the text of this case) has become perhaps the most quoted text.

The mission of the church is to be God's servant for liberation. The church cannot liberate the poor, but it can identify and suffer with them, look at reality from the same angle, work for justice, and provide enabling resources. Change will come when the poor take the necessary actions.

Individual conversion to Jesus Christ, as in the Gospel which Doug Williams preaches, is not sufficient for social change because it ignores the first two forms of liberation and the social impediments to the third in its concentration on the individual.

Liberationists are, of course, critical of Brazil's closed circle and the role TNCs play in it. There is some tendency to see TNCs as villains, but it is the overall injustice of the closed circle which is their target. TNCs do not figure in the vision of the liberated future because in the past TNCs have had so little to offer a process of change from the bottom up.

To executives such as Alan, liberationists might appear simplistic and utopian. They seem to underestimate the difficulty of accumulating capital and organizing the factors of production. Their criticism of TNCs overlooks the valuable contributions TNCs make in assisting rapid economic growth.

On a theological level, Alan will want to ask Paulo and Antonio if they are not subverting the church's traditional message of liberation from sin and replacing it with a political ideology. Alan will have to think through the charge that liberation theologians are guilty of reductionism—that is, that they reduce sin to social institutions, the Gospel to the struggle for justice, and Jesus' message to partisan politics. Finally, Alan must also ask questions about the use of Marx's thought. Is it compatible with the Gospel? Does it not at least carry the implication of leading toward violent revolution? How much does it control the theology?

It may be difficult for Alan and most North Americans to understand this perspective. What he can understand, however, is what he can see: the degrading poverty of Latin America which is the parent of liberation theology. Whatever he advocates to his two worlds, he cannot overlook this poverty without doing violence to his conscience.

Moderate and Reformist Christianity

This form of Christianity seems to be the vantage point of Benjamin Villaca. The case suggests that he comes out of what in the United States would be called a "mainline" denomination. Benjamin is clear on the mission of the church. Perhaps referring to Doug Williams, he rejects the individualistic escapism of conservatives and Pentecostals. But in the same breath, perhaps referring to Paulo de Souza and Antonio Cardosa, he dismisses the "ecumenical radicals." To his way of thinking they are tied to Marxism, too prone to violence, and finally irrelevant.

He then carves out for himself an evolutionary perspective. Implied in his understanding is a theological balance of individual and social dimensions and realism about the human situation. The persistence of human sin is assumed, and agents of both social change and the status quo must be carefully monitored.

The path of change is evolutionary and is best traversed along the route of education and evangelism. Indeed, those are the two main tasks of the church, although it would not be outside the bounds of his perspective for the church to engage in political action of a moderate, reformist type. He is encouraged by the liberalizations introduced by the government and would seem to support the return to a semblance of democracy.

Given the tenor of his remarks, he is probably in general agreement with the rapid growth policies of successive Brazilian governments, although he would no doubt be critical of the great inequalities and abuses of human rights which have accompanied those policies. Included in his support might also be general affirmation of TNCs and certainly the expectation that they would be open to reform and possibly even agents of a more human direction. He says as much when he asks for financial support.

As with the others, Alan needs to ask Villaca questions. Can the closed circle of Brazilian life be opened by reform? Would it not be better, Alan might think, either to let the current policies run their course with the hope that some benefits would trickle down to the poor, or to seek radical social change and some sort of socialistic alternative? The former might at least bring economic growth and the latter greater equality. Benjamin's reformist perspective runs the danger of achieving neither and being overwhelmed in the process by more extreme options. Finally, Alan may wonder whether Benjamin's perspective, like that of Doug Williams, does not implicitly support the status quo by claiming it is capable of reform.

ALAN JOHNSON'S PROBLEM

So whose worldview should Alan represent? What should he report to his colleagues at International Electric and what to his church's Social Concerns Committee? The same questions are, of course, directed to every North American Christian, if for no other reason than the massive influence of the U.S. government and economy in Latin America.

One thing for sure, Alan cannot return to the charity-based perspective which has dominated his wealthy church in the past. That perspective deals with symptoms, not causes, and is not very relevant to the massive suffering in Latin America. Likewise, business as usual at International Electric is not an option unless Alan wants to turn a deaf ear to the cries he has heard in Brazil. Alan hardly seems callous to the suffering he has witnessed, so it seems that he must either find a way for International Electric to become less of the problem and more of the solution, or resign.

Whatever Alan decides, one thing he can do is share his new insights. In his explorations he has shown great openness in seeking to augment his understanding with genuine dialogue.

In assessing Alan's dilemma and the many perspectives he has encountered, the Christian concern for the poor should play an important normative role. It is a concern with many dimensions: greater equality, political freedom, the correction of human rights abuses, the provision of basic necessities over the long haul, and participation in community. In showing concern for the poor it is not enough to be well intentioned. The task of building durable and equitable political and economic institutions must be added to right intentions in order for justice to be a reality in Brazil.

ADDITIONAL RESOURCES

Berryman, Phillip. *Liberation Theology.* New York: Pantheon; Oak Park, IL: Meyer-Stone, 1987.

Gutiérrez, Gustavo. *A Theology of Liberation.* Maryknoll, NY: Orbis Books, 1973; rev. ed., 1988.

Hewlitt, Sylvia Ann. *The Cruel Dilemmas of Development: Twentieth-Century Brazil.* New York: Basic Books, 1980.

Johnston, Bruce F., and William C. Clark. *Redesigning Rural Development: A Strategic Perspective.* Baltimore: Johns Hopkins University Press, 1982.

Newfarmer, Richard, ed. *Profits, Progress and Poverty.* Notre Dame, IN: University of Notre Dame Press, 1985.

Scheper-Hughes, Nancy. *Death Without Weeping: The Violence of Everyday Life in Brazil.* Berkeley, CA: The University of California Press, 1992.

United States Department of State. *Sustaining a Consistent Policy in Central America.* Special report no. 124, 1985.

Video: "Capital Sins: Authoritarianism and Democratization" (Program 2). Series title, *Americas.* Alexandria, VA: PBS Video. The entire series is relevant to Latin American issues.

Case

The Agenda: Preference
for the Poorest?

"The first item on the agenda is Don Brown's report from the Fundraising Committee on the capital campaign," declared Will Jennings, a black
Episcopal priest who, as chairperson of the Board of Trustees of the Community Land Trust, chaired its monthly meeting.

"Well, you'll all be pleased to hear that the capital campaign raised
$420,000 on the condition that we buy land and houses in the West End
south of Grant Street and build or rehab for $35,000 or less," said Don
proudly. "We had a large number of contributors, and eleven large corporate gifts. All six Committee members worked very hard. As you can see in
the written reports I am handing out, the Fundraising Committee suggests
that it become a standing committee of the Board, with its members Board
members."

At that Kitty Bailey, the attractive, middle-aged black woman who had
been executive director of the Land Trust for seven years, snapped to
attention. She had had several run-ins with Don since he assumed control
of the Fundraising Committee. Don had come to the Trust as a volunteer
through a social action project in his church. He had recently retired as
vice-president of a large multi-national corporation. When Kitty asked Don
to take on the much needed capital campaign, he recruited friends to fill
the other five positions on the Fundraising Committee. In Kitty's opinion,
the other members of the Committee were like Don—white, well-to-do
suburbanites. She was convinced, however, that they were neither familiar
with black urban poverty nor comfortable with the Trust's poor black
residents who, under the by-laws, made up the majority of the Board. Kitty

admitted that having spent twenty years escaping from the poverty of the projects of the West End, she was perhaps over-sensitive to slights to the poor black residents. But she suspected Don's proposal was a move toward a by-laws revision lowering the level of resident participation on the Board.

Before the applause died down for the extraordinarily high sum raised—more than twice the goal of the campaign—Frank Hart, the attorney on the Board, asked a question. Most of the other Board members had thought Kitty's recruiting of Frank when she first accepted the directorship was very impressive; he was a partner in the largest, most prestigious law firm in the city. Few knew that Kitty and her husband and Frank and his wife were good friends, or that Kitty and her husband were godparents to the black child adopted into Frank's and Tina's white family ten years before.

"Don, that's a fantastic amount you have raised," praised Frank. "But why the restrictions? Why only south of Grant Street, when you know that we have options on at least four properties north of Grant? And why the $35,000 limit on building and rehab costs? That's less than the last Audley Street house. Who set these restrictions?" asked Frank.

"The donors. No restrictions, no money," said Don.

"Don," said Frank, "I've looked through the report, and I don't see a donor list. How much money is restricted, by what donors, and why do those particular donors want us to work only south of Grant Street?"

Don replied, "The Committee made a decision to accept the restriction in order to qualify for large corporate donations. There is at least twenty years of work for the Trust in rehabbing and building low-income housing south of Grant, so the restriction is no handicap."

Morita Adams, the most outspoken of the resident members, declared, "Well, it don't take no brains to figure out where that restricted money comes from. Who wants to keep the Trust from buying parcels north of Grant? The developers, the big real estate companies, and their banks. I bet Koul Brothers Construction, Park Place Developers, and State Bank want to expand their Liberty Street project south."

Sarah Hawkins, a white Methodist minister and a new Board member, looked bewildered. "I don't understand. Those groups have lots more money than the Trust does, and can outbid us for any piece of property they want. Why should they worry about us? Property values all over the West End are so low that even outbidding us they can get anything they want for a song."

Will Jennings explained, "Developers need large tracts of land down-town, Sarah, because they build for the upper-middle class. They have learned that the white middle class will not buy into a neighborhood near poor black neighbors. For whites to move downtown, developers need large enclaves of exclusively middle-class housing. The Trust was set up in 1978 to stop gentrification in the West End of downtown, so that what remained of black low-income housing would not disappear, leaving blacks dispersed and homeless. When the Trust buys the land, it legally separates the land from the house and sells the house, retaining a repurchase option on any future sale. We only lease the land to the house buyer for $1 per year. Our low-income residents have decent housing, the security of home ownership, and the ability to leave those homes to their children and grandchildren. However, once the Trust gets a piece of property in the center of a neighborhood, the developers have to look elsewhere, because they won't ever get the whole area."

Don strenuously objected to Will's explanation. "Look, the developers aren't villains here. The city needs to develop the downtown ring in order to expand the tax base so it has the money to fund social service projects in places like the West End. The condos and townhouses, the new shopping areas, are good for the downtown and good for the black residents too. You make it sound like a good thing to have miles of rotting and abandoned housing that only the desperately poor would consider. If blocks of rotting, empty buildings north of Grant Street are torn down and replaced by new housing and commercial developments, then all the West End will be safer, more attractive, and more prosperous."

Kitty impatiently interjected, "But Don, how can it be a good thing for the poor black population to have their housing bought and torn down to build upscale communities where they can't live and where they aren't even welcome to walk because they are regarded as potential criminals? Last year when the Liberty Street development opened, I went up on my lunch hour to look it over. Two uniformed guards demanded ID, then followed me—only me, not any of the whites walking around—up and down the street. And I was a middle-aged black woman in a business suit. Imagine how they'd respond at night to young black men who wandered in for ice cream at the deli!"

Frank repeated his question about the amount of the total that was restricted. After hearing that $200,000 of the $420,000 was pledged on condition that the Trust abandon the West End north of Grant Street, Frank introduced a motion that the Board decline the $200,000 restricted donation and use the remaining $220,000 to implement existing Board policy and goals. To Don's obvious dismay, the motion passed nine to six.

SAFETY AND DEVELOPMENT: FOR WHOM?

Will Jennings nodded to Jim Meadows, the Trust's construction supervisor, as he addressed the Board. "The next item on the agenda is the building inspection campaign announced by City Council last week. Jim will tell us how it affects us."

"Well, as far as I can tell," said Jim, "if the city inspectors aren't on the up and up, we have some serious problems, especially the six vacant properties we recently bought and the fourteen on which we have options. Frank tells me city law allows the City to do just about anything it wants with buildings that are unsafe to live in. Being unsafe to live in can mean

anything from not complying with the latest building code to being struc-
turally dangerous. The worst case is that they condemn all our properties
and institute immediate demolition. Almost as bad would be to give us
thirty to sixty days to complete repairs or face demolition. We could rehab
from two to four houses in sixty days, but never all of them. If the City gives
us a year, though, we could rehab them all and continue much as we have,
with only a little more attention to the time between purchase and rehabbing."

Chairperson Will Jennings asked, "What do you mean, if the City is on
the up and up? Is there something fishy here?"

Kitty intervened to add, "There are strong rumors and suspicions in all
the low-income housing organizations downtown that City Council is
working with the developers on this one. Other low-income housing
groups have also been buying dilapidated and condemned buildings from
both private owners and from the City with the idea of keeping upscale
developers out of the West End. Due to a shortage of rehab money, three or
four buildings sit empty for every one that gets rehabbed and rented out to
low-income people. A lot of people think the City means to use inspectors
to mandate demolition of those buildings in the name of safety and face-
lifting the City. The real object would be to increase the tax revenues by
making the advocates for the poor give up properties that prevent upscale
development of poor neighborhoods."

Father Phil Cahill, a white pastor from St. Joseph's, the Catholic parish
in the West End, suggested, "Let's not get paranoid. We should follow the
law and assume that we will be safe."

Kitty responded, "The problem is, Father, we don't have the time to
follow all the building codes in the law. Most of the buildings in the city
aren't up to code because only new buildings have been inspected for
decades. Even now they are only going to inspect empty housing and
housing owned by non-profits. Does St. Joe's or the rectory have a sprinkler
system as required for buildings in which public meetings are held? An
electrical system with breakers, not fuses? Nothing we own now is up to
code; if it were, we would have sold it to a resident. In the year we need to
meet code, this campaign could demolish all the West End's low-income
housing before we can buy and rehab it. The irony is that despite City
Council's rhetoric about making downtown housing safer for the poor, few
of the real firetraps where the kids have lead poisoning, the furnaces don't
work, and the stairwells are rotted through, will even be inspected because
they are occupied and privately owned."

Will addressed the group. "Can we agree that until we have further
information, Kitty should employ as many paid and volunteer crews as she
can locate to rehab our buildings?" All nodded immediately, and Kitty
began a list of contacts to call.

Morita raised her hand asked, "I need to put my kids to bed in thirty
minutes. What's this last item on the agenda about target population?"

THE POOR, THE POORER, AND THE POOREST

Will responded, "Thanks, Morita, for calling us back to the time. Father Phil and Sarah wanted to address the Board concerning their unease at the change in the Trust's target population over the last few years. Father Phil, Sarah?"

Father Phil recalled, "There have been a lot of changes in the Trust in the last years. And I know that some of them were necessary. We weren't very organized before Kitty assumed the directorship. Seven years ago we had ten houses and three apartment buildings. Most of them were in terrible shape, and we didn't have the money to fix any of them. We were slum landlords, though we didn't make any money. We veterans on the Board reluctantly went along with selling the apartment buildings in order to concentrate on single-family home ownership. There are other organizations that concentrate on housing the elderly poor, the alcoholics, addicts, and mentally incompetent who can never be candidates for home ownership. *This* organization should stick with its stated purpose of providing home ownership to the poor. But in the last three years our average cost for houses at purchase rose from $1,500 to $6,000, and our average rehabbing cost rose from $15,000 to nearly $32,000. The Trust was begun as a form of Christian outreach to the poorest. But the poorest cannot afford monthly payments of over $200 for mortgage, taxes, and insurance, which is what we have to charge on these houses on twenty-year mortgages at 3 percent. Our ministry must be to the poorest of the poor."

Sarah added, "I know of two families in the West End who want to buy homes in the Trust but have been priced out by the increases. Some of our people just cannot afford more than $75-100 per month, because the family income is $600 per month or less. Many of them make only minimum wage. Most can't get forty hours of work a week. Those who do get forty hours still don't even bring home $150 per week. These people are the real poor, not people who make $900 per month or more and can pay $200 per month."

Morita waved her hand to speak, but before Will could nod another resident, Carla Hancock, who rarely spoke, burst into speech. "My brother bought one of those first houses for $16,000. Mine cost me $32,000, twice as much. But mine is a house to be proud of; it ain't falling apart like his. All his got was new windows and doors, the roof patched, and a new sink and toilet. Now his plumbing and electric fell apart, his roof leaks something awful, all the floors sag, and they's afraid to use the toilet for fear of falling in the basement. Lots of poor people can't afford houses like mine. But those first houses was a rip-off, 'cause poor people can't afford to both buy 'em and fix 'em decent. My brother Cass figures he got took again. He's still living in a slum, not a decent house. And he owe forever."

Frank Hart added, "Father, I agree that the price of the houses is an important issue, and that we can't let it get too high. But if we are ever going to help the West End become a strong, stable neighborhood with decent housing, we need to offer housing that continues to be both decent and affordable over the long run. Carla is right. Most of those early owners couldn't afford both the mortgage and the major repairs necessary. If we do the major rehab and reroof, rewire, replumb, brace the floors, replaster where needed, and put in a new furnace and replacement windows, the new owners will have ten to twenty years before they face major repairs. By then their income will have increased, if only by inflation, and the fixed amount of the mortgage will be a smaller part of their income. With really good housing available, those families who are making it are more likely to stay in the neighborhood, to fight to keep it free of drugs and crime, and to care about the schools and the parks. We have to find ways of making communities work, not just hand out leaky lifeboats to drowning people. That way we never get ahead, and they're never saved."

As the clock struck nine and the Board prepared to adjourn, Sarah suggested that perhaps the Trust should commit itself to helping as many of the "least of the brethren" as possible and trust God to make it work. Will announced that this issue would be the first agenda item next month. Each of them should think and pray to prepare for a decision.

Frank, who took turns with Kitty driving to the Board meetings, dropped off Morita and Carla at their homes near the Trust office, and then headed north toward Kitty's home. Once on the highway, he asked how she felt about the discussion on serving the poorest. "It's a real dilemma for me," she replied. "I really do believe there are individual and social obligations to serve those who are in greatest need. But I can't see overlooking the many who could take care of themselves really well if they just had a little help in the beginning. I could spend all our yearly budget on food and shelter and medical and psychiatric help for Dan, Morita's ex-husband, who is certainly among the poorest. But he's been so damaged by crack that he'll always be dependent. I'm not arguing that he should be ignored. It's just that I can't believe God wants us to ignore the Moritas who are left to raise the kids in order to serve the Dans of the world."

Frank responded, "I have always thought of this work in terms of long-term justice, of instituting a process that frees all the oppressed. But it seems to me that if two people have fallen in a hole, and I only have enough strength to pull one out, that I should pull out the one who is most likely to help me pull the other one out, and not the one who is weakest. But now I'm not sure we have looked at the whole picture. We can probably all agree that it would be wrong to focus on the hopelessly damaged, like Dan, and ignore the Moritas and their kids. But remember last year when you pointed out that our selection process for home ownership preferred welfare families over the working poor, because they often had as much or slightly more income, but also had Medicaid and income security that the working poor don't? Your concerns then weren't all that different from those raised tonight." Troubled, he added, "Perhaps Sarah is right, and I don't have enough faith in God. Maybe the real issue for me is that I'm not sure I could sustain hope if I worked only with the poor who seem the most hopeless."

Kitty nodded, "I know what you mean. I'm glad we have a month to think about it."

Commentary

The Agenda: Preference for the Poorest?

The participants in this case would probably disagree as to what the specific issues in the case are. Perhaps most could agree that racism is one issue here, but the explanations of where the racism is illustrated might be very different. For example, Kitty might point to the proposal to dilute the black resident majority on the Board with white members of the fundraising commitee as racist, in that it would prevent the residents from controlling their own community. Don might see resistence to such a proposal as racist, in that persons who would contribute more to the organization were rejected in favor of those who would do less, on the basis of race. Many people might see no evidence of racism in this case because no person or group seems motivated by hatred based on race.

Some social analysts have insisted that the very character of racism has changed in U.S. society. They argue that racial injustice is no longer best understood in terms of racist intent, but of consequences, and that the inequality of persons of color in U.S. society is maintained no longer by segregation laws but by impersonal economic structures and practices which have been responsible for the formation of an underclass of persons of color. Structural aspects of postmodern capitalism, especially a permanent surplus of labor and low rates of economic growth, they argue further, obstruct efforts to eradicate or escape from that poverty-stricken underclass. Thus one of the implicit questions is whether any of the proposed actions in this case is racist, or whether the black poverty in the case merely reflects the effects of past racism in U.S. society. This question forms one aspect of the central question that has already been framed by the Board in terms of Christian spirituality and ethics: who are the poor?

LOVING GOD WHO LOVES THE POOR

The basic obligation of Christians, according to Jesus, is to love God with all our heart, all our soul, and all our mind, and to love our neighbor as ourselves. (Matt. 22:37-39) To love God is to commit ourselves to the fulfillment of God's intentions for creation, in which love of neighbor is central. It was Yahweh's action of rescuing the Hebrews from slavery in

Egypt that revealed the nature of Yahweh's love. In the same way, Jesus later taught that love of neighbor is demonstrated through meeting the needs of our neighbor, which thus gives a priority to the needy neighbor. To come to the aid of the needy takes precedence over formal worship. Jesus declared the good neighbor to be the Samaritan who stopped to aid the robbery victim. The priest and the Levite had passed by without helping because they were unwilling to risk the ritual uncleaness that would temporarily bar them from temple worship.

Many scriptural scholars note that Jesus' warning that it is easier for a camel to pass through the eye of a needle than for the rich to enter the realm of God may not have referred to the eye of a sewing needle, but to the pedestrian gate of a city, which was also called the "eye of a needle." The implication is clear. It would be difficult for a camel to enter the pedestrian gate. It might require kneeling, and it could not be done if the camel were carrying a full load on its sides. But it was certainly possible. The issue is not the size of the camel, but the attitude of the camel and how much unnecessary burden the camel carried. The implication, then, is that a radical conversion to a humble, unencumbered condition is necessary if the rich are to enter the realm of God. Part of that conversion involves aiding the needy. Members of the Community Land Trust Board agree that they, and all Christians, are called to a preferential option for the poor. That preference for the poor does not exclude love of other persons who are not poor, but does give priority to the needs of the poor because of their need.

The Board is called to reflect on what a preferential option for the poor means in terms of both the goals and the strategies to be pursued. Following their goal of "as many families as possible in home ownership," Don and the Fundraising Committee were willing to make compromises to restrict housing development to a limited section of the downtown West End. This is, of course, a worthy goal, but it assumes an understanding of poverty solely in material terms. Such thinking fails to understand that these people lack not only decent housing, but the ability to exercise responsibility for their community. They need better homes, and they need to build and direct their own community. Living in poverty over time robs individuals and communities of the ability to make choices, to control their own lives and communities. Unless poverty is actively resisted by communities, it makes persons powerless and dependent. Inevitably this powerlessness and dependence wear away feelings of both dignity and self-worth and the ability to feel beloved by God and other persons. Without these, communal bonds weaken and break. Involuntary poverty is sinful and affronts God our Creator/Parent because it kills and maims bodies and souls, individuals and communities.

The requirement that the black residents form the majority of the Board was undoubtedly chosen as part of a larger attempt to restore to individual poor black residents their ability to make decisions and control their lives and community. The requirement is, of course, not enough by itself to effect that goal but is part of a wider vision that aims to restore power and autonomy. At the Board meeting, the residents seem for the most part passive. Though they constitute a majority of the Board, only two speak. No resident is identified as chair of a committee. On the one hand, if this level of contribution to meetings is typical of the residents on the Board, it is not surprising that Don and his Committee may think they have more to offer the Community Land Trust Board. On the other hand, if the ravages of poverty are to be overcome, there must be a process in which the residents learn to discern and articulate the interests and aspirations of their community and then go on to achieve them. That process has the potential for providing the needed individual dignity and communal autonomy to reassert control over their lives and community.

JUSTICE AND CHARITY

Although the Fundraising Committee probably does not see itself this way, its goal seems to be more akin to traditional notions of charity than to social justice as understood by many Christian churches today. One of the most obvious differences between justice and charity is how power is distributed. Justice distributes power so that the weak become stronger and better able to care for themselves. Charity meets people's immediate needs in ways that keep them dependent. Members of the Fundraising Committee are well intentioned, and they are attempting to alleviate the poverty of their black neighbors by providing opportunities for home ownership. They undoubtedly see their own relationship to the black residents who benefit from the Land Trust as based in love. But real love is effective. In this case, effectiveness would include empowerment of the residents. The Fundraising Committee could have accompanied their bid for Board membership with a proposal to expand the number of residents on the Board to preserve the majority, or with some alternative aimed at preserving resident responsibility. The effects of the proposed deal—$200,000 for a Land Trust retreat from north of Grant Street—work against empowerment by dividing the existing West End community, benefitting the Trust by the sacrifice of that part of the community north of Grant Street.

HONESTY IN POLITICS

The City Council decision to inspect residential property in the greater downtown area, if it is followed up so as to force owners to fix unsafe buildings or forfeit them, is an ambitious undertaking with the potential to improve the living standards of many poor residents. But a policy is only as good as its procedures. The procedures guiding implementation of this new policy are not clear. As Jim Meadows says, the new policy could force the Trust to speed up the process between purchase and rehab. This would mean the Trust and other low-income organizations would have fewer empty, rotting buildings to become eyesores or havens for drug dealers and gang violence. This effect of the inspection policy would greatly benefit the West End. The new policy could also be implemented in ways that demolish whole neighborhoods and encourage rebuilding of upscale, rather than low income, housing. Whatever procedures are implemented must, in order to be just, be imposed upon all groups equally. If Kitty is right that the inspection will only include vacant buildings and those owned by non-profits, the inspection would be discriminatory and would undermine its supposed intent to protect the poor.

The interest of the City Council in expanding the tax rolls through bringing more middle-class persons downtown is understandable. Since the late sixties, the shift of the middle class to the suburbs, the move of many industrial plants to developing nations, and the relocation of many corporate headquarters to smaller cities or to suburbs of large cities have severely shrunk the tax base of many cities. The decaying infrastructure of many large U.S. cities—their bridges, sewers, subways, streets, and harbors—also began to demand increasingly large infusions of capital.

Growing unemployment, gentrification trends, and federal cuts in welfare and food stamps have increased the need for low-income housing at precisely the same time that cities are hard pressed to continue basic services such as fire, police, street repair, and schools. The tremendous rise in crime and the consequent rise in the expenses of the criminal justice system, added to the expanded medical costs of both the AIDS epidemic and illegal drug use, have brought many large cities to the breaking point. The federal government has also contributed directly to the housing crisis faced by the poor. Under the Reagan administration, the low-income housing projects in the federal Department of Housing and Urban Development's planning and implementation pipeline dropped from just under five hundred in 1980 to fewer than seventy-five in 1988. Those few projects that were implemented under the Bush administration were disproportionately restricted to the elderly and the disabled.

Few cities are able to take on the increased burden of funding sufficient low-income housing to accommodate those in need. Many cities see luring middle-class persons back into the city as the only path to a tax base sufficient to allow the city to continue to provide hospitals, police and fire services, street repair, and garbage service. Housing for the poor cannot be dealt with in isolation from these other issues. Protecting the integral existence of poor communities so that empowerment can take place within those communities entails an ongoing tension with pushing for gentrification. The City Council may be legitimately torn between the two; nevertheless, inspection procedures should be just and not unduly favor one group.

The Trust might do well to reject the paranoia Father Phil warned against and join with other concerned organizations in publicly negotiating with the City Council for reasonable renovation schedules for inspected buildings below code. Kitty and members of the Board might use their media contacts to encourage TV and newspapers to investigate dangerous privately owned housing in order to generate support for expanding the inspection program. A local TV news report filming broken stairways and furnaces, peeling lead-based paint, and grill-less windows in buildings exempted from inspection could be very powerful. Such actions should be understood not just as savvy politics, but as part of an effective strategy for implementing a preferential option for the poor.

One of the issues in the inspection that does arise in the Board discussion is the effect of the inspection on homelessness. Organizations such as the Land Trust face a dual problem—the overall lack of low-income housing, which is the major cause of the rise of homelessness in the 1980s and 1990s, and the destruction of low-income, often minority, communities in old center cities. Inner city poor have been dispersed for decades to government housing spread around large metropolitan areas. While many of the intentions behind this dispersal were benign, its effects are not. The dispersion has produced the disintegration of communities and neighborhoods, followed by the failure of many new recipient communities to welcome or include the new residents from the clearly demarcated "projects." The poor in the project become excluded from political decision making. Their former leaders, who no longer represent a coherent community, are silenced.

A vigorous inspection program would improve the quality of available low-income housing, especially if it includes occupied, privately owned units. But the more effective an inspection program is in raising the quality of housing, the more likely it is to lower the number of available units of low-income housing. Some owners will be either financially unable or unwilling to invest in the necessary repairs and will abandon the buildings. Other owners, forced to invest in their property, will evict low-income tenants before the rehab process and upon completion will rent to middle-class tenants from whom they can recover their investment. Not all of the non-profit organizations will be able to renovate all their units in a timely manner, and some units will be demolished. Without new low-income units, homelessness will increase. Here, too, it is necessary to decide which poor to aid: those whose safety and comfort will increase due to an inspection policy, or those who would be forced into homelessness by an inspection policy.

WHICH NEIGHBOR?

Housing is a complex avenue into the contemporary phenomenon of poverty, in part because low-income housing is dependent upon issues such as employment and wage levels. Under full employment and what Catholic social teaching has called a "just wage" (a wage that supports a worker, a spouse, and children and allows for saving toward property ownership), homelessness would cease to be a major social problem. But modern society has not enjoyed, and does not soon expect to again enjoy, full employment. Nor do all workers enjoy wages that meet the requirements of a just wage.

Low-income housing presents some interesting situations for examining the consequences of various interpretations of the preferential option for the poor. Father Phil and Sarah interpret the preferential option to mean that the poor are favored over the rich, and the most poor over the least poor. Is such an interpretation accurate?

Since the Gospels do not pass down to us any discourse by Jesus regarding this question, we must look to the activities of Jesus himself. On the one hand Jesus did seek out the "poorest," though these were not always the most materially poor. If we ask what groups Jesus championed in his ministry, it would be accurate to answer that he championed the cause of the most marginated, the most afflicted, and those most discriminated against. The poor, the crippled and sick, the dying, women and children, and even the despised prostitutes and tax collectors all received special treatment from Jesus.

On the other hand, it would also be accurate to say that it was not Jesus who sought out these "poorest" of Israel, but they who sought him, and he who responded to them. The geography of Jesus' wandering ministry and his directions to the disciples he sent out in his name make clear that he directed his ministry at the settlements of the Jewish inhabitants, farmers and fishermen, not at the wealthy trading communities of the Gentiles (Matt. 10:5-6). The Gospels tell us again and again that within the Jewish communities the sick and the children were "brought to him" and that tax collectors, prostitutes, and those begging favors sought him out.

Perhaps the speech of Jesus that most directly speaks to this issue of preference for the poorest is the story of judgment in Matthew 25. Jesus concludes that the Lord will say to the righteous, "Come, you who are blessed by my Father, inherit the kingdom prepared for you from the foundation of the world, for I was hungry and you gave me food, I was thirsty and you gave me to drink, I was a stranger and you welcomed me, I was naked and you gave me clothing, I was sick and you took care of me, I was in prison and you visited me." And when they ask when they did these things, the Lord will say, "When you did it for the least of these who are my family, you did it to me." All these different needy make up the group of the "least" of the Lord's family; there is no attempt to rank caring for the sick compared to giving a drink to the thirsty, and no attempt to rank the different degrees of sickness. In Jesus' own ministry he exorcised demons, cured the sick, defended the children; in short, he responded to a variety of needs.

The members of the Land Trust have concentrated their energies on providing housing, and, in fact, providing home ownership. In doing that they have already determined that they will not be working with the most needy individuals within the community of the poor, for the most needy are not ready for the level of responsibility that home ownership demands.

The most needy are those who are the furthest away from Jesus' model of fully human persons able to accept the costs demanded of disciples to extend themselves in unconditional love of neighbor. The most needy are those who no longer have hope for salvation, who have accepted the world's judgment that they are not worthy of the love of God. Support for the most needy must be offered in small doses, demanding smaller efforts, lest the poorest become discouraged at their failures and reinforce their despair.

This is not to say that Father Phil and Sarah do not have a point in calling attention to the rising costs of Land Trust homes. If home ownership programs are not appropriate for many of the most poor, perhaps the Trust should more carefully attempt to aid the poorest among those capable of home ownership. On the one hand, it would be a mistake to use the resources of the Land Trust to aid a group which would be able to effect the same step into home ownership by themselves, though on less favorable terms. On the other hand, the finances of the poor are very fragile. Luck has much to do with the ability of poor families to keep up mortgage payments in programs like the Land Trust: sickness and accident, burglary or vandalism, car breakdown, fire and many other misfortunes can send poor families into bankruptcy. They do not have insurance to protect them from the financial effects of misfortune. For this reason it is sometimes not so helpful to stress the differences between families with $600/month and families with $900/month. Factors such as the size of the family, the health of the family, and even the strength of the family's support network can all make the "richer" family the truly poorer one. Perhaps a compromise could be worked out, in which the Land Trust would continue to reach out to its present family pool, but incorporate some families who look like good prospects for home ownership despite their lesser incomes. The cost of homes for such families could be partially subsidized by the Land Trust on a sliding scale.

Using Land Trust funds to subsidize some of the rehab costs for some of the poorer families is better than the Land Trust's earlier policy of doing less than total renovation. The already precarious financial situation of the poor, their lack of savings, and their lack of insurance make the risk of buying a house that may soon need major repairs too high. What is the effect on new homeowners of discovering that their houses need a new furnace, or a new roof, or that unless they replace the windows they cannot afford to heat the house? One effect is material: because the down payment used every penny of savings, the replacement cannot be done. Meanwhile a faulty furnace endangers the lives of the family, as well as the value of the house. Another effect is more spiritual. Persons whose lives are spent in poverty in minority communities that are deteriorating and spilling over with crime and pain have a difficult time sustaining hope. A common defense in the lives of the poor after a certain amount of suffering is to refuse to hope, lest the repeated disappointment of hope completely undermines their ability to cope. To raise the hope of the poor, only for them to see that hope dashed due to inadequate renovation, is cruel. It is to place stumbling blocks in front of the hope of the poor:

> If any of you put a stumbling block before any of these little ones who believe in me, it would be better for you if a great millstone were fastened about your neck and you were drowned in the depth of the sea. Woe to the world because of stumbling blocks! Occasions for stumbling are bound to come, but woe to the one by whom the stumbling block comes! [Matt. 18:6-7]

The most likely objection to a compromise that uses Trust funds to subsidize costs for lower-income families is that it would lower the number of families who could be helped into decent, affordable home ownership. Because Kitty as executive director is involved in the lives of residents and their communities, she could undoubtedly tell horror stories about the lives of persons on her waiting list for homes: mothers bringing new babies home from the hospital in January to buildings with no heat, children whose levels of blood lead are dangerously high from eating flaking lead-based paint from the walls, and handicapped elderly people on walkers and canes negotiating rotted stairs without handrails. How does the benefit of including some lower-income poor in the home ownership pool weigh against the disadvantage of delaying the move to safe, affordable homes for familes like these?

CONCLUSION

Perhaps the tension on the Board could best be dealt with through a communal retreat experience. The Board might invite the members of various committees that report to the Board, as well. The fact that the Board members seem to have a self-consciously Christian identification and share a theological tradition, even though there may be differences of interpretation, gives them a decided advantage over many other groups which must engage in translating values and norms from one religious or moral system into another. Since Will Jennings, Don Brown, Phil Cahill and Sarah Hawkins are connected with churches, the Board should have many resources for finding an outsider trained in leading groups in reflection on the implications of Christian faith for specific pastoral praxis.

A retreat could not only help ground greater understanding of, and respect for, the pespectives of others, but could also remind the Board members that the meanings of love and justice and the identity of the poor of the Gospel must always be interpreted. Those meanings will be different in different social locations in different historical periods, and they will appear differently to different persons. We have no way of knowing whether the "true interpretation" (God's) corresponds to one particular human interpretation, to no human interpretation, or somehow incorporates and/or transcends them all. There are no easy choices in this case, no clean answers. Prayer and reflection by Christians in this case should help create a spirit of humility and openness which facilitates and does not paralyse action on behalf of justice. Recognition that each of our perspectives is limited should make it easier for the non-residents on the Board to support a process which aims at the residents not only chairing the Board and making up the majority of its members, but also taking full responsibility for the future of their larger community. As Christians who lead by serving, the role of the non-residents should be a self-consciously temporary one, aimed at their own superfluity.

ADDITIONAL RESOURCES

Cone, James H. *Martin and Malcolm in America: A Dream or a Nightmare?* Maryknoll, NY: Orbis Books, 1991.

Gudorf, Christine E. *Victimization: Examining Christian Complicity.* Philadelphia: Trinity Press International, 1992.

Holland, Joe, and Peter Henriot, S.J. *Social Analysis: Linking Faith and Justice.* Maryknoll, NY: Orbis Books, 1983.

Lefkowitz, Rochelle, and Ann Withorn, eds. *For Crying Out Loud: Women and Poverty in the United States.* New York: Pilgrim, 1986.

Fuller, Millard. *No More Shacks!* Waco, TX: Word Books, 1986.

Peter-Raoul, Mar, Linda Rennie Forcey, and Robert F. Hunter, eds. *Yearning To Breathe Free: Liberation Theologies in the U.S.* Maryknoll, NY: Orbis Books, 1990.

PART III

VIOLENCE/NONVIOLENCE

Case

Vietnam's Children

"What should I say to Chris?" Martin Paxton questioned himself. "Should I remain silent, press my ideas on my son, or merely point out the options? What Christian perspective makes sense in a world of fifty thousand plus nuclear weapons?"

Then Martin's memory, or perhaps it was his conscience, began to work. The images of his own Vietnam experience came flooding back like an ever-flowing stream. He is "gun boss" on a U.S. Navy destroyer with six five-inch guns. Routine mission: to shell "Vietcong positions" from two miles off the coast of central Vietnam. "Battle stations," booms the ship's public address system. The radio crackles the coordinates of the target. One round on its way. The spotter over the target in a light plane responds with a "left four hundred yards, down two hundred yards." Another round, another spot. Then in an electric voice the spotter yells, "You've got 'em on the run. Shoot! Shoot!" A quick correction to fire control, then the command, "Thirty rounds, fire for effect!" The noise is deafening. The shock shakes loose the accumulated dirt of twenty years from the pipes overhead. The spotter's voice returns even more excited, "You got 'em, you got 'em!" The combat center erupts with cheers. The captain races back from the bridge to congratulate everyone. Back slapping, hugs, and handshakes follow. God, it feels good! Until the wee hours of the morning, that is. Then the small voices began to work: "Why did the gunners want to paint coolie hats on the sides of the gun mounts? Why did you hesitate? Why did you finally say, 'No, I don't think coolie hats are appropriate'? What are you doing here in Vietnam? Why did you enjoy killing the Vietnamese so much? Who are you anyway, a killer, a Christian, or both? Why didn't anyone prepare you for Vietnam or killing? Why didn't you think these things through before you got here?"

This case was prepared by Robert L. Stivers. Copyright © The Case Study Institute. All names have been disguised to protect the privacy of the individuals involved.

The questions never were answered. Discharge, graduate school, an occupation, several jobs: life has a way of intervening to block introspection just as the decisions of one's children have a way of releasing it. Chris, his son, was almost eighteen and required by law to sign up for the draft.

Martin's question to his son as he was on the way out to a basketball game was innocent: "What are you going to do about the draft?" The reply was quick and without reflection: "Sign up, I guess, and declare conscientious objection, whatever that is." The door slammed and the sound of Chris dribbling the ball down the walk faded away as the old questions reasserted themselves.

Martin was not without resources for the questions and the new context of Chris's decision. A recent adult education class in his church had studied Christian views on violence and nonviolence. The class had helped him sort out a few things. The early church, he learned, had been pacifist, and a continuing tradition had carried the option of nonviolence to the present in what Ronald Smith, the class instructor and professor of religion at the local college, had called "the way of the cross."

A Mennonite from the local area, Jacob Kaufmann, visited the class on the first Sunday and explained his own pacifism. He identified with the position represented by *Sojourners Magazine* and spoke of how important the community of the church is to the way of the cross. "The church," he said, "takes its cue from the nonviolent but socially active model of Jesus in the New Testament." He went on to explain that the early Christian community followed Jesus and his nonviolent ways not because Jesus demanded it, but because faith motivated it. "When Christ is truly in you," he said, "nonviolence is your automatic response. Love engenders love. That is the message of Jesus. I can never be a soldier."

Martin's friend Jim Everett had pressed Jacob in the question period which followed. "How can I follow the way of the cross in a fallen world?" he asked. "What would you do if your wife and children were attacked?" Obviously Jacob had heard these questions before because without hesitation he replied, "We are called to follow Jesus, not make the world turn out right. Ultimately, we are called to suffer before we inflict suffering. And in any case, we do not need to kill the attacker. There are other alternatives."

Jacob's assurance had a certain appeal to Martin. The way was simple, straightforward and seemed to fit Jesus' radical call to discipleship. Jacob himself was active in the community on justice issues in the tradition of Gandhi and King.

Still, Martin was not convinced. "Justice is as important in the way of the cross as nonviolence," he thought. "On occasion a large measure of justice might be gained for a small measure of violence. Why prefer nonviolence to justice in these situations? And who does the dirty work of keeping order in a violent world?"

The next Sunday Ronald Smith presented a position he called "Christian realism," out of which comes the doctrine of the justifiable war. Historically,

Ronald explained, this position emerged after the emperor Constantine converted to Christianity in the early fourth century and the church achieved a favored position. Christians took political office and became responsible for the general welfare. The ethical and political task for Christians of this view, Ronald continued, is not perfection or the literal following of the way of Jesus, but the use of power to push and pull sinful reality toward the ideal.

"Not best, but better," he insisted, "because best is impossible in a fallen world. The way of the cross may be lived personally, but it is not immediately relevant to politics. We in our freedom can ignore the power of God in our midst and alienate our neighbors. God doesn't set things right or organize them for us. We have been given dominion and are responsible for the use of power. To serve one's neighbor, to steward resources, and to achieve higher levels of justice in a sinful world mean a Christian must compromise and occasionally use means which are not consistent with the way of the cross. This is how anarchy is avoided and tyranny prevented. This does not mean the way is irrelevant and God does not work in the world. God acts like a magnet pulling us out of sin and moving us to higher ethical levels, and we have a limited capacity to respond. God's power and this capacity are the basis of hope and make 'the better' a constant possibility. Simply put, those of this view are realists because of sin, and Christians because there are resources for making this a better world."

Ronald went on to draw the justifiable war tradition out of this realistic perspective. "Nonviolence is the norm," he insisted, "but on occasion violence is permissible if it clearly meets certain criteria." He then set forth the criteria and indicated that they make both violence and selective conscientious objection moral possibilities. He also observed that if every nation took the criteria seriously, all war would cease. He paused and added, "but that is a big 'if'."

Martin remembered leaving the class attracted to this position as well. But he was also troubled. How can realism be consistent with the picture of Jesus in the New Testament? Does not the idea of a justifiable war open the flood gates to misuse? Even Hitler claimed his cause was just, not to mention what Martin himself had been told in Vietnam. And how about nuclear war which would always violate one or two of the criteria? The very thought of a just nuclear war is preposterous. Religiously, do the realists take the power of sin too seriously and the power of the Holy Spirit not seriously enough?

The next Sunday a Salvadoran refugee offered still another position, called liberation theology. Her name was Maria, or at least that was how she was introduced without further explanation. Martin found her difficult to understand because of her Spanish accent, but her perspective was clear enough. Maria spoke of centuries of oppression in Central America. In emotional terms she related the violence done to her family in San Salvador by right-wing death squads. She described her own participation in a "base community," and how a grass-roots movement of the poor is spreading through Latin America. She insisted the movement was Christian and spent most of her time linking it to liberation themes in the Bible.

"Yes," she admitted, "we use Marxist analysis to understand our situation. We also seek an alternative to the dependency created by international capitalism and the oppression of political and religious oligarchies." Maria concluded with a passionate plea for justice for the poor and an end to violence fomented by the rich against the poor.

When asked if she advocated violence in response, Maria looked down, paused, and slowly replied, "Sometimes there seems to be no other choice. I feel called to relieve the suffering I see and reluctantly to fight for liberation."

Martin was deeply moved by Maria, whose position seemed to be a variation of the justifiable war tradition, but with important differences, of course. Still Martin was bothered by her references to socialism and Marxism. The former did not seem very efficient as a way of economic organization, and the latter not much help when it came to creating something new. What both attracted and bothered him most, however, was her passion. He worried that passion easily yields to fanaticism and fanaticism to new forms of tyranny.

The final week of the class Ronald Smith explained the crusading tradition in Christianity, but without much enthusiasm. He had not been able to locate anyone to represent the position. This does not mean the crusade is dead, he suggested, only that few are willing to state it in its classic form. The best example is the willingness on the part of many Christians to use violence in putting down "godless communism."

In the Christian tradition, he went on, crusaders base their violent actions on the holy war texts in Deuteronomy, Joshua, and Judges. They see as God's clear command the call to stamp out evil and the designation of themselves as God's agents. Serving in the army of the righteous is a Christian responsibility.

Ronald dismissed the position by claiming it improperly literalized the biblical texts and then misapplied them. Faith in God is the real significance of the texts, and they are hardly directly relevant to modern warfare with all its destruction. He added that the portrayal of God as commanding violence was incompatible with the biblical witness taken as a whole and that crusaders often fail to see their own sin. He concluded by observing that crusades are usually the bloodiest kinds of wars. He cited the religious wars of the seventeenth century and the Iran-Iraq conflict as examples.

Martin agreed but reflected on the depth of the good/evil dualism in each of us. "Wouldn't we all like to stamp out evil if we could?" he mused. "And how like us it is to represent our own cause by our best ideals and our opponents' by their worst deeds!"

Martin sifted through the options one more time. "I might be able to quiet my own conscience, but what do I say to Chris? Should I advocate the way of the cross and conscientious objection? Should I suggest a more realistic option which allows for justifiable wars in oppressive situations and selective conscientious objection in others? Or should I tell him to sign up, do his duty, and serve his country as millions have before? After all, that's what I did."

Martin had now been in thought for over an hour. He was drawn out of those thoughts by the sound of Chris dribbling a ball back up the walk. Chris entered the house and asked, "Dad, you wanted to talk about registering for the draft?"

Commentary

Vietnam's Children

A generation has matured since the Vietnam War. It knows little about My Lai, the Tet offensive, Khe Sanh, or the final capitulation. The troubled waters stirred up by injustice, massive demonstrations, rhetorical flourish, and challenges to traditional authority have stilled. But beneath the surface, currents of conscience and unresolved identity created by the Vietnam War still run deep. Like the powerful currents which circle in the great ocean basins, these undercurrents of conscience circulate without resolution. Martin Paxton, on the occasion of a chance question to his son, Chris, finds himself in one such current of conscience with a chance to break out and simultaneously to help Chris make a decision about conscientious objection.

To see that Vietnam and Chris's decision about conscientious objection are related is important. They are related on the personal level through the exchange of thoughts and feelings between father and son. They are also related through the four Christian perspectives on violence presented in Martin's adult class. Finally, they are related through the education Chris has received in the Paxton family. Martin's conscientious ambivalence, which includes his lament about not being prepared for killing, has no doubt been communicated to Chris. Vietnam's children, whether they realize it or not, are now making decisions about draft registration with their parents' and their society's moral perceptions of the Vietnam War as important ingredients.

CONSCIENTIOUS OBJECTION

Chris's disconcerting and quick reply to Martin's question about signing up does not make clear whether Chris objects to all wars or merely to unjustifiable wars. This may just be a lack of information in the case. More likely, Chris does not himself know the difference between conscientious objection and selective conscientious objection, and how the law treats each.

From 1948 through 1972 the U.S. government used a combination of draft and voluntary recruitment to fill the ranks of its armed forces. In 1971 the draft was put on standby status and voluntary recruitment became the sole source of new soldiers. Draft registration continued until 1975 when it was suspended. In 1980 registration was reinstated.

That is the status of the law today. All males ages eighteen to twenty-six are required to register by filling out a form available at the post office. Failure to register can result in a fine, imprisonment, or both. After registration, the name of a registrant such as Chris is entered into a computer for possible future use.

To make use of these names to induct draftees into the armed forces would require an act of Congress with the signature of the President. In an emergency a law to classify and induct could be passed on very short notice accompanied by all the emotions of nationalism which cloud clear thinking.

Were such legislation enacted, local draft boards would quickly form, classify all those who are registered, and begin calling individuals for induction, first from the twenty-year-old age group according to a rank order of birthdays determined by lottery. Once Chris was classified 1A and his name came up, he would receive an induction notice and have ten days to report. It is within this ten-day period that he would have to set in motion the machinery for deferment or exemption on grounds of conscientious objection.

Once Chris made application for conscientious objection, the draft board would postpone induction and set a date for a hearing where he could present his case. His application would be judged on the basis of three criteria: (1) that he is opposed to participation in war in any form; (2) that his opposition is by reason of religious training and belief; and (3) that he demonstrates sincerity.

If the application were successful, Chris would be reclassified in one of two conscientious objector categories. If not successful, the local board would have to declare in writing the reasons for its rejection, which Chris could appeal.

The vast majority of conscientious objectors are registering for the draft, but a number of alternatives exist, including refusal to register and the indication of conscientious objector status in the process of registration. The task for Chris is to think through the ethical implications, decide if he is a conscientious objector and what type, and make his decision about registration. If he elects to be a conscientious objector, he should seek the advice of a draft counselor and begin preparing his supporting material.

THE VIETNAM WAR

The Vietnam War is not over. The hand-to-hand combat has long since ceased, but the meaning of the experience has not been settled. The Vietnam upheaval has never been adequately worked through, and as time passes, it looks more and more as if it never will be. Americans either cannot or will not come to terms with it.

Martin appears bothered by two things. The first is the destruction of a social myth about the United States, the second the destruction of a personal myth about himself. For Martin and many other Vietnam veterans the destruction of their social and personal myths and the lack of adequate replacements have resulted in lost identity and the inability to comprehend what they went through.

The 1950s saw the apex of American power. Victorious in World War II and economically unrivaled, Americans had reason to be content with themselves in spite of serious unresolved social problems. They also had a vision with roots. American social mythology depicted a new city which is set on a hill free from the cynical entanglements and imperial ambitions of old and decaying Europe. Stories of the American frontier told of rough but moral and hard working pioneers pushing back the frontier and bringing civilization in their wake. Those who resisted were pictured either as uncivilized and in need of American technology and virtue, or evil and in need of a crusade.

The frontier closed in the nineteenth century, but its mythology remained open-ended in spite of changing conditions and rude shocks such as the Great Depression. The mythology was skillfully manipulated by politicians like John F. Kennedy with his New Frontier. It was exploited by those who saw the spread of communism in Asia as the latest evil in need of a crusade, and the Vietnamese as candidates for American technology and virtue.

In the end this pervasive social mythology was not able to carry the day for an entire nation. The harsh realities of racial violence and the injustice and inconclusiveness of the Vietnam War combined to explode the myth for a vocal minority. For men and women such as Martin Paxton the bell is now cracked and no new bells have yet been cast.

Martin could not have avoided participation in this mythology. He would have been brought up on westerns, war movies, and patriotic instruction. The path of least resistance would have led him to the conclusion that for the first time in history, here was a moral nation. Because he was brought up in a middle-class America that almost without question saw itself as morally right, he probably saw himself and his nation as inheritors and purveyors of that morality. Abundance would have shielded him from the violence of poverty and class conflict. Entering the Navy was probably as natural as a trip to Disneyland.

That beneath the mythology of the American dream and his own peace in it lay a different reality would only have been dimly perceived. It apparently was not the injustice of Vietnam or the oppression of racism which revealed this reality to him, at least not initially. Rather it seems to have been his participation in and apparent enjoyment of killing and the acids of uncomfortable dreams stimulated by a vigorous conscience. The combat center erupted with the "happy" news of death, killed Martin's false consciousness, and left him with a good dose of guilt.

In a like manner Vietnam blew the top off the dormant volcano of the American dream. Martin's crisis is the nation's crisis. The problem for both Martin and other Americans is how to build new mythic mountains to give order and justice to their landscapes. Martin may be building one in his Christian journey.

In Christian terms the problem is repentance and new life. Repentance must be the foundation of his building. The first stone is to realize that he is one of those individuals who is capable of killing and enjoying it. Such an admission is hard for most individuals. It forces the sacrifice of the proud self and produces vulnerability. For modern nations it is much harder because pride is so strong and so central to national identity. For corporate America with its glowing self-image and righteousness to admit that the Vietnam War was unjust may be too much to expect.

The guilt Martin feels and the continuing discussion about Vietnam are signs of God's judgment and first steps toward repentance. But the recognition of judgment is not the end of the story. God forgives and this forgiveness opens the door to new life. As soon as Martin goes through the door of repentance, the process of coming to terms with his role in Vietnam will begin. There are indications this process has already started.

The prospects for America in its continuing mental struggle over the Vietnam War are not as good. Nations have far fewer resources for coming to terms with their own injustices. Continuing infatuations with nuclear weapons and armaments do not improve the prospects. The church will have an important role to play in whatever rethinking takes place, for it has resources for announcing judgment, for coming to terms with guilt, and for moving beyond it.

Any rethinking that goes on must address Martin's question and lament: "Why didn't anyone prepare me for Vietnam or killing?" That question points up a shortcoming in the education of children in the United States. Experiences differ, of course, but a child of Martin's generation would normally have been exposed only superficially to peace education. History texts of his generation emphasized kings and great victories. The pacifist side of the Christian tradition was a well-kept secret, even in Sunday school. The media glorified violence and past wars much as they do today.

It is no wonder Martin found himself on the firing line before he had thought things through. His option, stated at the end of the case, was "sign up, do your duty, and serve your country." Is it not a problem that the state sees its internal cohesion as so important that it tries to make certain that this is the only option which can receive a hearing? Has the church failed to present the full range of options out of its own traditions? Or is the failure to question, to explore, and to reflect Martin's?

The answer is yes to all three, and from an ethical perspective the point is that those who are forced to make life and death decisions ought to be exposed to moral perspectives on violence. The state's need for compliance with its will and certainly the church's role in supporting the state do not warrant the exclusion of such perspectives. Young men and women have the right to have access to the different options.

CHRISTIAN OPTIONS

Available to Christian thinking on conscientious objection and the Vietnam War is a normative tradition of great variety and richness. No less than four distinct options are presented within the case itself. The Mennonite Jacob Kaufmann offers the pacifist option. Professor Roger Smith discusses both the crusade and Christian realism, which includes the justifiable war tradition. And finally, Maria presents liberation theology in its more militant form. Liberation theology may or may not be a fourth option. Its theology is certainly distinct, but on the use of violence its proponents are not in agreement. Some are pacifists, while others see violence as justifiable as a last resort in oppressive situations.

Pacifism

Pacifism appears first in the case. Christian pacifism is linked with what is called "the way of the cross." Jacob Kaufmann presents a modern version of this very traditional perspective, a version often associated with theologian John Howard Yoder.

The way of the cross starts with and stresses what it takes to be the New Testament view of Jesus Christ. According to this perspective, Jesus unambiguously models and calls Chris and Martin to one radical option which is normative for life in society. No other options are valid, no other path but discipleship that is authentically Christian.

This radical option takes its cue from Luke 1:46ff. and 4:5-8. In these texts Jesus is announced as an agent of radical social change who scatters the proud, puts down the mighty, exalts those of low degree, and sends the rich away empty. These texts portray Jesus in a new light. Jesus introduces a nonviolent but politically active way of life for Chris and Martin to live in the midst of the world. This way is best seen in the cross where Jesus stands up to Pilate but does not resort to mob violence or coercive political power to achieve his ends.

The way of the cross is not a new law. It cannot be forced on Chris or Martin, for its essence is freedom. It must be chosen by the disciple with recognition of its true costs, the ultimate being readiness to suffer. While all are called, few will follow because of the high costs. The few who follow will gravitate to small, sharing communities, for the church is the essence of the way.

The way of the cross almost always runs counter to the prevailing culture because the world cannot bear its ethical rigor. No compromises with secular values are brokered. A distinct lifestyle emerges. As disciples, Chris and Martin are called to live simply, bear hostility, serve others, and to be dominated by God's self-giving love.

The way is emphatically nonviolent. Violence is antithetical to God's love even when some other good seems to justify it. Jesus makes clear that an authentic witness to the world is possible without resort to violence.

Nonviolence is not passive nonresistance. Jesus did not condone sin. He resisted it at every turn. Nor did he give in to the power of Rome. Likewise Christians are to resist up to the point at which they would have to use violence to continue resisting. At that point resistance takes the form of suffering. Gandhi, King, and the tactics of nonviolent resistance offer a model for those who choose this option.

Finally, the way involves a radical break with calculations of consequences, power balances, and prudence. As followers of the way Chris and Martin would not be responsible for getting results, making things come out right, or moving society to some higher level of moral endeavor. If good results come, fine. If not, then they persevere. They are called first, last, and always to the way.

For Chris the way of the cross points unambiguously to conscientious objection. To Martin it calls for repentance and in the future active resistance to all forms of violence.

Christian Realism

Roger Smith presents the second option, Christian realism, which is presumably his own. In our time the best-known exponent of this position was the American theologian Reinhold Niebuhr.

Christian realism has its roots both in Luther's two realms doctrine and Calvin's call to transform society. The nomenclature reveals the essence of the perspective: the holding together of idealism and realism.

Idealism is a disposition to be loyal to norms or to some understanding of goodness or right. Christian idealists usually look to the Bible and the tradition for their normative understanding and stress adherence to the rules and principles which they find in these sources.

Realism is the disposition to take full account of sin and other elements which frustrate the realization of the ideal. It starts with the way things are and stresses the brokenness of history, limitation, and the pride of individuals and groups. Instead of pushing single-mindedly toward the ideal, the realist asks: "Where do we go from here?"

In Christian realism Chris and Martin must keep the ideal or normative pole of the tradition together with the realistic pole of the way things are. Realism without vision degenerates into cynicism; idealism without a sense of sin abstracts into illusion.

Chris and Martin are called in this view to live in freedom on the knife edge between idealism and realism and to act politically to move the present situation toward the ideal without the illusion that they can or must achieve the ideal. The political task for them is not the rigorous following of the ideal, however important the ideal may be, but the use of political and sometimes even military power to establish the most tolerable form of peace and justice under the circumstances.

The idealism in this perspective comes from an understanding of God's work in Jesus Christ. Jesus Christ reveals the wisdom and power of God to be self-giving love untainted by self- or group-interest. This ideal is not achievable by Chris or Martin because of their own sin. Nevertheless, approximations of the ideal are possible for them because God's power of love is constantly at work in human affairs and their lives.

God's love judges and convicts Chris and Martin. It breaks their pride and prevents illusion. It brings humility and repentance. As a result, Chris and Martin can undertake political tasks motivated by God's love but with a healthy sense of their own sin as well as the sin of others.

The cross and resurrection free Chris and Martin to work in the midst of horror and contradiction and to serve without need of reward. God's love is also a power at work in the world. It creates the possibility of justice and peace and sustains Chris and Martin against the power of sin.

The realism in this perspective comes from an analysis of human sin. Sin is the inevitable alienation which results from self- or group-centered attempts to gain security against the anxieties of the human condition, for example, using guns or waging war in response to political frustrations. This tendency to seek security in and through the self or the collective is strong in individuals, stronger still in groups. While the individual has a limited capacity for repentance, for shifting from self to God, and for relationships with other persons, this potential is greatly reduced in groups. It is impossible, for example, for groups to love each other.

Such realism does not lead to pessimism and withdrawal. Rather it leads to a new awareness about groups. Different norms apply. If groups cannot love, then the appropriate norm is justice under law. Groups can achieve some semblance of mutual regard and justice by balancing power against power.

This view of groups as having a different set of norms than individuals is called the two realms doctrine. In it the earthly realm is governed by justice, law, rules, and the sword; the divine realm by love, the Gospel, and sensitivity. Chris and Martin, provided they find their center in the divine realm, are freed by the cross and resurrection of Jesus Christ to live and work in the earthly realm and to get their hands dirty as soldiers.

Indeed, the task for Chris and Martin is to serve in the earthly realm doing within reason what is needed to make it a better place to live. They are called to exercise power and insofar as they are able to move the inevitable power balances which are prematurely called justice to higher levels of freedom and equality.

The call to exercise power in as ethical a manner as possible leads to the principles of the justifiable war. In the best of times Chris and Martin should work for justice and peace using nonviolent means. In the worst of times, when neither justice nor peace is possible, violence is sometimes the lesser of evils.

In such situations Christian realism considers violence, if not good in itself, at least acceptable as long as certain conditions are met. There are seven conditions or criteria for a justifiable war:

1. Last resort: All other means to achieve a just and peaceful solution must have been exhausted.

2. Just cause: The reason for fighting must be the preservation or restoration of a morally preferable cause against a clearly unjust adversary.

3. Right intention: The intention of violence must be the establishment or restoration of peace with justice.

4. Declared by legitimate authority: Only legitimate authority may declare war. Private, self-appointed defenders of justice are disallowed.

5. Reasonable hope of success: While success does not have to be guaranteed, the useless sacrifice of soldiers no matter how just the cause is ruled out.

6. Noncombatant immunity: Civilians without direct connection with the opponent's war effort must not be intentionally attacked.

7. Proportionality: The force used should be proportional to the objective sought. The good sought should exceed the horrible evil of the violence.

This perspective puts pressure on Chris and offers several alternatives on Vietnam for Martin. Christian realists do not reject military service out of hand, but are prepared to resist fighting in an unjust cause. Unfortunately, the current draft law does not allow for selective conscientious objection, which is the logical outgrowth of the perspective. Realists must therefore either serve or take the legal consequences in the event resistance is conscientiously selected.

Martin, should he accept this perspective, must decide on the justifiability of his own involvement in Vietnam and what to advise Chris. If he sees his involvement as unjustified, which seems to be the case already, he should seek forgiveness and new life in Jesus Christ. He should also relate to Chris the lessons he has learned over the years as his conscience has reacted to his experience in Vietnam. For the future he should be prepared to support just and resist unjust causes. His advice to his son probably should be to register for the draft and to be prepared for selective objection with all of its ambiguities and perils.

Liberation Theology

Maria offers the third option, liberation theology. What is distinctive about this theology is its perspective—its constant touchstone is the concrete reality of the oppressed poor. In order to understand the causes of that oppressive reality it employs a variety of tools, among them the biblical witness and the social sciences, including some elements of the social theory of Karl Marx. Liberation theologians must work to understand the political and economic causes of poverty and oppression so that they can better help the poor in eradicating those causes. Liberation theologians also employ the social sciences to give factual insights to the biblical witness, the essence of which they argue is commitment to the poor.

Using the social sciences, liberation theologians have scrutinized historical developments in Latin America from Spanish authoritarianism to liberal democracy, to the current control exercised by the military in most countries. What emerges from their reading of history is a long train of abuses. Economic elites have combined political, economic, and military power with other-worldly, pietistic expressions of Christianity to exploit the Indians, mixed-bloods, peasants, and Afro-Americans of the region.

Today the combination of transnational corporations and local elites, buttressed by the military might of the United States and marching under the ideological banner of economic development and conservative Christianity, is continuing the oppression begun under the Spanish. The oppressed majority, awakened by their new consciousness of this situation, have two options: continued bondage under the status quo or liberation.

Liberation theology enters at this point as a challenge to conservative theologies and as the Christian basis for seeking liberation. The incarnation places Chris and Martin squarely in the midst of life, not in some idealized spiritualized realm apart. An incarnational approach affirms Jesus Christ as the measure and power of God's work. It also affirms history as the place where God's work of making and keeping life human will reach fulfillment. The key for interpreting God's presence and hence for setting social priorities is social justice for the poor.

Liberation theologians see the essence of the Gospel in the struggle for liberation on three levels. The first level is the elimination of social, economic, and political injustice. At a deeper second level liberation is historical. It expresses the struggle of the poor to come to a new consciousness about history, rejecting what has been mediated by ruling classes and realizing the liberating power of Jesus Christ. This second level is concerned with freedom, specifically the freedom of the poor to determine their own destiny. The third level is theological. It is liberation from sin through faith in Jesus Christ. It is also the most fundamental level, for sin is the root of all oppression.

These three interdependent levels are played out in the Bible in concrete historical situations. Liberation theologians see the beginning of God's act of liberation in the Exodus, which becomes the paradigm for all levels of liberation. The Israelites were freed from Egyptian political and economic bondage and came to a new sense of identity as a people. This activity of God continued in the work of the prophets who challenged the unjust social conditions and reigning ideologies of their times.

In Jesus Christ something new is added. God takes Israel's place as the suffering servant and reveals a willingness to suffer that humanity might be fully liberated. Jesus sets human understanding on a new course of justice and liberation. Jesus himself rejected perverted forms of kingship and the role of the messianic leader of an armed revolt, but not the use of human power itself. Jesus incarnates God's just and liberating rule creating a new consciousness of liberation which is to be carried out by Chris and Martin in their own situations.

The relevance of Jesus' ethic is direct. The realm of God is not merely foreshadowed, but actually present and operative in historical struggles for liberation. Thus liberation theology would challenge Chris and Martin first to try to understand the perspective of the oppressed and then, working from that perspective, to determine how best to participate in the fuller realization of the kingdom as it breaks in to transform society.

Liberation theology does not offer a distinctively new perspective on violence to Chris and Martin, since all of the traditional options are found in it. Instead it asks them how they can participate in God's so-called preferential option for the poor. For Chris this means close scrutiny of U.S. military involvement in the Third World and preparation to resist or support such involvement depending on a new criteria: how it hurts or helps the least advantaged. For Martin it presents a new view of Vietnam through the sights of the poor instead of those of his ship's guns and his own culture. Finally it calls both to a new, topsy-turvy biblical awareness and to action in cooperation with the world's poor.

Crusade

The final option presented in Martin's class is the crusade, which historically has been an option but does not appear to be so in this case. One reason the crusade has been popular is its simplicity. It divides reality into good and evil. The crusader is always on the side of the good, the enemy always the incarnation of evil. God wills the eradication of evil, hence the crusader is justified, even commanded, to kill. Another source of its popularity is its compatibility with tribalism, that seemingly natural human inclination to favor one's own group and accept without question its rituals, perspectives, and aggressions.

The crusade has had its moments in Christian history. It was at work in the conquest of the Promised Land by the Hebrews. Pope Urban II used it successfully in the Middle Ages to rescue the Holy Land temporarily from the forces of Islam. Today in some Christian circles it is encountered in the call to oppose "atheistic communism."

In the case study the crusade is seen as foreign to the teachings of Jesus. Its dualism of good and evil is simplistic in the extreme, especially in its naiveté about the sin of the crusader. Its embrace of violence is so alien to the central Christian experience of faith as to make a mockery of it. For these and other reasons Ronald Smith, the teacher, was correct in dismissing it as an option. It is out of the normative bounds of Christianity and offers no guidance to Chris or Martin. Its ethical importance today is that of an historical artifact and an example of what to avoid.

ADDITIONAL RESOURCES

Bainton, Roland H. *Christian Attitudes toward War and Peace.* Nashville: Abingdon, 1960.

Bell, Linda A. *Rethinking Ethics in the Midst of Violence: A Feminist Approach to Freedom.* Lanham, MD: Rownan and Littlefield Publishers, 1993.

Gray, J. Glenn. *The Warriors.* New York: Harper & Row, 1959; rev. ed., 1967.

Gutiérrez, Gustavo. *A Theology of Liberation.* Maryknoll, NY: Orbis Books, 1973; rev. ed., 1988.

Kolko, Gabriel. *Anatomy of a War.* New York: Pantheon Books, 1985.

Míguez Bonino, José. *Doing Theology in a Revolutionary Situation.* Philadelphia: Fortress Press, 1975.

—————. *Toward a Christian Political Ethics.* Philadelphia: Fortress Press, 1983.

Niebuhr, Reinhold. *The Children of Light and the Children of Darkness.* New York: Charles Scribner's Sons, 1944.

Sider, Ronald J., and Richard K. Taylor. *Nuclear Holocaust and Christian Hope.* Downers Grove, IL: InterVarsity Press, 1982.

Stone, Ronald H. *Reinhold Niebuhr: Prophet to Politician.* Nashville: Abingdon, 1972.

Yoder, John Howard. *The Politics of Jesus.* Grand Rapids, MI: William B. Eerdmans, 1972.

Case

To Our Own Land

"Why don't you people just dig up the bones and take them with you?"

Saki Monnakgola listened to his brother Amos as he repeated the white farmer's angry words. Saki had not gone with family members on their annual pilgrimage to their ancestors' graves for several years. Each year, however, Amos managed to travel to Soweto from his home in Bophuthatswana to tell Saki about the journey. The two brothers talked long into the evening about the land.

Saki had been only two years old at the time and had no clear memory of the forced removal twenty-five years earlier. Amos, who had been eight, had vivid memories of the day their possessions were thrown on a military truck and their home destroyed by a bulldozer. Along with the wider community of two hundred families, they were forced onto trucks, driven many kilometers north, and dumped on the slopes of rocky hills in Bophuthatswana. Their goats, chickens, cattle, and fruit trees were left behind. Acres of ripening maize were left in the fields.

BACKGROUND

The 1913 Land Act and the 1936 South African Development Trust and Land Act, supporting a policy of "separate development," divided the country by racial identity. The legislation designated reservations, later named "bantustans" and then "homelands," which were disconnected rural areas reserved for the black African population. After 1948, when the Nationalist Party came into power, additional apartheid policies were enacted. The Group Areas Act of 1950 designated all of South Africa's

This case was prepared by Alice Frazer Evans, Plowshares Institute. Copyright © 1994, The Case Study Institute and distributed by Yale Divinity School Library, 409 Prospect Street, New Haven, CT 06511. All names and places have been disguised to protect the privacy of those involved in this situation.

residential and trading areas for the exclusive use of one of four racial groups: Black, White, Colored (mixed race), and Asiatic (Asian or Indian). The 1950 Population Registration Act further divided black South Africans into ethnic and language groups.

Between 1960 and 1982, over three million Blacks and a smaller number of Coloreds and Asians—over 10 percent of the population of the entire country—were forcibly removed by the South African State from areas designated for other racial groups. Many of those removed held titles and land deeds which were invalidated by the new laws. A small number of rural Whites were also forcibly removed. The various land acts called for black South Africans, who made up roughly 75 percent of the population, to live on 13 percent of the land. Eighty-six percent of South Africa, including the cities and prime agricultural and mining lands, was granted to Whites, who were some 12 percent of the population. Blacks were not permitted to own land outside of the "homelands" and were to hold "citizenship" and voting rights only in these areas that the government considered independent national states.

AMOS AND SAKI

During the years following his family's removal, Amos continued to live in Bophuthatswana near his parents. With no formal schooling, he used his natural ability with engines to become a motor mechanic. He found work wherever he could, often leaving his wife and children for weeks at a time. Amos's family and the other members of the community lived in make-shift corrugated metal shacks. There was no electricity in the community, no tarred roads, and very little arable land. While there were two water taps, they were usually dry. The only reliable water was sold in a nearby village and had to be carried in by hand or on donkeys. There were no schools or clinics within walking distance. Once when Saki was a small boy, he asked his mother why they didn't gather stones and build stronger houses. He never forgot her reply: "We want to go back to our own land. We will not build houses here."

Saki, like most of the community youth, left the barren settlement when he was in his early teens. While many of the young people who left and were able to find work became migrant farmers, Saki moved to the township[1] of Tembisa to live with his mother's sister. He completed his secondary education and obtained a job as a clerk with a European firm in Johannesburg. He had recently moved to a more responsible position with a South African business. Saki was also active in the local politics of the township. Saki returned to the settlement occasionally for family events such as funerals or weddings.

Amos continued telling him about the most recent pilgrimage to the family's traditional land. The previous year the farmer had denied them access to the land. He told them they were dirty, they had left rubbish behind, and had not closed the pasture gates when they left the year before. While the farmer allowed them on the land this most recent trip, he reminded them that his father had legally bought the land from the government. Now that his father was dead, the farmer told them that he had inherited full legal title to the land as the oldest son. The only reason he let them come back was because his father had allowed it. As he grudgingly climbed out of his pickup truck to unlock the outside pasture gate, the white farmer said, "The land was used improperly by you lazy Blacks. You'll never know how to make the land productive."

Amos continued, "Saki, I looked into the back of the farmer's truck, and I saw Daniel Ncube sitting there. He and his family were forced off the land when we were. Now he's a laborer on the land where his father and grandfather were born. We both looked away." Amos paused before saying, "Other images strike me about this last visit. I held my youngest daughter's hand as we walked across the pastures to the grave sites. It is very important that she understand that we do not return to visit the old home sites, but the graves. We go to clean the ground, pull weeds, and give thanks to our ancestors that we have been preserved to return for another year. As we were leaving, we passed the neatly fenced graveyard of the white farmer's family. The old man's grave has been there about three years, but there is also a new, very small grave there now. It is painful to realize that we are forced to put grave against grave in our land."

A CHANGING SOUTH AFRICA

Saki had listened quietly. He responded slowly. "Amos, the laws in South Africa are changing faster now than we could ever have imagined. Since the 1991 Abolition of Racially Based Land Measures Act was passed, many communities have begun to press the government for their land. The people of Mogopa who were forcibly removed have already been granted some of their land by the courts. For the first time there is a real possibility that you and the community could return permanently, not just on difficult pilgrimages."

Amos was silent for several minutes. "Saki, I'm not sure how to begin to reclaim our land or even if it would be best for my family. Even with the money you send each month for our parents, we have only enough to keep the family alive. Where would we get stock, or plows, or seed? I've watched the small farmers struggle for survival even when the land is fertile. I would need the labor of all four of my children in order to work a farm successfully. The children have seen you succeed by moving to the city. Would it be right to make them stay on the land with me?"

"Amos, I can't say what your children should do," Saki replied. "But I know you've got the determination and ability to make a living on the land. Remember the stories our grandfather told us about the agricultural prizes he and the black farmers won before the time of combines and tractors? I read an article that confirmed that throughout South Africa in the 1920s and 1930s, black Africans were much more successful farmers than the Boers."[2]

"That's not the only thing that worries me," said Amos. "A lot of our people who are migrant farmers are coming back to the community with no work. They say that many whites are losing their farms to the banks and other creditors. The farmers who are failing say it's because the government has stopped supporting farm programs and is using funds to help Blacks instead. I am certain that many of those farmers wouldn't hesitate to kill us if they thought we were returning to claim the land. The AWB [3] fans the violence with predictions of a 'blood bath' as black Africans increase their role in government. I have heard that in mining communities where black and white miners are competing for jobs, AWB members say, 'Our fingers are itching to kill the kaffirs.'[4]

"Even if I were convinced that the most important thing for our family was to return and that our people were willing to risk their lives to do so, I need some hope that we could succeed. I once believed the ANC [5] would take the land away from the Whites and give it back to us. But I don't hear that talk any more except from the PAC."[6]

Saki agreed that many people had become disillusioned about nationalizing the land. "State ownership of farms in the 'bantustans' has been a disaster under corrupt leadership, and it has been a failure in Eastern Europe and Mozambique. After strong pressure from a coalition of communities seeking to reclaim land, the government established the Advisory Commission on Land Allocation. One of the most difficult problems is how far back to go to restore land that was taken unjustly. The PAC says that the land is ours, and we should be willing to fight for it. The Boers say the land didn't belong to the Bantu[7] people in the first place, but to the Khoi-San,[8] who are all dead. Other Whites say we should begin today as a republic of free people living together. They say that since the government scrapped the Land Acts, Blacks are free to buy the land. But that argument is ridiculous: most of our people are so impoverished they have no possibility of buying land."

Saki reminded Amos, "Before 1948 some of our people sold their land to Whites. How do we move into a new society and deal justly with those Whites who see themselves as legitimate land owners? I worship in a church with Whites who have fought apartheid for years and risked their jobs and personal relationships to challenge state policies. Some live in homes inherited from their grandparents. It was wrong for the government to take our homes from us; would it be less wrong to demand the homes of these people? I have met other Whites in my work who are so deeply afraid that a 'New South Africa' means they will lose everything they have that they strike back with blind hatred and anger. The land touches the deepest emotions in all of us."

LAND IN THE NEW SOUTH AFRICA

"Amos, I am convinced that how we deal with the land may be the most decisive factor in building a new society. Hope for some solutions may lie in the church, which worked with business leaders to get political parties to sign the Peace Accord.[9] South Africa is the only country I know that has a government and a nationally supported structure to reconcile community disputes."

Amos replied, shaking his head, "I know you've talked about the church and how important it has been for you. But I don't see the church doing much more for our people than talking. 'Peace' and 'reconcile' are cheap words. Will the church be as supportive of fighting for our rights when the cost is much more than words?"

Saki didn't have an answer for Amos. In the stillness that rested between them, Saki wondered why it was so important for him that Amos try to reclaim the land. The farmer's obscene suggestion to "dig up the bones" was unthinkable. There was a bond with the land Saki could not explain either to Amos or to himself. It had to do with identity and dignity. What political and economic strategies could bring restitution for those who had been brutally dispossessed yet not destroy the possibility of a new and just South Africa? Friends who were members of PAC were strong in their belief that reliance on market forces would never justly redistribute the land. Saki tended to agree with them, but their proposals to expropriate the land might be short-sighted. Saki realized the truth in his warning to Amos— that the land evoked the deepest emotions. Many of the white farmers were arming themselves, and the AWB was provoking violent confrontations. Any attempt to reclaim their land would surely bring the community into open conflict with the white farmer. Saki believed he could count on some brothers in his community to fight with the people if their struggle became a symbol of the black struggle to recover land. But could he encourage this approach for his family?

Saki realized that another very difficult question was whether he was willing to join Amos in an active struggle for the land. He was one of only a few Blacks in the company where he worked, and he was aware of how threatened many of his white colleagues were by black majority rule. If he became a strong public advocate for land redistribution, his new job would be seriously jeopardized. The personal cost of any attempts to reclaim the land would be high for everyone concerned. To be successful, Saki, Amos, and the community would need allies as well as strategies.

NOTES

1. Townships such as Tembisa or the more well-known Soweto are residential areas set aside for black South Africans on the outskirts of white

urban areas. Between 1959 and 1991, Africans could live in the townships legally only if they had proof of employment in the area; those considered residents, as opposed to hostel-dwellers who were considered temporary laborers, were permitted to own houses but were not permitted to own land in the townships.

2. Boers is an Afrikaans word which literally means "farmers." It is often used to refer to all Afrikaners, descendants of Dutch settlers who first came to South Africa in the mid-1600s and who have led the Nationalist government since 1948.

3. The Afrikaner Resistant Movement (*Afrikaner Weerstandbeweging* in Afrikaans) is a militant, right-wing, pro-apartheid movement formed in 1973 by Eugene Terre Blanche, a former policeman and farmer.

4. A highly derogatory term.

5. The African National Congress was established in 1912 as the South African Native National Congress. This major African political organization was banned in South Africa in 1960 along with its president, Nobel Peace Prize winner Albert Luthuli. The ANC was again permitted to operate legally in South Africa in 1991. Nelson Mandela became leader of the ANC after his release from prison.

6. The Pan Africanist Congress, an African nationalist political organization favoring greater militancy, closer black African unity, and national pride, separated from the ANC in 1959. The PAC was also banned in 1960.

7. Bantu is a group of related languages spoken by central and southern African peoples; the term is used by some South Africans to refer to all Blacks.

8. The Khoi and San were Southern African nomadic aboriginal people who no longer existed as an identifiable group after the arrival of European settlers.

9. The National Peace Accord was initiated by church and business leaders and signed in 1992 by most political parties. The Accord agreed on rules of conduct for political parties and police, established a special investigative unit (the Goldstone Commission) and special courts to handle violations, and authorized development of national, regional, and local peace structures to assist in conflict resolution.

Commentary

To Our Own Land

Many ethical decisions focus on a conflict of values in a specific context. The case "To Our Own Land" calls on most North Americans to enter a culture and an historical context very different from their own. The background paragraphs of the case and the commentary provide factual information about the laws which led to the "forced removal" of the Monnakgola family, their community, and more than three million other South African persons of color from their homes. It is particularly challenging, however, for those of other cultures to comprehend the devastating effect the forced removals had on those involved.

The presenting problem in this case is whether or not Saki should encourage and support his brother Amos in gathering the original community members and proposing a return to their land. A decision to attempt to reclaim the land is one that the community would ultimately need to make. It is clear from the case, however, that Amos, as a community leader who has continued to take the people on the annual pilgrimage back to the land, would have significant influence with his people. Saki's concerns about encouraging Amos are compounded by the facts that efforts for land reclamation could further endanger the community and that Saki's new job in Johannesburg would be jeopardized if his support of land reclamation became known to his employer.

Beneath the personal dilemma of whether or not Saki should encourage Amos lies the challenge of discovering the most appropriate and effective strategies to reclaim the land and the dignity of the people. Because the case study "Oil and the Caribou People" deals directly with issues of land and identity, this commentary will focus primarily on strategies for liberation that include violent and nonviolent approaches. Amos and Saki note the possibility of enlisting the support of the Pan Africanist Congress, which advocates violence to meet goals when other approaches are not successful. In the eyes of the "third world" residents of many bantustans, taking up arms to recover land they consider stolen may be not only just retribution but an issue of survival. Ethical considerations involve the legitimacy and the effectiveness of a strategy of violence or "counter-violence" in this particular context. With this in mind, however, Saki poses a critical question facing South Africa and many other nations: how can past injustices related to land be redressed without jeopardizing future stability of the country?

Finally, even if Amos, his family, or any members of the community are able to regain ownership, would they be able to survive by returning to their land? In many cases in Zimbabwe and several Latin American countries, for example, simply turning over title or deed to landless people does not enable them to become self-sufficient. The people also need access to credit and the means to make the land productive.

The *context* of the dilemmas in this case is the unique circumstances which have led to this particular time in the history of South Africa. The reader is challenged to consider the Christian *norms* that would inform Saki and Amos's responses. And both the effectiveness and appropriateness of Saki's response involve the authenticity of his *relationship* with his family, his church, and the people with whom he works. Saki has established a life in an urban township and is part of an interracial religious community, but he also feels a commitment to his family and their community. He is struggling with the meaning of solidarity with them in the struggle for human dignity and self-determination. Context, norms, and relations all affect the decisions for Saki and Amos and ultimately for all of the members of the global human community who are committed to addressing the destructive effects of unjust national policies.

The case challenges the reader to empathize with a view from the "underside of history." This is an understanding of history in which God is active and where, in the words of liberation theologians from around the world who authored the 1987 Lusaka Statement, " . . . civil authority is instituted of God to do good, . . . under the Biblical imperative all people are obligated to do justice and to show special care for the poor and oppressed." It is from the perspective of the poor and oppressed, with whom God has already demonstrated solidarity, that the appropriateness of a forceful retaking of the land will be evaluated. The context will demand for many readers that they attempt to "see with new eyes" and "hear with new ears" the cry of these people.

CONTEXT: THE CONDITION OF THE PEOPLE

Hundreds of thousands of people of color in South Africa live in staggering poverty, malnutrition, and unemployment. Most of these people live in the bantustans or in squatter camps on the outskirts of apartheid-established black townships. The reality of their lives stands in stark contrast to the proportionate wealth and privilege of the vast majority of South Africans previously classified as White. The inequality is illustrated perhaps most shockingly in that a black child dies of hunger every fifteen minutes in what is acknowledged as the most prosperous African nation in terms of agricultural and natural mineral resources. The infant mortality rate in rural black South Africa is ten times that in white areas.

Allan Boesak, a prominent "colored" South African leader, describes the bantustans or homelands as "human dumping grounds." A bantustan such as Bophuthatswana, where the Monnakgola family lives, consists of numerous disconnected areas of land. Some of the allotted land is fertile, but the majority is barren. There are relatively few paved roads and minimal rail transportation. Unemployment in many of the bantustans is over 50 percent; in some areas 25 percent of the children die before their first birthday. While the laws that created and sustained the bantustan system were abolished in 1991 and 1992, there is little evidence that conditions of impoverishment have changed.

Prior to repeal of the apartheid laws, the apartheid system was based on several "pillars of apartheid." These included the Population Registration Act and the Group Areas Act, which sustained the system of segregation. Domination by four and a half million Whites who were eligible to vote was legally guaranteed, while twenty-six million black Africans were assigned to bantustans and consequently deprived of any meaningful voting rights. The Land Acts of 1913 and 1936 developed "reservations," allocating 13 percent of the land for Blacks and 87 percent of the land for Whites. The National States Constitution Act of 1970 decreed that all Blacks were citizens of one of ten ethnic bantustans and granted "independence" to these areas. Following this legislation, forced removals of Blacks from areas designated for either Whites, Coloreds, or Indians were intensified. Not all relocations were into the bantustans. Renewed application of the 1950 Group Areas Act forced sizable numbers of Indians (a South African designation for people of Asian descent) and Coloreds (persons of mixed race) from their urban homes to the periphery of cities and towns throughout South Africa. With no Bill of Rights and no functionally independent judiciary, people of color were severely limited in opportunities to appeal to the courts for recourse.

The financial and social ramifications for those who were forcibly removed from their homes, communities, and livelihood are incalculable. Most people of color in South Africa have lived for decades in a society which severely limited their access to employment, health, and education and legally stripped them of their citizenship and the basic human right to self-determination. The most serious deprivations were usually experienced by those who were forcibly removed to remote areas of the bantustans. A substantial number of people such as the Monnakgola family and their community were moved from agricultural lands where they were self-sufficient to barren areas where they were barely able to survive.

Analysis of extensive interviews with residents in nineteen relocation areas conducted in 1983 by the Surplus People Project (SPP) of South Africa (*Forced Removals in South Africa*, Vol. I [P.O. Box 187, Cape Town, 8000, RSA], p. 18.) concluded that even more significant than the material deprivation suffered by those who were removed were the "social and psychological effects inflicted on communities and individuals."

For most people the process of being relocated is one that only serves to emphasize their lack of personal control over their lives, over their families' lives. . . . The dominant mood in relocation areas is often one of passivity and helplessness in the face of the enormous problems and the hidden bureaucracy that controls people's lives. Organization is generally (though not always) very poor, particularly in the very isolated areas—relocation can be seen as a process of disorganization, as well as dispossession.

SPP interviewers reported that one of the most frequent responses to a question about who people believed would help them with their problems was basically "they put us here, they must do something, " but with little or no expectation of any help. The most frequent responses to questions about what people could do themselves were, "Nothing" and "I don't know." Insight into the passivity and disempowerment of persons who were forcibly removed may help readers understand why it is Saki and not Amos who proposes recovering the land. While conditions in the group area townships are poor, with inadequate services, a lack of infrastructure, and a high cost of living, the further away a relocation site is from a metropolitan area, the more desperate the living conditions are. The poorest areas, with crude cardboard or tin shelters, pit latrines, and few if any water sources, were the areas to which "the poorest, least skilled, most marginalized groups of relocated people were moved." (SPP, *Forced Removals*, p. 20.) By having the opportunity to move from the rural community to live with his aunt in the township, Saki was empowered by education, by consciousness of national political changes, by his active role in community politics, and by the sense of self-worth which came with being a provider for himself and his parents. Saki has control of his life in ways that Amos has never experienced. Retaking the land could be a significant step for Amos and the community toward recovering not only a lost identity with the land, but the dignity that comes with taking control over one's life.

In 1991, via the Abolition of Racially Based Land Measures Act, the government of President F. W. de Klerk repealed the Land Acts which had provided the legal framework for expropriating land to further apartheid. This Act opened the way for the purchase of land by anyone, regardless of race. Following very vocal criticism from a number of anti-apartheid organizations, the government amended the legislation to include the creation of an appointed Advisory Commission on Land Allocation to deal with land claims. While several organizations representing communities that had been forced from their land objected to the unrepresentative composition of the Commission and were concerned that the Commission had only an advisory status, numerous communities were willing to submit claims to the Commission. In the first two years, however, only four of the twenty claims submitted to the Commission were heard, and only two of these were successful. The Commission makes no provision for inhabitants of those communities which once held the land in common and were dispersed to different areas, making cooperative claims to recover their land almost impossible.

While there is in place a legal structure to adjudicate land claims, the system appears to be cumbersome and has been severely criticized by claimants and their legal counsel. Land, homes, and livelihoods were violently taken by the government in power. Violence was also done to human dignity as a dominant culture abused and seriously misunderstood the cultural heritage of people whose identity was tied to the land. Violence to persons of color has been direct, structural, and pervasive. A perspective "from below" might well justify counter-violence through forced reoccupation of the land as an ethically responsible form of self-defense. This is the perspective voiced by the Pan Africanist Congress, alluded to in the case, which advocates resorting to force when that appears to be the only option to reverse the destructive legacies of the apartheid system.

South Africa is in a dramatic transition from white minority rule to black majority rule. Within this context most South African Whites exist in virtual isolation from the human conditions of most Blacks, with contact often limited to domestic servants and shopkeepers. Isolation is reinforced by the media, with prominent stories of "black on black" violence featured regularly. The white population seems increasingly dominated by fear. Political forces to the right and left of the government denounce even modest reforms as either sellouts to white South African minority rights or manipulative gestures that are "too little, too late." The constant pressure of fear and anxiety, plus the loss of power and privilege, make it difficult for many Whites to hear and believe the assurances of the majority of black leaders that white minority rights will not disappear.

Ironically, if the white minority manages to block all restoration of land—a move that will sustain unjust land distribution, enshrine privilege based on color, and entrench the results of human rights abuses—this approach could well drive the landless to violent repossession of land. All property ownership in the new South Africa could become vulnerable, and those who obstruct an equitable process of restoration would ultimately be undermining their own security. The "white farmer" in the case study who holds title to the land once occupied by the Monnakgola family and their community may have done more to jeopardize his control of the land by his single rejection of the people on their annual pilgrimage than all the years in which his father opened the gates for the community to return to clean the graves. The farmer's fear of losing control and his tragic misunderstanding of the people's relationship to the land and their ancestors are significant barriers to peaceful resolution. For a growing number of Whites, the illusion of the restoration of peace and order without a radical change in the condition of the majority of South Africans is just that—an illusion. Whether that change will come about through dialogue and peaceful means or through violent confrontation is still to be determined.

There is already warfare in South Africa. The question is not how to avoid violence but how to contain it. Frank Chikane, Executive of the South African Council of Churches and author of *The Church's Prophetic Witness Against the Apartheid System in South Africa* makes it clear that the debate on issues of violence and nonviolence can continue only when there is a "space" where the participants experience no immediate threat to their lives. "People in the black townships of South Africa consider [discussion] 'a luxury' of which they have been deprived," declares Chikane. Those dominated by the society can no longer participate in an illusory debate because a state of war has already been declared, and a great deal of "space" has been eliminated. The Reverend Chikane observes, "Faced with this reality one can either run for one's life or fight back in self defense.... There is time only for responding to the violence of the system."

The view "from below" makes it clear that the war is between economic classes that are defined primarily along racial grounds. South Africa is engaged in a struggle for liberation by the poor against the non-poor. This struggle is not limited to South Africa. In South America, Central America, North America, and Australia, for example, poor and marginalized peoples, often aboriginal people, have been robbed of their lands by dominant cultures.

THEOLOGICAL RATIONALE

Seventy-two percent of South Africans claim to be Christian. Those on different sides of the conflict about land call on different components of the Christian Gospel to support their positions. The Dutch Reformed Church (DRC), the largest Christian denomination of white South Africans, traditionally justified apartheid through biblical interpretation. The term apartheid is an Afrikaaner word meaning "separateness." While the DRC has formally renounced its support of apartheid, the denomination continues to take a strong stand against violence toward the state and offers theological justification for actions deemed necessary for the preservation of law and order. A confessional statement from South Africa entitled the Kairos document identifies this view as "state theology." "State theology" gives "divine" authority (Romans 13:1-7) to the state in the name of "law and order" and renounces all violence toward or criticism of the state. Some argue that as majority rule by black South Africans becomes the accepted norm, many black churches will adopt "state theology."

Many other South African Christians, including millions of Blacks in independent African churches, while condemning the results of apartheid, refrain from any direct political involvement in the struggle. They advocate a clear division between issues of church and state. The Kairos document describes this position as "church theology." "Church theology" does not involve any analysis of society and applies traditional themes of reconciliation, justice, and nonviolence while supporting a blanket condemnation of all that is called violence.

Saki Monnakgola appears to have rejected both of these positions. He seems to be viewing the world from the perspective of those who are struggling for liberation. The theological norms that might inform his reflection on whether or not and how to support Amos and the community are influenced by the view of a theology or Christology "from below." This view from the "underside of history," the view of oppressed people, may challenge traditional theological norms on violence and nonviolence. Church historians remind contemporary Christians that in pre-Constantinian days the church was identified with the poor and outcasts of society. Christians were known as "dangerous subversives." In the centuries following Constantine, the church became identified with the ruling classes and with Western civilization. In a conflict of values, the church came to identify with the dominant values of ruling regimes and frequently legitimated the use of violence by these regimes while opposing revolutionary violence to overthrow them.

There is another theological tradition, one that distinguishes between oppressive state violence and the use of violence in self-defense against aggressors and tyrants, which may be helpful to Saki and Amos. This perspective, sometimes known as the "just war" tradition, allows for a theological understanding and at times a theological legitimization of force. This understanding supports not only the theological right to resist tyranny, but the theological obligation to do so in "obedience to God." Although nonviolence is still normative for the church, the alternative just-war tradition has been rediscovered by numerous liberation theologians, including the framers of the South African Kairos document.

The Kairos document takes its name from the Greek word meaning "the present time" and conveys a sense of crisis (Luke 12:56). Seen by many as one of the most important theological documents of the twentieth century, the document was developed by an interracial group of over one hundred fifty professional theologians, lay theologians, and church leaders as "a Christian, biblical, and theological comment on the political crisis in South Africa." The document was intended to stimulate discussion and action. While the Kairos document was written prior to the dramatic legal changes in the early and mid-1990s that removed the legislative structures upholding apartheid, the document continues to speak to the critical need to address the entrenched effects of apartheid.

The Kairos document rejects both "state theology" and "church theology" while proposing a "prophetic theology" that views apartheid or any forms of discriminatory separation as heresy and the effects of apartheid as evil. This particular theological position is based on an interpretation of the Christian Gospel that establishes a method and several norms for decision and action.

A social analysis of any particular "kairos" is the first step in the process of developing a prophetic theology. The methodology employed is one of "praxis" which involves dialogue between experience and theological reflection and which begins with the experience of the people. The social analysis of South Africa in the Kairos document reveals a "conflict between oppressor and oppressed" with "irreconcilable causes or interests." The "far right," identified in the case with military movements such as the AWB, seeks to sustain at all costs systems of power and privilege. Amos clearly expressed his concern about the militant farmers who are arming themselves to protect their farms from occupation. The "far left" identified in the case with the position of the PAC, seeks at all costs to change the structure of society and eliminate the role of the white minority in political decisions. Proponents of the far left see legal reforms as attempts to insure that the system is not radically changed. Through his relationship with Whites in a Christian congregation, Saki has become sensitive to the perspectives of those who have strongly opposed the apartheid system but who would suffer, perhaps unjustly, if their homes and land were taken by force. If the community decides to mobilize and reclaim the land, neither of these confrontational approaches may offer hope for long-term resolution of land distribution.

The case raises the quandary of "how far back" one should go to establish legitimate claims to the land. Many militant black Africans consider all of the land in South Africa to belong to Blacks whose ancestors lived throughout Southern Africa. These ancestors did not adhere to western concepts of land ownership. While much of the land was taken by colonial military power, other areas were seen by European settlers three to four hundred years ago as "unoccupied" and in no way "owned" by nomadic tribal groups whom they saw as only occasionally passing through the territory. Other land was bought from African tribal leaders. More recently South African lands were taken by the Nationalist Government under the category of "eminent domain" for dams, transportation systems, schools, or other public projects. Vast areas designated as game parks or military reserves have also been cleared of residents. The original farms and grazing lands no longer exist. Force, coercion, and unjust laws were also used to place land control and ownership in the hands of Whites, to a lesser extent in the hands of Indians and Coloreds, and to assign the poorest areas to Blacks.

Over sixty South African communities that were forcibly removed from their land in the past forty years have formed a coalition to support the Land Restoration Campaign. This group has identified eight different groups whose land claims they support. The first group that forms the core of the campaign is former land owners who held deeds to their land. Other groups include those who did not have title but who lived for many years, often generations, on government land before being forced off; tenants and farm workers who had been given small pieces of land in exchange for work but were later evicted by the farmers; and owners who lost part of their land by encroachment of white farmers. The issues and claims are very complex; a long-term solution to just land distribution will not easily be found. Christians, however, may call on several norms to inform responsible and just strategies.

1. *God is the liberator of the oppressed.* The Bible makes this clear in the Exodus story telling of the liberation of the Israelites from bondage in Egypt (Ex. 3:7-9), and in the Gospels with Jesus' identification as the one prophesied by Isaiah to bring " good news to the poor, . . . release to the captives, . . . and to set at liberty those who are oppressed" (Luke 4:18-19). Oppression is seen as a basic category of biblical theology, and God has taken sides. God is concerned about the rich who benefit from oppressive structures and God calls them to repentance, not simply to compromise or reconciliation. The first norm is to name and resist oppression and support God's liberating activity in the world.

2. *God calls us to seek justice* (Micah 6:8). Since tyranny is the enemy of the common good of all the people, it is the enemy of God and must be eliminated. There is a moral right and an obligation to resist tyranny because it violates the image and likeness of God in the people. What the tyrant or tyrannical structures do to the least of the people is done to God (Matt. 25:49). Christians are called to love their enemies (Matt. 5:44); the way to do this is to eliminate oppression for the sake of the oppressors as well as the oppressed. Several methods of eliminating oppression are suggested in the Kairos document as a challenge to action: taking sides as God does with the oppressed; participating in the struggle for liberation and justice; transforming all church activities as a sign of solidarity; civil disobedience; and providing moral guidance on the duty to resist oppression and to curb excesses. There is no specific recommendation on violence or force in the document, but it is clearly not condemned in prophetic theology. The second norm, then, is to identify and resist tyranny and to seek justice through concrete action.

3. *The hope of Christ is confidence in a realm of love, justice, and peace.* Faith means hope. Tyranny and oppression cannot last forever. Real justice, authentic peace, and genuine reconciliation are assured by God's grace in the coming of the realm which Christ initiated. The struggle will be difficult, costly, and conflictual. But, the Kairos document declares, "At the very heart of the Gospel of Jesus Christ and at the very center of all true prophecy is a message of hope." The third norm is to act with confidence that hope for liberation and justice is already a reality in Jesus Christ and the Kingdom of God.

4. *God calls for the respect of human dignity.* The dignity of the human person has its source in the doctrine of creation, the understanding that each person is created in the image of God, the mandate to see Christ in the other, and God's plan for the redemption of each person. In the words of American Roman Catholic bishops, "Every human being possesses an inalienable right that stamps human existence prior to a division into races or nations

and prior to human labor and human achievement." The fourth norm is to recognize and ensure basic human rights and the self-determination of peoples.

5. *God's power redeems the whole creation.* God's power to redeem points to the end of poverty and the restoration of the land. God's will is for every person to have sufficient resources to meet basic needs and for all species and ecosystems to be sustainable. The fifth norm makes it the responsibility of all social institutions to assist in meeting basic needs and protecting the land.

UNDERSTANDING OF "VIOLENCE"

Understanding violence is crucial to Saki and Amos's decisions. It is sometimes helpful to distinguish between the "force" of the state and the "self-defense" of the oppressed. Violence, however, is generally understood as an "all inclusive act of compulsion or restraint," according to South African scholar Charles Villa-Vicencio, who suggests several propositions that may clarify issues of violence within the particular context of South Africa.

1. *Some form of violence is an inherent part of the political process.* From Mahatma Gandhi to Martin Luther King, nonviolent resistance to the force of the state did not guarantee restraint on the part of authorities. Peaceful demonstrations by children in Soweto in 1976 resulted in their killing and imprisonment. By definition, the state is the holder of the final means of force. Regardless of tactics, some degree of violence is inevitable.

2. *There is a difference between state violence and tyranny.* A state that genuinely represents its people may resort on occasion to the use of force. When a state lacks the consent and respect of the governed, however, it becomes an illegitimate regime or a tyranny and maintains its power by the use of violence. Repeal of apartheid laws and the enfranchisement of the black majority have propelled South Africa into the tumultuous process of moving from an illegitimate to a legitimate representative government. Unless and until any new government is able to respond to the needs of its landless and marginalized citizens, however, it is not likely to have the legitimacy that comes from support of the majority of its people.

3. *Revolution is an inevitable response to state tyranny.* Liberation is a human desire; history suggests that people will eventually resort to violence if necessary to gain freedom. The church must be as concerned with the morality of indifference as with the morality of violence.

4. *Not all violence is revolutionary violence.* Most frequently overlooked are institutional and structural violence such as dehumanizing laws, poverty, and the resulting hopelessness. There is the direct violence of vigilante groups but also the anarchic or purposeless violence that can occur in the struggle for liberation.

5. *The spiral of violence needs to be broken.* Violence and counter-violence

will not change the structure of a society like South Africa. The need is to build a different kind of society that is more equitable and sustainable.

RELATIONSHIPS: INDIVIDUAL AND COMMUNITY

Saki faces ethical decisions in the context of a nation at a distinctive historical turning point. The context determines the boundaries of the path Saki and Amos take in their decisions about the land and the struggle for self-determination. The norms for the work of liberation, justice, and human dignity provide a series of signposts along the way with which they can check-in to reorient the trip. Saki's ethical decisions are not determined by either the context or the norms, but one hopes he will be informed by both. The relational dimension of Saki's decisions may be as important as the context and norms.

Saki's cultural relationship to his older brother Amos demands respect. Saki is also indebted to Amos as his connection or bridge to the family and the land. The traditional roles were reversed, however, when Saki became a provider for the wider family, especially his parents who depend on his monthly checks. Should Saki lose his job because of his involvement in a campaign to reclaim the land, the family's minimal security may be threatened.

As an urban community leader, Saki has the support of many friends in the township. There is a subtle distinction in most South African townships between "elected officials," who have often been selected and supported by the Nationalist government, and "civic" or community leaders who have often taken strong stands in opposition to apartheid structures. The case implies that Saki, who has friends in the PAC, is a community activist with strong ties to others engaged in the anti-apartheid struggle. These relationships will be very helpful to Saki if his friends decide to join him in reclaiming the land. Saki is aware, however, that if strong political assistance is secured, his and his family's needs may become less important than the cause of reclamation.

A third set of relationships which appear to have an impact on Saki's perspective are those formed in his church. As part of an integrated congregation, Saki has met Whites who have taken personal and professional risks to join black South Africans in the struggle to abolish apartheid structures. There may be white colleagues in the congregation who would not only be willing but who have special skills to support Amos and his community in an effort to reclaim the land. The congregational relationships may have also contributed to Saki's questioning the justice of taking land from those Whites who were not involved in the violent acquisition of land.

Amos, as the older brother with dependent elderly parents, is assumed by his community to be the family leader. While Amos is surely grateful for Saki's support and goes out of his way to keep in touch with his brother, he may find the family's dependence on Saki's job in Johannesburg difficult to accept. The normal cultural pattern is also for the oldest brother to advise those younger. It will also be difficult for Amos to accept Saki's advice and assistance, particularly since Saki's urban experience and sophistication give him greater ability to deal with the complex issues involved in land reclamation.

Saki must be extremely careful that he not put his own agenda on Amos. Amos and the community in Bophuthatswana are those who will be most affected by any attempt to reclaim the land, and only they can make the final decision. Saki's concern is to support his family and the people of the community if they decide to reclaim the land. Seeing his decision "from below" as he does suggests two primary avenues of action: counter-violence and active nonviolent resistance.

OPTION: COUNTER-VIOLENCE

Historically, the church, while regularly condemning violence, has frequently supported it in defense of the state or the state's right to maintain law and order. The church supports violence by the state when it identifies primarily with those in power. Identification with minority voices is quite difficult because the dominant ideology is usually determined by those in power. Voices "from below," from people in a subjugated class and culture who seek to control their own destiny, are difficult to hear, especially when they speak in terms of violence. If Saki seeks an alliance with his township friends in the PAC, they will likely seek to justify counter-violence as an act of self-defense. They will argue that there is both the right and the obligation of Christians to resist tyranny for the sake of liberation.

It is not clear that Saki has come to terms with his own conflict in class values. While Saki is marginalized and disadvantaged when compared to South African Whites, he has nevertheless benefited from the economic and social structures of apartheid. He himself is being challenged to face the contradiction of protected privilege and counter claims of solidarity with his people. Since the question in this context is not just about the morality of violence but also about the morality of a struggle for liberation, his decision is all the more difficult.

OPTION: ACTIVE NONVIOLENT RESISTANCE

Identifying with oppressed people calls for solidarity with their interests and causes, but it does not always mean one responds by complying with specific requests. Amos has made the assumption that reclaiming the land will involve direct, open confrontation with the farmer. There may be, however, creative nonviolent ways for Saki and his colleagues to support the community.

Some black South Africans have declared that concepts such as "nonviolence" and "reconciliation" have come to be hated as much as "apartheid."

Amos scornfully announces that " 'peace' and 'reconciliation' are cheap words." The suspicion is pervasive and not unjustified that the repeated calls for nonviolence and reconciliation were tools of the dominant pro-apartheid minority to maintain the status quo. "Reconciliation," when interpreted as capitulation to a stronger force, can become an instrument of oppression.

An alternative social analysis would suggest, however, that expropriation or forced retaking of the land are not the only viable and effective means of changing the status quo. Taking up arms could lead the people to participate in the spiral of direct violence for which many current land owners are better armed. In other words, to engage the enemy of the people on their own grounds, while it might be theologically justifiable, would be a tactical error in the legitimate struggle for liberation. An armed encounter could invite a disastrous loss of life on both sides.

There are other ways for Saki to demonstrate his solidarity with the people. One of these could be through a creative, sustained program of active nonviolent support of land reclamation which may have more hope of recovering the land and transforming South African society than the use of direct force. While the Land Restoration Campaign, begun in 1990, continues to support the approach of directly reoccupying land, members of the campaign support multi-party negotiations; educating dispossessed people about their rights; forming local, regional, and national land organizational structures; and "mass action." Mass action entails marches; pickets; "stay-aways;" sit-ins; lobbying churches, foreign embassies, the trade unions; using the media to educate the public; and establishing a People's Land Claims Court. Many of these approaches were used effectively throughout the late 1980s and early 1990s to bring about the dramatic reversal of apartheid legislation.

While the Land Restoration Campaign supports reoccupation of land by former owners or tenants, the campaign does not advocate the use of military force. With a deep distrust of the predominantly white South African Defense Force which was used to suppress them, many black South Africans have resisted giving up the military wings of numerous anti-apartheid organizations such as the PAC. Some see the separate military forces as the only means to regain control of the land. To counter this resistance and promote a nonviolent means of dealing with the separate military units, South Africa has instituted the unique approach of the Joint Peacekeeping Unit. The establishment of this unit, a concept originally proposed by Stanley Mogoba, the Methodist bishop of Southern Africa, holds promise as a nonviolent way to bring about peace. Representatives of competing military forces form single units that are trained in skills of conflict resolution. These interracial, multi-lingual units hold the potential of building the nation's trust in ways which polarized military units could never do. The use of joint forces builds on the recognition that non-racialism is the only viable option for the new South Africa.

The Land Claims Court was proposed as a nationally elected body. It will be an extremely difficult and long-term task to bring dispossessed black South Africans to trust the judicial system. Growing confidence in the court system as fair and unbiased will depend not only on a history of balanced rulings but on the development of a representative judiciary. At the time of the first national election in April 1994, all jurists in South Africa were white males, with the exception of one white woman. Movement toward a multi-racial civil service, especially in the judiciary, is a critical step toward the long-term stability of the just society that Saki hopes for.

The success of small units emphasizing conflict resolution represented in the Land Restoration Campaign makes clear that negotiation is an important tool to reclaim the land. Successful negotiations were also promoted by the National Peace Accord. As noted in the case end notes, the accord was initiated by church and business leaders and signed in 1992 by most political parties. The accord established rules of conduct for political parties and police, a special investigative unit (the Goldstone Commission), and special courts to handle violations. It also authorized development of national, regional, and local peace structures to assist in conflict resolution. While the regional and local structures, or Peace Committees, have not been successful in all situations, there have been remarkable successes in negotiating resolutions to many potentially violent confrontations. South Africans have developed a strong culture of negotiation at every level of the society.

Finally, if the land is taken by force without employing democratic structures, tenure by those who occupy the land may be short-lived. Amos is keenly aware that he and the community do not have seeds or plows. To be sustainable, any land distribution program must build in support structures. Farmers need access to credit, training in modern agricultural techniques, adequate roads, and access to markets. These support structures can be supplied throughout the country on a fair and non-racial basis by the strong backing of democratically elected Parliamentary representatives. Black and white South African leaders have concluded that the country cannot prosper unless mutual interests are met. This inescapable reality brought an end to apartheid and must be the cornerstone of new legislation to bring about equal justice.

ROLE OF THE CHURCH

Amos perceptively asks, "Will the church be as supportive of fighting for our rights when the cost is much more than words?" Churches must not only talk about nonviolent resistance but actually engage in it. Nonviolent resistance draws on a theological tradition different from that of many liberation theologians prominent in Central America. It calls for a rediscovery of the work and thought of Mahatma Gandhi, who began his life work in South Africa. Another source is what Martin Luther King, Jr., called "active love" in a civil rights movement profoundly rooted in the Christian tradition. Nonviolence was for King, as for Gandhi, first of all a way of life; to use it as a technique is the first step in one's own transformation. King confessed, "I believe that unarmed truth and unconditional love will have the final word in reality." Many proponents see this form of active nonviolent resistance as reducing the future danger of continued militarization of the state and the glorification of violence as a form of oppression under a new government.

Nonviolence, as developed in the biblical tradition, is a commitment that is not passive but active, not careful but costly, and not safe but suffering. It is especially identified with Jesus. A fresh understanding of scriptural passages such as "turning the other cheek" and "going the second mile" (Matt. 5:38-41) need to be reappropriated.

Saki might try to mobilize his congregation, both clergy and laity, to support the land claim of his brother's Bophuthatswana community. But the church in South Africa is challenged to take a much broader view of the struggle for land distribution than to support individual cases. Christians may be called not only to join those involved in mass action but also to become actively involved in negotiations about land. Many church leaders and committed grass roots community lay leaders are acquiring training in skills of mediation and negotiation to equip them for a more active role. Christians may also be called to challenge their individual denominations to look seriously at past histories of unjust land appropriation and to consider the most faithful use of thousands of acres of fertile land owned or controlled by churches throughout the country. Just distribution of church lands would be a dramatic step toward breaking the cycle of injustice.

Historically, South Africans involved in the struggle against apartheid tended to force a choice between violent and nonviolent responses to apartheid. In the struggle to end the unjust effects of entrenched apartheid policies, both positions may have a place, but those who engage in counter-violence to reclaim the land must seriously consider the effects of violent confrontations on long-term land ownership and the shaping of a new non-racial society.

THE CALL FOR ACTION

Signers of the Kairos document called for discussion, debate, reflection, prayer and, most of all, action. In South Africa, where ultimately the issue of just land distribution will be settled by South Africans themselves, there are arenas in the spheres of counter-violence and nonviolence that are yet to be tested. Conflict, suffering, and death are unlikely to diminish immediately with either approach. Signs of hope rest with nonviolent tactics such as those undertaken by the Land Restoration Campaign, local and regional peace committees, a growing force of trained grass roots mediators, and the Joint-Peace-Keeping Force.

An ethical response to an ethical debate might appropriately follow with the moment of truth (Kairos) for South Africa and the world community. Allan Boesak, a colored South African church leader, and Alan Brews, a white South African Methodist clergyman, reflect the spirit of the multi-racial gathering in Harare when they conclude, ". . . for the majority of oppressed Blacks the issue is not violence but liberation." This perspective from the "underside of history" challenges those in power in the global community to respond to the dilemmas of land distribution and the building of a new society in South Africa with new eyes.

ADDITIONAL RESOURCES

Boesak, Allan A., and Alan Brews. "The Black Struggle for Liberation: A Reluctant Road to Revolution," in *Theology and Violence: The South African Debate.* Charles Villa-Vincenio, ed. Grand Rapids, MI: William Eerdmans Publishing Company, 1987.

Evans, Alice Frazer, Robert A. Evans, William Bean Kennedy. *Pedagogies for the Non-Poor.* Maryknoll, NY: Orbis Books, 1987.

"Forced Removals in South Africa: General Overview," Surplus People Project Report, Vol. I, P.O. Box 187, Cape Town 8000, South Africa

From South Africa: A Challenge to the Church. Theology in a Global Context Program, 22 Tenakill Street, Closter, NJ 07627. Contains the Kairos Document and the Harare Declaration.

Land Update, a regular publication of the National Land Committee, P.O. Box 30944, Braamfontein 2017, Johannesburg, South Africa.

Villa-Vicencio, Charles, ed. *Theology and Violence: The South African Debate.* Grand Rapids, MI: William B. Eerdmans Publishing Company, 1987.

Wink, Walter. *Violence and Nonviolence in South Africa: Jesus' Third Way.* Philadelphia, PA: New Society Publishers, 1987.

PART IV

THE ENVIRONMENT

Case

Snake in the Grass

Erica Mann sat in her den still working at 10:30 P.M. after a long Friday at her office in the Federal Building in downtown Phoenix. At thirty-eight, Erica was a respected research biologist and conservationist, even though she had earned her Ph.D. in zoology only three years earlier. She was proud of her success, which she felt was the result of hard work, self-sacrifice, and high ethical standards.

Erica was the Endangered Species Coordinator for the Western Division of the Federal Wildlife Agency (FWA). A unit of the Department of the Interior, the FWA had a congressional mandate to enforce and carry out the provisions of the Endangered Species Act (ESA) of 1973, which directed federal agencies not to carry out, fund, or authorize projects which jeopardize a threatened or endangered species or destroy habitats critical to their survival. Erica's job was to identify threatened and endangered species in her district, see that they were listed in the Federal Register, and enforce the ESA. Another of her agency's functions was to assess the likely effects of proposed federal construction projects on any endangered species. These assessments normally were included in a project's Environmental Impact Statement. Her job of protecting endangered species had not been made any easier by a 1978 amendment to the ESA which provided for a seven-member review committee to grant exemptions to the strict provisions of the act if economic benefits were substantial.

Erica was also the chair of the Conservation Committee of the International Herpetological Society (IHS), a worldwide organization of over 2,200 herpetologists. Although the society's chief role was the promotion of scientific research on reptiles and amphibians, it also provided information for public education and conservation purposes. Erica's involvement with the society reflected a love of reptiles stemming from her childhood infatuation with dinosaurs.

Until recently her dual roles as FWA Endangered Species Coordinator and IHS Conservation Committee chair had blended smoothly, combining the best aspects of vocation and avocation. Now it looked as though a national environmental group, the Environmental Preservation Club, was preparing to sue the federal government over a case in which the IHS and the FWA were involved on opposite sides.

The problem had arisen the previous July when Erica proposed that the Sonoran desert snake be listed as an endangered species. The snake was already listed as endangered by the Arizona State Wildlife Office and was threatened with extinction because it has a restricted habitat, and there was a possibility that that habitat would be destroyed. This species could be found in only a few isolated places in the desert near the Bailey River, a tributary of the Colorado River in western Arizona. An independent study conducted for the FWA by a biological consulting firm had documented previous local extinctions of the Sonoran desert snake due to flooding of the habitat by dams along the river. The investigators had concluded: " . . . the real hazard posed by any new dam is a large increase in the probability of total extinction of the species."

In September, the U.S. Bureau of Inland Waters presented the FWA with plans to build Blevins Dam on the Bailey River to provide water for irrigation, recreation, and the projected growth of industry and new homes in the area. The bureau requested an assessment of the Sonoran desert snake for the Environmental Impact Statement. Erica's FWA report, delivered to the Department of the Interior in December for approval, had ended with the following statement:

> There are no known measures which can be implemented in conjunction with the Blevins Dam to avoid jeopardizing the Sonoran desert snake or adversely modifying its natural habitat. Our advisory recommendations are that the water supply needs of the area be met through the development of an alternate water supply source. We considered the possibility of improving the survival outlook for the snake through creation of an artificial habitat in the area adjacent to the proposed reservoir. However, we determined that this alternative is not viable because detailed knowledge of the habitat requirements of the Sonoran desert snake does not presently exist. Such information would require several years of extensive and intensive field and laboratory study to obtain.

In May Erica was shocked to read the Bureau of Inland Water's Environmental Impact Statement for the Blevins Dam:

> Artificial habitats that will allow the species to carry out all phases of its life cycle can be created and maintained. Areas adjacent to the new

lake could be planted with vegetation species endemic to the areas in which the Sonoran desert snake occurs naturally. A team of biologists could then engage in extensive trapping of the Sonoran desert snake in areas threatened with inundation as the lake fills and relocate the species to the new artificial habitat. Long-term commitments to best management practices within the newly created habitat would be maintained by all parties concerned (i.e., the U.S. Bureau of Inland Waters, the Federal Wildlife Agency, the Blevins County Municipal Water Management Authority, and the Arizona State Wildlife Office) to facilitate successful colonization of the Sonoran desert snake in these areas.

Stunned by the bureau's reversal of her FWA recommendation and the twisting of her analysis, Erica called Susan Winston, a friend who worked for the FWA in Washington, D.C. "The word through the grapevine," Susan said, "is that Senator Elder promised his constituents that the project would proceed even if he had to gut the entire Endangered Species Act to do it. He seems willing to call in every political debt to get this dam built. You know he has been in the Senate for over twenty years and served two House terms and as governor before that. If you ask me, it looks fishy. Orders probably came down from the secretary as a result of pressure from Senator Elder, and your report was misrepresented accordingly."

Not long after talking with Susan, Erica received a telephone call from David Miller, the country's leading snake biologist. "Erica, the top is about to blow off the Sonoran snake issue," David said with authority. "I was just at a meeting with lawyers from the Environmental Preservation Club, and they are saying it could be the test of the Endangered Species Act they have been waiting for. The Blevins Dam project is so clearly in violation of the act and the plans for that artificial habitat are so patently weak that they are sure they can win. Everyone knows that no new field studies were conducted on the snake between your December report and the reversal in the Environmental Impact Statement in May. There is absolutely no biological basis for building artificial habitats, and no reason to think that the snake can survive in them. The IHS leadership wants to throw the full weight of the society behind the Environmental Preservation Club. As IHS Conservation Committee chair, we are expecting you to take a leading role in this."

Walter Jackson was District Director for the FWA and Erica's immediate superior. He had held the position as Endangered Species Coordinator before his promotion to director two years ago. Walt was a close friend and a respected colleague. It was he who had suggested that Erica apply for the vacant coordinator position. Walt approached Erica in the Federal Building cafeteria at lunch. "I am as upset as you are at having to swallow that new report," Walt had said, "but sometimes we have to forgo fighting a battle when we will lose the war, Erica. You and I know that the Environmental Preservation Club is crazy to think they can make a case on this one. No judge or jury in any Western state will ever defend a snake against the water needs of humans. Worse, you are clearly faced with a conflict of interest if this thing goes to court. I would hate to have you lose your job over a lost cause. You are a good coordinator, Erica, and we will need your help to fight other battles we can win. Stick with the agency on this one and then you can help me go after that timber company operation that is threatening the eagle nests up north."

Dick Gilsey, professor of environmental ethics and Erica's teacher in college, called after reading Fight for Wildlife, the Environmental Preservation Club's activist newsletter. "Erica, you know that each of God's creatures exists for a particular purpose, even if that purpose is hidden from us. Remember the Rosy Periwinkle, that inconspicuous tropical flower you learned about in my course. Who could have guessed that it could provide drugs for treating childhood leukemia and Hodgkin's disease? The loss of genetic diversity means the loss of opportunities for future generations— for medicine, industry, and agriculture. There is the possibility, no matter how remote, that this snake holds some irreplaceable value for our health and welfare. I admit we do not know what it does out there in the desert. Maybe it will never have any direct value for us at all. But at the very least it fills some functional role in the ecosystem, even if we do not yet understand what it is. In any case, does dominion over the earth mean that we have the right to destroy other species that inhabit this planet with us, or does it mean that we have the responsibility as God's stewards to care for them? Extinction is forever, Erica. Once that snake is gone, its functional contribution to the ecosystem, its genes, and its potential gifts can never be brought back."

Erica sat back at her desk and thumbed through the Environmental Impact Statement for the Blevins Dam Project, stopping at the section entitled "Local Involvement: Citizens, Groups, and Individuals." The many letters from local residents appended to the report were nearly unanimous in their support for the project. She read aloud excerpts from several of the letters:

Animals are sacrificed in laboratories for science. If the Sonoran desert snake has to be sacrificed for the sake of water for human beings, I see no difference.

If the environmentalists had to have their water supply rationed in the heat of the summer, maybe they would agree that we cannot live without water.

This is what the Bible says about the value of a snake in Genesis 3:14: "So the Lord God said to the serpent, 'this is your punishment: You are singled out from among all the domestic and wild animals of the whole earth to be cursed.' "

I hope there are enough good people with good common sense to outweigh those radicals with all their priorities in the wrong place.

We desperately need water in this state to support mining and agriculture. I am reminded of the Book of Genesis, Chapter 1, verses 26-29, where God gave human beings dominion over the earth and "over every creeping thing." Gentlemen, I am concerned about protecting our environment as much as the next person, but this issue of the Sonoran desert snake borders on the ridiculous when it comes to the survival of the mining and agricultural industries of Arizona.

Closing the report, Erica picked up the letter she had received two days ago from Jack Knight, president of IHS. After glancing at the clock, she reread the closing paragraph:

Conservation issues are important for the Society. It is important to protect natural populations from catastrophic habitat modification and inappropriate exploitation. Although I appreciate your uncomfortable position as an employee of the federal government, I must know for certain whether you will stand with the IHS on this issue. I will call this Friday night at 11 P.M. for your decision.

As Erica put the letter on her desk and glanced at the clock again, the telephone rang.

Commentary

Snake in the Grass

The problem is deceptively simple: the snake or the dam. Given the arid Southwest's thirst for water and the low status of snakes since Genesis 3:14, all the makings for a quick decision are present. Why not cave in to Senator Elder and the compromisers? Over against the great benefits to people of water on otherwise useless land, what is the worth of the insignificant Sonoran desert snake?

Actually, the snake has considerable worth as a symbol, as a contributor to human welfare, and as an intrinsic good. As symbol, this snake represents the rapid extinction of species resulting from the destruction of fragile ecosystems worldwide. The snake is a potential contributor to human welfare because its irreplaceable genetic material might afford options for scientific efforts to improve human health and to increase the food supply. As for the intrinsic good of the Sonoran desert snake, the authors of Genesis 1 are quite clear that God created it and all other species good.

Moreover, an additional dam in the desert of western Arizona may be difficult to justify. Dams have their uses: irrigation for an increased food supply, flood control, recreation, electricity for homes and industry, and clean water for drinking. But this dam may not be well suited for these purposes, and the costs of construction and maintenance may be greater than the financial benefits. There is even a certain amount of foolishness in encouraging settlement in the arid Western United States where only limited numbers are sustainable unless huge, expensive, and complex transfers of water between river basins are undertaken.

When the deeper ramifications are considered, the simple snake versus dam arithmetic becomes a more complicated calculus. The task is to see the Sonoran desert snake in terms of this more complicated calculus.

The Christian tradition, especially as it developed in Western Europe, is not without problems in all of this. Since the Industrial Revolution, a utilitarian view of nature has dominated this tradition. The command to take dominion of the earth in Genesis 1 has generally been interpreted as license to use nature willy-nilly for human purposes. The side of the tradition which sees nature as intrinsically good has been muted. Today species extinction, environmental degradation, and new questions about sustainability call into question this dominant utilitarian view and invite Christians to consider alternatives.

This case also raises two ethical issues which have appeared in other cases.The first is the dilemma of sticking to principle or seeking effective compromise. Should Erica rigorously follow the ethical and professional instincts which brought her in on the side of the snake, or should she work responsibly within the federal bureaucracy and understand that politics is the art of the possible and that giving in to special interests now may yield important dividends in the future?

The second question has to do with those special interests themselves, symbolized in the case by Senator Elder and the distortion of Erica's report. The history of water projects in the United States, particularly in the South and West, is one in which special interests and pork barreling have been pronounced. The Sonoran desert snake has no voice, and the few who will come to its defense seldom have anything to gain and are chronically underfunded. Were it not for a strong love of nature among Americans, the snake would not have a chance.

SPECIES EXTINCTION

The extinction of the Sonoran desert snake would not be an isolated event. It would be just one of an unprecedented number of species extinctions resulting from human destruction of habitats.

Scientists have estimated the total number of species may be as many as 30 million or more. This remarkable diversity is a result of 3.5 billion years of evolution. Perhaps as many as two-thirds of all animal species that ever existed are now gone. Historically as many as six periods of mass extinctions can be documented in fossil remains, most induced by climate changes. These periods have lasted as long as two million years, as was the case with the extinction of dinosaurs.

Unlike earlier periods, in the last 100,000 years human beings have increasingly been the cause of extinctions. Today the contraction of biological diversity is proceeding at a faster rate than ever before, or so the fossil record seems to indicate. This is cause for alarm. Especially worrisome is the loss of tropical rain forests which cover only 7 percent of the world's land area but host about 40 percent of species.

Humans cause extinctions through such activities as hunting, forest clearing, conversion of virgin land to agricultural use, the pollution of air and water, the construction of dams, and the control of predators. Hunting works directly, the other activities indirectly through destruction of habitat.

Some species are already well along in a natural process of extinction which human intrusion only hastens. Others are well suited to their environments but do not possess traits which allow adaptation to human interventions. Still others reproduce slowly and cannot bounce back from a rapid loss of numbers. Finally, there are those with narrow habitat requirements, usually having to do with feeding, which are doomed when their narrow habitat is disrupted. Without further information it is difficult to determine to what extent these factors are at work with the Sonoran desert snake. The threat of human intrusion is obvious, however—flooding the snake's habitat with a dam will have a major impact upon the snake's environment.

PRESERVATION?

The case for and against preservation rests on four considerations: the usefulness of the snake for humans, the usefulness of the dam for humans, the Christian tradition's view of nature, and the goodness of the snake in itself.

Usefulness of the Snake

So what is the usefulness for humans of the Sonoran desert snake? For one thing the snake is part of a functioning ecosystem which could be destroyed with the loss of a particular species. This dire outcome is unlikely given the rarity of the snake, but in its own fragile system the snake plays some roll as predator and prey. Humans have much at stake in the preservation of healthy ecosystems. Whether this particular snake and this particular system are of great significance is not the point. They represent something very precious. Healthy ecosystems are the very foundation of life.

Second is the matter of genetic diversity which is contracting at an alarming rate. Again the Sonoran desert snake represents something larger than itself. As total genetic diversity decreases, so does the genetic pool for further evolution. More significant for humans, new techniques of genetic manipulation make even the most insignificant species potentially important. Rare plants and animals often provide the genetic material which can be spliced into more common varieties to enhance survival, increase productivity, and provide new raw materials for further developments.

In agriculture genetic manipulations have already led to new or much-improved strains of many plants and animals. One foundation of the so-called green revolution is the capacity of geneticists to develop new strains which vastly increase productivity. This capacity in turn rests on the availability of hitherto undiscovered genetic potential. This is also true in medicine where rare species regularly provide the genetic material for life-saving drugs. In short, to preserve this potential, the genetic diversity should be maintained. No species should be thoughtlessly destroyed.

Third, plants and animals have more direct uses in agriculture, industry, and medicine. None of these uses is indicated in the case, but until the species is thoroughly studied nothing can be assumed. In medicine even apparently rare and useless species have proven significant. The Rosy Periwinkle mentioned in the case is a classic example.

Fourth, plants and animals are important to a clean environment and to climate. Some species, for example, break down pollutants. Tropical rain forests are sources of oxygen and influence the amount and pattern of rainfall.

All these factors add up on utilitarian grounds alone to a substantial argument in favor of conserving biological diversity and preserving endangered species. The strength of this utilitarian argument will vary from species to species and system to system, but it always should be a factor in decisions about endangered plants and animals.

Usefulness of the Dam

Unfortunately for the Sonoran desert snake the good for humans has another dimension in this case: the utility of an ample water supply provided by the dam. The potential usefulness of an obscure and seemingly useless snake is pitted against the known usefulness of the best dams.

Water is essential to the mining and refining of metals, to the manufacture of chemicals, to the production of oil, pulp, and paper, and to food processing. A dependable water supply can make the desert bloom, increasing the amount of land producing food for a hungry world, boosting yields per acre, and giving peace of mind to farmers with huge capital investments. Municipalities use water for drinking, cooking, bathing, washing, and other activities. Dams can also harness water's energy in order to generate electricity. Hydroelectric power is clean, efficient, and wastes very little water.

All these uses add up to a considerable benefit and to heavy and increasing demand, in this case fueled by Arizona's population growth rate of 30 percent per decade for the last thirty years. It is no wonder that planners want to build a new dam.

From the resulting sum of benefits must be subtracted the costs, however. As the best dam sites are used, and generally they have been in the Southwest, the number of cost effective sites diminishes and the price of projects goes up. At some point costs exceed benefits and the dam is not worth building on economic grounds alone.

Irrigation in the desert is no panacea. High evaporation rates mean lost water and increasingly salty soils. Reservoirs behind dams silt up. As they do and high costs rule out dredging, benefits are reduced and eventually the dam must be abandoned.

The costs in terms of extinct species such as the Sonoran desert snake must also be counted. Unfortunately, because this cost cannot be quantified with precision, it tends to be overlooked and the lost species undervalued.

Finally, the addition of new dams in arid regions has a circular effect. If the water resources are not priced at their true cost, which they have not been in the Southwest, inordinate numbers of new settlers are attracted and come to assume sufficient supplies at low cost as a natural right. Officials who do not supply ever-increasing amounts of cheap water are viewed as irresponsible and quickly lose favor at the polls. So an increasing amount of water is supplied and this in turn attracts even more settlers with the same expectations.

Unless this circle is broken with a pricing policy which makes the consumer instead of the American taxpayer pay the cost, the nation more and more will squander its resources. There is little reason to subsidize expensive irrigation projects when overproduction in more humid regions is a problem. At some point the Southwest will be forced to live within its means, that is, unless Senator Elder and others continue to be successful in transferring costs.

The preceding considerations and the role of Senator Elder in this case force a discussion of politics. In the United States the control of water, especially in the West and South, has been a well-documented combination of Byzantine intrigue and pork-barrel politics. These things are clear: (1) water for irrigation is priced to the farmer at a fraction of its total cost, the difference being paid by the taxpayer; (2) projects with costs exceeding benefits, some because costs were purposely underestimated and benefits inflated, are regularly undertaken; and (3) endangered species have been undervalued and even ignored altogether.

The process which produces these results is also clear. Water flows toward power and money. Members of Congress from states where water is a key issue secure appointments on relevant water committees. Powerful congressional delegations trade projects off or authorize just enough projects to secure majority support for their projects. The branches of the executive concerned with water resources take an interest in their own appropriations and join ranks to promote projects even to the point of making cost/benefit analyses "come out right." Witness what happened to Erica's report in the case.

Conservatives who otherwise denounce socialism and government spending readily join the party. They know just as well as their more liberal colleagues that the costs will be paid by politically unaware outsiders and the benefits enjoyed by their knowing constituents.

The Colorado River basin is an excellent example of this phenomenon. After many years of nice and not so nice political give and take, portions of all the waters of the basin have been assigned to a variety of groups. Still the population of the region continues to expand. There are more endangered species in the basin than in any other region of the country. Traditional interests still compete for water. Impoverished Native Americans press for their rightful share. Industry, agriculture, and municipalities vie for greater shares. Seven states tussle continually over relative allocations.

In all of this Arizonans have tended to get less than an equitable share of the water in the basin. Their response has been the Central Arizona

Project, a mammoth project designed to bring water for irrigation to the Phoenix and Tucson areas, which are rapidly exhausting their groundwater supplies. To give the project some semblance of cost effectiveness, high dams were originally proposed on the Colorado River. These dams would have flooded portions of the Grand Canyon outside national park boundaries. Eventually, after a long and bitter political battle led by environmentalists, the dams were rejected, but not the project itself, which continues to receive appropriations in spite of highly dubious cost effectiveness.

It is not clear whether the dam being considered in the case is part of the Central Arizona Project, but it is important to remember that issues such as those raised in this case continually reappear in the charged political context in which decisions about water are made. Focusing on the data given in the case itself, it would seem that the combination of high costs, dubious benefits, endangerment of a rare species, and the need to come to terms with the realities of desert life, economic expansion, and a flawed political process adds up to a compelling case against the construction of the dam. Senator Elder may have the votes to carry it through, however, and a sympathetic judicial process may concur. It would be a mistake to think that rational analysis will automatically win the day.

To sum up, it would seem that in the short run the benefits of building the dam might outweigh the preservation of one species, but if the issue is viewed from a long-range perspective, the preservation of the Sonoran desert snake may well be much more important for human beings and the earth than the short-range benefits from the dam.

Nature in the Christian Tradition

The Christian basis for weighing the usefulness of the snake for humans over against the benefits of the dam comes from a distinctly utilitarian view of nature which has developed in Christianity. Thus in order to round out the discussion of usefulness it is important to consider this view of nature and the norm of stewardship which emerges from correctly interpreting it.

The authors of Genesis 1:26-28 state that God gave the first humans dominion over the earth and ordered them to subdue it. Out of this gift and demand has developed a perspective which sees nature as an "it" to be utilized for human benefit. This perspective has been especially strong in Western Christianity, and since the Industrial Revolution has dominated all other perspectives.

This view originally gained currency in Israel's competition with its neighbors. The Canaanites and others in the region worshiped nature gods. Although there were many variations, nature was generally seen as sacred in the worship of these neighbors. Nature had a life of its own and that life was divine. In contrast stood Israel with its faith based on history. God had made a covenant with Israel and continued to act in human history in accordance with the promises of this covenant. Nature was not sacred. It was a created good to be used, a thing with no divine status whatsoever. Israel's neighbors were idolatrous in confusing nature and God.

To this view was later added a significant insight, the combination having tremendous consequences, according to historians. The insight was that since nature is a divine creation, it reflects the mind of God. Exploring it will increasingly remove the shroud of mystery which covers God's work in the world.

All the ideological ingredients for the rise of science and the unleashing of technology are there. Discovering the mind of God provides the motive and the encouragement. The utilitarian character of nature removes the restraint which comes from the fear of incurring the wrath of nature gods. All that is needed is for the fruits of modern science and technology to descend from heaven like manna. Senator Elder's dam is the last in a long train of such fruits, or so he would have his constituents believe.

The rise of modern science and technology is much more complex than this, of course, but the link to religious ideas is there. Judaism and Christianity contributed to this rise and generally both have supported or at least acquiesced in the rapid economic expansion which has resulted.

So as not to get carried away in celebration of science and technology, however, it is necessary to add that economic expansion and the philosophy of growth long ago shed their religious mantles. There is now considerable worry that dominion has come to mean unlimited exploitation. Indeed, if many of the goods of modern life are to be attributed to science, technology, and the ideology of growth, then so also must the detriments which go under the name of the environmental crisis. The combined effects of rapid population growth, depletion of natural resources, pollution, extinction of species, and the turning of people and nature into things to be exploited are producing a crisis which will not go away. The plight of the Sonoran desert snake is a microcosm of this crisis.

In light of this a return to the biblical texts is instructive. Dominion in Judaism and Christianity does not mean exploitation. Misuse of nature and people should be labeled with its true name, sin. Dominion in the Hebrew texts means careful and loving stewardship. In Genesis 1:26-28 dominion is given to humans as God's viceroys. The viceroys have authority, but the earth belongs to God, and the viceroys are to pattern dominion on God's loving and caring rule. This God of the covenant has declared nature good and works within it to redeem both humans and creatures. This God is concerned for the whole creation, not just for one part of it.

Stewardship is one key. Daughters and sons are to receive the earth from their fathers and mothers and pass it on in no worse and hopefully better shape than they received it. And as shepherds are accountable for the sheep in their care, so humans are accountable for their stewardship of nature. Misuse of nature is sin and will be judged as such.

The significance of the utilitarian view and its companion norm of stewardship is twofold. On the one hand, it gives warrant to calculations of utility in Christian ethics. The usefulness of the snake may be weighed against the usefulness of the dam. On the other hand, the norm of steward-ship, when applied in the context of Western materialism and misuse of nature, encourages far better care of the earth, and, by implication, the Sonoran desert snake. The Christian understanding of sin adds weight to the position that advocates that humans must carefully scrutinize the consequences of the way in which they use nature. While nature may be used in a way that benefits all, humans will be prone to misuse, a sin which requires repentance.

The Goodness of the Snake

Beyond the norm of stewardship, which still places nature in the hands of humans, there is a muted but very important tradition which sees nature as a good in itself apart from humans. This is not nature worship, and the brutalities of nature are not ignored in it. It is rather a tradition which sees nature as personal, alive, and subjective. Examples of it are found in the Hebrew scriptures in Job 31:38-40, Exodus 23:10f., Leviticus 25:1ff., and Psalm 96:11f. St. Francis in his "Canticle of Brother Sun" is another example. And today the love of nature which is so strong in many Americans who are Christians is still another.

This tradition has one of its bases in God's gift of aesthetic sensitivity. Most humans are incapable of turning nature into an "it," and rightly so. An equally important basis is found in the declaration by the authors of Genesis that God created nature good. The Sonoran desert snake is good because the hand of God is somehow linked to its existence. Together these norms give warrant to the preservation of the Sonoran desert snake as a good in itself, not just as something which might be used by humans for their own good.

Are there degrees to this goodness? Is the preservation of the rhinoceros more important than that of a snake? Given the snake's "bad press" it would be a temptation not to care about it and maybe even to see extinction as good. But this is the same kind of thinking which can permit categoriza-tion of humans into classes and the oppression of so-called "inferiors" by their self-appointed "superiors." Goodness is goodness, even to the least of God's creatures.

ETHICAL CONCLUSION

In many ways this case is complementary to the cases "Rigor and Responsibility" in part 1 and "Oil and the Caribou People" in this part. What all three have in common is a new ethic of ecological justice. Promi-nent in this ethic are three norms: justice, sustainable sufficiency, and participation.

Justice means fairness. In the biblical witness the touchstone of justice is the welfare and liberation of the poor and the care of the land. In this case study justice calls for both the provision of a sufficient and sustainable energy and water supply to humans in the region and the preservation of the Sonoran desert snake.

Sustainable sufficiency means good stewardship. It refers to the long-range capacity of a system to supply energy and food for basic needs at a reasonable cost to society and the environment. This norm would certainly call into question the building of more dams in such an arid region. The costs are high and the sustainability of a large human population under such conditions is questionable.

Participation is having a say in decisions which affect one's life. In this case it leads to the mandating of an open political process where the needs of both people and the environment are heard and taken into account. The special interest politics which seem to be at work in this case should not go unchallenged. Finally, does this norm call for a statewide or regional referendum on the dam? If so, the snake would surely lose. But the answer to the question is "no"—the federal government with its environmental protection laws and power of appropriation for dams has made this a national issue, and in fact in many ways all environmental matters are international issues.

These three norms and the Christian views of nature are the basis for understanding and coming to grips with the decision of whether or not to build the dam. Beyond this, Erica Mann must make a personal decision. The case leaves her about to receive a phone call during which she will be asked where she stands. For Erica the decision involves a basic question of character. Will she stand on principle and resist efforts to eliminate the snake in the name of human progress, or will she seek to make compromises in hopes of future effectiveness in saving other species? Further, will she permit herself to be dehumanized by a bureaucracy which thinks so little of her professional integrity that it feels free to distort her report without even consulting her? The distortion of her report may only be a trivial matter; but at some point, always difficult to determine, the degree or frequency of compromise makes a mockery of principles. Some compromises so violate principles as to invalidate them. Instead of exceptions to principle, compromises can become the rule, and a person can lose direction as expediency becomes normative.

The case does not permit entry into Erica's conscience. How much a matter of principle the decision is to her is not clear. Nor are the total benefits of the dam to the people of the region known with precision. Erica might agree to the sacrifice of the snake and a little of her integrity if the benefits substantially outweigh the costs.

What is finally being weighed is the value to humans of the God-given goodness of the snake over against the value of the dam to humans. This is the ethical calculus. But tacked on, as it usually is, is a matter of character. Who Erica is as a person is as much a question as what to do about the dam.

ADDITIONAL RESOURCES

Bruggemann, Walter. *The Land*. Philadelphia: Fortress, 1977.

Buchholz, Rogene A. *Principles of Environmental Management: The Greening of Business*. Englewood Cliffs, NJ: Prentice-Hall, 1993.

Hoage, R. J., ed. *Animal Extinctions*. Washington, DC: Smithsonian Institution Press, 1985.

Mather, John R. *Water Resources*. New York: John Wiley, 1984.

Nash, James A. *Loving God: Ecological Integrity and Christian Responsibility*. Nashville: Abingdon Press, 1991.

Reisner, Marc. *Cadillac Desert*. New York: Viking Penguin, 1986.

Rolston, Holmes III. *Environmental Ethics: Duties to and Values in the Natural World*. Philadelphia: Temple University Press, 1988.

Ruether, Rosemary Radford. *Gaia & God: An Ecofeminist Theology of Earthhealing*. San Francisco: Harper, 1992.

White, Lynn, Jr. "The Historical Roots of Our Ecological Crisis." *Science* 155, no. 3767 (March 10, 1967).

Wilson, Edmund O. *Biodiversity*. Washington, DC: National Academy Press, 1993.

Case

Oil and the Caribou People

Ron Blanchard had eagerly accepted the invitation from Bill Sanders. As head of social ministries at church headquarters, Bill had invited Ron to represent the Church and Society Committee of their denomination at the clan gathering of the Gwich'in people during mid-June in northeastern Alaska. Ron had never been above the Arctic Circle in mid-summer. The prospect of visiting such a remote place and learning more about native American culture seemed like high adventure and something good for his social studies teaching at Western High School in Seattle.

Now that the trip was over, he had to produce a report on the gathering for the Church and Society Committee. Bill Sanders had also asked for Ron's recommendation on proposed oil drilling in the Arctic National Wildlife Refuge (ANWR) on the north slope of Alaska's Brooks Range adjacent to the Gwich'in reservation. Bill indicated that sixteen other religious organizations and thirty-two Native American groups had already endorsed Gwich'in opposition to the drilling. The Gwich'in, it seemed, were interested in gathering further support and so had invited Bill to send a representative.

The Gwich'in are Athabascan people with a population in the range of five to seven thousand. They live primarily in northeastern Alaska and northwestern Canada. Legend and archeological evidence support a long human presence on the lands now inhabited by the Gwich'in. Traditionally, the Gwich'in roamed the boreal forests of the region as hunter-gatherers in bands of six to eight families. They lived a harsh life in an unforgiving land with cool summers and long, frigid winters when starvation was an ever-present danger.

Over the past seventy years or so, the rigors of life had been radically

---

This case was prepared by Robert L. Stivers. Copyright © The Case Study Institute. All names have been disguised to protect the privacy of the individuals involved.

modified by a regrouping in larger social units in small villages. These changes were occasioned by the coming of Episcopalian missionaries, the building of schools, and the acceptance of modern technology, in particular the rifle and the snowmobile.

Ron learned that Gwich'in opposition to oil exploration stems from the threat they perceive to their main source of subsistence, the Porcupine Caribou Herd, and to the culture and spirituality they have developed in relation to the herd. The Porcupine Herd, with almost 180,000 animals, is one of the largest herds of caribou in the world. It winters south of the Brooks Range on Gwich'in lands. In spring a great migration takes place. First the females and then the males trek through the passes of the range onto the north slope, where calving occurs almost immediately, reaching its peak in early June.

The herd migrates to the north slope to take advantage of the rich tundra vegetation in the brief but fertile Arctic summer, to avoid its natural predators who seldom venture onto the slope, and to gain respite from the hordes of mosquitoes in the winds off the Arctic Ocean. Beginning in late summer, the herd makes its way once again south of the range and disperses across Gwich'in lands to endure the winter.

For centuries the herd has been the primary source of food for the Gwich'in's subsistence economy. The Gwich'in have harvested animals from the herd in sustainable numbers and developed a culture closely bound to the herd and its migration patterns. The herd continues to do well in this habitat, with its numbers increasing since 1979. The Gwich'in in turn have survived as a people, though not without considerable hardship.

To prepare himself for the trip, Ron had read scientific reports on the potential effects of petroleum development in ANWR and an anthropological study that described the ancient ways of the Gwich'in. The scientific reports were tentative, Ron thought. Twenty years of experience with oil production at Prudhoe Bay and its effects on the smaller Central Arctic Herd were inconclusive. Numbers in the Central Arctic Herd were stable, but lower birth rates in recent years and the tendency of the caribou to avoid feeding grounds near production facilities worried scientists. Would the same thing occur in ANWR, where the best feeding grounds are slated for drilling? Would the caribou of the Porcupine Herd seek other, less-nutritious feeding grounds more populated with predators? One thing the reports made clear was that reproductive success depends on summer weight increase and the avoidance of predators. The scientists urged caution.

From the anthropological study, Ron learned about the traditional nomadic way of life of the Gwich'in, their main food sources, and their relation to the caribou. He understood intellectually their concern for the loss of both their primary food source and their traditional culture. He was not prepared by his study, however, for the degree to which their traditional culture already seemed to be in jeopardy, something he learned after arrival at the clan gathering. He was not sure he understood enough about these people, the technology of oil, or the ecology of the north slope to make a recommendation on drilling in ANWR. To make any recommendation might well be an exercise in disinformation, harmful to meeting the nation's energy needs, or worse, harmful to these people who had so kindly hosted him for five days.

Throughout his stay during the clan days, Gwich'in tribal elders had been eager to recount the old days and their experiences. Barbara Frank, whose age was difficult to judge but who looked to be in her seventies, told about the old days and of summer movements in small family groupings. The warm days added nuts, berries, and fruits to their steady diet of moose and small animals. In winter she remembered a harsh life in crude shelters and a diet of caribou and whatever other animals trapping produced. She expressed in deeply spiritual terms the close relationship of her people to the caribou. Although she spoke with nostalgia, she never once urged that the modern comforts of the village be abandoned for a return to the wilderness.

Another elder, John Christian, remembered the coming of the missionaries and the schools they established. He related how his parents and grandparents were attracted to the village that grew up around the church and school. They were fascinated by the new technologies that added a margin to subsistence in the Arctic and the amusements which brought variety and diversity. His family was subsequently baptized. They abandoned their given names for Christian names and assumed the superiority of the new and the inferiority of the old.

Alongside these private conversations were daily public gatherings with starting times that baffled Ron. It was confusing to have no schedule, no appointed time to begin. Things just happened. The sessions began when the spirit moved and ended when there were no more speakers. Other more experienced visitors dismissed his confusion as "Gwich'in time." There was no set agenda. An elder kept order and transferred to each speaker the large decorative staff that gave the right to address the assembly.

The general topic for the first public gathering was oil exploration in ANWR. Moses Peters, an important tribal elder, spoke in English and presented his assessment of the situation. He reviewed existing production procedures at Prudhoe Bay and the shipment of oil through the Alaskan pipeline. He claimed that operations at Prudhoe Bay had adversely affected the smaller Central Arctic Caribou Herd that summered in the vicinity. While the herd's numbers had remained stable in the early years of production, he felt that the lower birth rates and higher calf mortality over the past few years were signs of stress. The herd, he asserted, was reluctant to cross the pipeline and did not graze in the vicinity of the wells.

Moses went on to say that the oil companies expect their next big find will be in ANWR. "Already two of the biggest companies have sunk exploratory wells," he said, "although they have not made their results public." He feared that the one hundred miles of pipeline, four hundred miles of roads, the gravel pits, the production facilities, and air strips would seriously disturb the migration routes of the Porcupine Herd at a crucial time in its annual cycle. "Caribou survival," he insisted, "depends on being born in the right place at the right time, and all of the caribou depend upon these summer months on the north slope to rest and restore food reserves. It is this period of predator-free resting and feeding that prepares the caribou to reproduce and to survive the winter."

Moses handed the staff to his daughter, Mary, who added: "Oil waste and burn-off would contaminate the tundra. The caribou would not be able to eat." She concluded with alarm: "We will starve again as it happened before, but this time it will be worse."

Mary returned the staff to her father, who concluded by saying that they needed to continue to press for the permanent protection of ANWR. "The refusal of the U.S. Senate a few years ago to consider energy legislation that includes developing ANWR for oil is not enough. The oil companies will keep the pressure up. Once the price of oil increases as supply dwindles in coming years, gas-hungry Americans will make known their demands for new sources of supply. Environmentally conscious senators may not be able to withstand all this pressure. We must get permanent protection now. The caribou is our main source of life, our survival. We can't live without the caribou. All our traditional skills, our whole way of life, will be lost if there are no caribou."

Ron was impressed by the sincerity of these appeals and the efforts of the Gwich'in to secure reliable scientific evidence. He was troubled, however, by some of their conclusions. He also recalled his conversation with Glen Stone, a friend who worked as an engineer at Northern Oil. They had discussed the issues prior to Ron's departure for Alaska. Glen had talked about his own involvement on the north slope at Prudhoe Bay. He painted a rosy picture of the benefits of oil production to all Alaskans. "Oil money," he said, "builds schools, roads, and other public-works projects. It keeps personal taxes low, and enables the government to pay each resident a yearly dividend. The native Americans benefit too, perhaps most of all."

Glen went on. "Production at Prudhoe will not continue forever. We need ANWR to maximize investment on the pipeline and to keep these benefits rolling to Alaskans. There may be as much as nine billion barrels there! Why lock up such a valuable resource? As for the ecological concerns of the environmentalists and the Gwich'in, I think they are wrong about the effects at Prudhoe. The Central Arctic Herd is in fine shape. Modern construction and containment techniques minimize negative environmental impacts. Believe me, we take great precautions. The Gwich'in have little to worry about."

Glen continued by pressing one of his favorite themes, the coming energy crisis. "Oil, gas, and eventually even coal will be so expensive in the future that we will have to shift to alternatives. Appropriate alternatives are not in place and will require considerable development. In the meantime, we will need all the fossil fuels we can get our hands on. Otherwise production of goods and services will decline and unemployment increase. It won't take long under those circumstances to unlock ANWR. We can be patient; it's just a matter of time."

Glen ended the discussion by pointing out that other native groups in Alaska, in particular Inupiat on the north slope, have far fewer problems with exploration than do the Gwich'in. He wondered out loud why the Gwich'in were so troubled but offered no opinion since he had not been in contact with them. Ron wondered too, especially about Glen's evaluation of the scientific evidence at Prudhoe and his claim that oil revenues had benefited groups such as the Gwich'in.

As the days of talk continued, Ron thought he detected something deeper at work. Oil exploration seemed to be symbolic of the invasion of modern technology and the threat it presented to traditional Gwich'in culture. It was an obvious enemy: alien, capitalist, consumer-oriented, and potentially destructive to the environment. What really seemed at issue was Gwich'in identity.

The little that was said about oil exploration after the first day seemed to support this conclusion. Instead, the question of identity dominated public sessions. Speaker after speaker decried the erosion of Gwich'in culture. Some in prophetic voice condemned the erosion outright. Others reflected their own personal struggle to preserve the best of the traditional culture while adopting chunks of modern life.

The speakers focused their concern on language. Mary Peters reported through a translator that in some villages only 20 percent of the children understand the Gwich'in language. She was troubled that the local schools taught English as the primary language and, worse, that some schools ignored native language altogether. For the most part she herself did not speak in English, believing that speech in her native tongue was a mark of integrity.

As he thought about it later, Ron certainly agreed that language was crucial. But the matter seemed to run deeper. He reflected on the one school in the village that was hosting the clan gathering. It was by far the largest, best equipped, and most modern structure in the village. Built with the wealth acquired by oil-boom Alaska in the 1970s and 1980s, its facilities were state of the art. Villagers could not avoid making comparisons between it and their own humble dwellings.

Even Ron, a total stranger, made the comparison, although he had not taken time during the meeting to explore the implications. As he thought about it later, it seemed odd that Gwich'in from other villages and non-Gwich'in like himself were not housed in the school but were put up in make-shift tents. He thought about his own backpacking tent and the mosquitoes that were so big the villagers were said to build bird houses for them. How much easier it would have been to lay his pad on the floor of the school, away from the swarms of mosquitoes and in easy reach of flush toilets and showers. How much easier indeed! He too could understand the attractions of modern technology.

Ron's reflections returned to the village itself and the things he had observed while hanging out and wandering around. Snowmobiles, while out of use for the summer, were everywhere in storage. Satellite dishes for television reception were common. The table in the laundromat was covered with glamour magazines. The teenagers roamed the village in groups without apparent direction, much like teenagers roam malls throughout North America. Joy riding and kicking up dust on big-tired, four-wheeled vehicles was a favorite pastime.

Perhaps the most obvious symbol of all this was the five-thousand-foot gravel runway that ran like a lance through the center of the village. As the place where visitors, fuel, mail, and supplies entered, it was in fact the center of town.

Although wary of his untrained eye, Ron concluded that the matter of oil exploration on the north slope was also a matter of the invasion of an alien culture and ideology. Yes, saving the caribou herd was important. Yes, teaching the kids the language was also important. But the deeper question in these deliberations seemed to be how can caribou and language survive the onslaught of modern technology and thought? How could a traditional people maintain their identity when much of what has attracted them comes from a more powerful and alien culture and seems to make life easier and more interesting? The problem for the Gwich'in was not just the oil on the north slope. It was also the school, the runway, the motorized vehicles, the glamour magazines, and maybe even the churches.

The Gwich'in gave the last day of their gathering to stories of flight and return. A procession of witnesses including Mary Peters testified to the horrors of migration to the outside. Lost identity, alcoholism, drug addiction, a final bottoming out, and then a return to roots were common experiences. But for each witness, Ron had wondered, how many were lost in the bars of Fairbanks?

Ron had been impressed with the integrity of those who testified. They were no longer innocent about modern culture. They seemed to have returned much stronger for their trials and with a healthy respect for tradition, the land, and the ambiguities of their situation. Perhaps these survivors and their children were the hope for a future that would be both easier and more satisfying. Maybe a new and stronger identity was being forged right before his eyes. He was moved to tears by Mary Peters' concluding remarks, this time in English:

> It is very clear to me that it is an important and special thing to be Gwich'in. Being Gwich'in means being able to understand and live with this world in a very special way. It means living with the land, with the animals, with the birds and fish, as though they were your

sisters and brothers. It means saying the land is an old friend and an old friend your father knew, your grandmother knew, indeed your people always have known. . . . We see our land as much, much more than the white man sees it. To our people, our land really is our life.

Ron's attention turned to the present and his report and recommendations to the Church and Society Committee. Should he merely report what he saw and write in pious, uncritical generalizations? Despite his ignorance as an outsider, should he try to state his misgivings about what is happening to this alien, but very rich, culture? Should he accept Glen's optimistic assurances about environmental impacts and benefits or mention the Fairbanks taxi driver who condescendingly observed that the controversy over ANWR was so much Indian smoke and mirrors to exact higher royalties from the oil companies? Should he recommend that the church support further oil exploration on the north slope or take up the cause of the Gwich'in, feeling as he did that more was going on with these people than a dispute over exploration? And how should he factor in his own strongly held attitudes about social justice for traditional peoples and his conviction that Americans were consuming far too much energy in the first place?

Commentary

Oil and the Caribou People

Under similar conditions fifty years ago, North Americans would have ignored this case. Led by the oil companies and backed by federal, state, and local governments, they would have moved in with little hesitation to tap the resource. They might even have done to the caribou herd and the Gwich'in as they did the buffalo and the Plains Indians. The Gwich'in would have been silent, and observers such as Ron would have noted little out of the ordinary, much less question their powers of discernment.

Today corporations and government are often more sensitive, a new breed of environmentalist is crying for the preservation of species and ecosystems, the Gwich'in are speaking out, and observers are questioning their own assumptions. Oil demand remains high, however, and with the depletion of reserves this demand may have the last word.

AN ETHIC OF INTEGRITY

To understand this case, a new appreciation of an old virtue, integrity, is helpful. The word *integrity* comes from the Latin, "tango," meaning to touch. The past participle of tango is "tactus." Add the preposition "in," and the English word *intact* emerges. Further consideration yields other relevant related words: integration, integer, and, of course, integrity.

The Christian tradition speaks of the immanence of God, of the God who is revealed in Jesus Christ and continues to relate to the world through the Spirit. In an ethic of integrity, God is the power of integrity that creates and sustains in three distinct but related dimensions of existence: (1) personal integrity, (2) social integrity, and (3) nature's integrity. Jesus Christ is the image of integrity, and the experience of integration may be named salvation or redemption. God's power of integrity is experienced consistently as an integrating force that creates the will in humans to act in accordance with their highest moral principles.

Personal integrity, the first dimension, is a harmony of act and intention in persons as they relate in community to God, other persons, and nature. Internal harmony is both the end product of integrity and its foundation.

It is the peace and unity of will, mind, and emotion that gives the freedom to act in accordance with intentions.

For Christians, intentionality is informed by norms derived from the Bible, the traditions of the church, and the personal experience of the Spirit. Sin is the power of disintegration that blocks integrity. Sin results from the refusal of the self, others, or the community to receive the power of integrity and is experienced as something done to a person or something the person does willfully. The continuing power of sin prevents the full realization of integrity. The presence of God in the midst of sin provides the resources for partial integrations and the assurance that the full realization of integrity is God's final aim. Integrity is dynamic, something that is partially realized, lost, to be hoped for, and received again.

Personal integrity is part of Mary Peters's reluctance to speak English in the public gatherings. She apparently sees speaking in her native tongue as an important element in the reinvigoration of Gwich'in culture and wants to match her words and deeds.

Ron Blanchard's personal integrity is also an issue in this case. Given his limitations as an observer, how is he to report his experience and make recommendations so that his intentions for the well-being of the Gwich'in, his own society, and the Porcupine Caribou Herd are realized?

Social integrity, the second dimension, is the harmony of act and intention in a community. Communities have integrity when peace and justice are foundational ethical concerns. While communities have fewer resources than individuals for receiving and acting on the power of God's integrity, peace and justice are deep wellsprings. To the Greeks, justice was the harmony of a well-ordered community where equals were treated equally, unequals unequally. For the Hebrews, shalom and righteousness resulted from keeping the covenantal relation with God and following the guidelines of the law. They included a special concern for the poor. For both Greeks and Hebrews, peace and justice fed on each other and together nourished social integrity.

Christians melded Greek and Hebrew traditions, emphasizing basic equality in Christ and seeing in the person of Jesus the model and the power for both peace and justice. These understandings of peace and justice have developed further in Western traditions with the norms of equality and freedom emerging as regulatory or judging principles of social integrity. The integrated society is one with substantial equality and common agreement as to basic freedoms. In the present day, liberation theologians have carried on this tradition. Returning to the special concern of the Hebrews for those at the margins of society, they speak about a preferential option for the poor, by which is meant political and ideological freedom and basic economic sufficiency for all.

The emphasis liberation theologians place on economic sufficiency for all exposes something else about social integrity. While peace and justice are the spiritual and ethical foundations of social integrity, they presuppose the provision of basic needs. The equal sharing of poverty can be as disintegrating as war and injustice. The definition of basic needs is notoriously difficult, of course. Clear in the extremes of absence and excess but vague at the margins, the concept of basic needs is useful for setting floors to poverty and discriminating about levels of consumption. As the commentary on the case "Rigor and Responsibility" makes clear, the norm of sufficiency establishes a floor below which a just society does not let its members fall. On the upside, it calls into question non-sustainable consumption and efforts to justify environmentally destructive projects on the grounds of sufficiency.

Basic also to peace and justice are elements of a common culture. No society can long remain integrated without some minimum of shared understandings, symbols, values, and traditions. A culture can become so fragmented by invasion from without or conflict within as to lose its identity.

A consideration of social integrity is central to this case. From the side of the Gwich'in, the integrity of their culture appears to be in jeopardy. Their way of life depends on the land and subsistence on the Porcupine Caribou Herd that needs special summer habitat in order to flourish. Their identity as a people depends on the maintenance of their language and respect for their traditions. Sensitivity to their situation calls for an understanding of the difficult changes they are facing, changes from the outside that may be too rapid for them to preserve that basic minimum of common culture.

From the side of the wider North American society, the Gwich'in and other native peoples deserve respect. In Christian perspective, this respect stems from the love of neighbor that stands at the center of the tradition and the norm of justice. There is also a need to address the dependency of industrial societies on the consumption of copious amounts of energy. Can such consumption be justified on grounds of economic sufficiency? Is it sustainable? Is it really integral to North American identity? These are questions North Americans should address before drilling begins in the Arctic National Wildlife Refuge (ANWR).

The third dimension is the integrity of nature. While human integrity and nature's integrity are separated in many people's minds, they are related because humans are a species in nature like any other species. As a consequence they must use nature as a resource to survive. They are distinct because other species do not exercise intentionality, at least not in the same way or to the same degree. Therefore it is incorrect to speak of a harmony of act and intention, justice, or sin in the rest of nature. These terms apply only to humans. Still, the concept of integrity may be even more relevant to nature, considering the root meaning of the word.

The integrity of an ecosystem or species is its intactness, its capacity to evolve dynamically or sustain itself so that a variety of individuals and species may continue to interact or fit together. What comes first to mind is a pristine (untouched) wilderness. This is too static a concept, however, and today a rare exception as humans have made themselves at home in an ever greater number of the earth's systems. Rather than some abstract, pristine ideal, it is better to speak in terms of the norm of sustainability. This norm allows for human participation in and use of nature without endorsing activities that cause the disintegration of systems and species. Such activities should be named for what they are—sin.

Maintaining the integrity of ecosystems is not solely a prudential matter for humans. Nature in biblical understandings has more than use or utilitarian value. It also has intrinsic goodness, at least in the understandings of the writers of Genesis 1, where God sees nature as good independently of humans, and in Genesis 9, where God makes a covenant with all of creation. In Christian perspective, nature is much more than a resource, or backdrop, or something to be overcome. Nature is to be cared for (tilled and kept in Genesis 2:15) as Jesus himself cared for others and sought their fullest realization. Humans are called to be good stewards in the image of God as that image is revealed in Jesus Christ. God will eventually redeem the whole creation (Romans 8). Nature's integrity is represented in this case by the Porcupine Caribou Herd. Oil drilling in its summer range has the potential to degrade habitat critical to the herd. The integrity of the herd is threatened and with it the social integrity of the Gwich'in.

ENERGY AND AMERICAN INTEGRITY

The era of cheap and abundant energy is almost over. The oil and gas currently supporting industrial societies are being depleted rapidly and are not renewable. Both will be in short supply and very expensive sometime in the next century. Already production at Prudhoe Bay adjacent to ANWR is declining and will be a mere trickle of its former self by 2015.

Coal reserves are sufficient to last several hundred years, even with increased consumption. Of great concern, however, are the serious drawbacks to the use of coal, notably air and water pollution, degradation of the land with strip-mining, global warming, and eventual depletion.

In terms of supply, the prospects for nuclear energy are brighter, but the environmental impacts of present technology are as bad or worse than coal. Energy from the fission of heavy atoms is more or less on hold because of economic costs, worldwide concerns about safety after Three Mile Island and Chernobyl, and the vexing problem of waste storage. Energy from the fusion of hydrogen atoms holds great promise but may never be commercially available due to the difficulties and dangers of containing the great temperature and pressure necessary for a sustained reaction to take place. It is also likely to be very expensive.

Unless fusion is harnessed at a reasonable cost, nations will eventually need to meet their energy needs from sources that are sustainable over a long period of time, essentially renewable resources. Solar power is frequently mentioned in this regard. Conservation, the name given efforts to save energy either by cutting back or by producing with greater efficiency, will also be essential.

The realm in which renewable sources of energy and conservation reign will be markedly different from the present realm where economic growth, as measured by the Gross National Product, governs. Sustainability and sufficiency will necessarily guide energy decisions, not growth, at least not growth of energy and resource-intensive production and consumption.

Between this realm and the one to come there will be a difficult period of transition that is already beginning and whose duration is difficult to predict because the rate of technological innovation cannot be known. The realm to come can be delayed if limits to growth are aggressively attacked with the so-called technological fix, that is, a commitment to find technological solutions to resource constraints.

Certainly new technology will have a role to play, but if the shape of human communities and the distribution of costs and benefits are disregarded in the rush for technological solutions, the new realm will hardly be worth inhabiting. Groups like the Gwich'in, if they can continue to exist in such a climate, will be peripheral. Social scale will be large and structure complex, with hierarchical, centralized, and bureaucratic administration. Materialism accompanied by great disproportions of wealth will continue as the reigning philosophy. In short, social integrity will be under severe pressure from the demand to find "fixes" and to pay those who can.

Alternatively, a society geared to renewables and conservation will bring pressure on everyone to live sustainably and to be satisfied with basics. It will be a society where appropriate scale, simplicity, a greater degree of decentralization, and greater equality will prevail.

Energy choices are social and value choices. If a critical mass of North Americans decide on lives that consume large amounts of energy and natural resources, or, alternatively, to live sustainably, they will simultaneously choose the economic and political structures to organize and sustain such decisions.

The decision to explore for oil in ANWR is thus much larger than meets the eye when technological and economic calculations are the only factors. In its largest dimension the question is, what kind of society do present stewards of the earth want for themselves and their children? And beneath this lurks basic questions of social identity and character. Who are North Americans as a people? What should be the center of their common culture?

The question of basic identity goes even deeper. In the commentary on the case "Rigor and Responsibility," two normative Christian traditions governed the analysis—rigorous discipleship and responsible consumption. The amount and style of energy consumption currently enjoyed by North Americans is difficult, if not impossible, to justify in terms of either tradition. Energy sufficiency can certainly be endorsed and a case made for oil as necessary in any transition, but the unnecessary and wasteful consumption of the present not only violates the norm of sustainability but also the model of frugality and simplicity seen in the person of Jesus Christ.

In sum, Christians will have difficulty justifying exploration in ANWR even before they consider environmental effects. Yes, oil will be needed in the transition to a more sustainable society, but until North Americans reduce their high levels of consumption and consider their identity in a world of limited resources, all the oil in ANWR will make little difference. The worst possible outcome stares them in the face: further depletion of oil reserves, no long-range alleviation of supply problems, and loss of the Porcupine Caribou Herd with its consequent impact on Gwich'in culture.

GWICH'IN INTEGRITY

The view of the Gwich'in in this case is through the eyes of a non-native on a short stay who is unfamiliar with their culture and has no formal training as an observer. Any one of these limitations might skew his observations.

While caution is warranted, a few things are clear. First, the Gwich'in are deeply concerned about the Porcupine Caribou Herd for reasons of subsistence and social integrity. Their history is tied nutritionally and spiritually to the herd. Were the herd to lose its integrity, the Gwich'in would receive another rude shock to their identity.

Second, Gwich'in culture, like most native cultures in the Americas, is in jeopardy. Ron wonders whether there is enough common culture left to maintain social integrity. The Gwich'in worry about this too, but also express words of hope and show signs of reinvigoration.

One way to approach the situation is to advocate closing ANWR to exploration and to pursue a policy of disengagement, leaving the Gwich'in to work out their own future. Such an approach has its attractions, given past injustices. The perceived need for oil, the many linkages between cultures in Alaska, and the intermingling of peoples on the land, however, make disengagement all but impossible.

Alternatively, policy makers could continue to pursue the two patronizing approaches that have governed United States policy in the past. The first of these approaches pictures Native Americans as backward savages in need of superior Western technology, social institutions, and culture. While still widely held, this picture must be dismissed outright and confession made for the expropriations, massacres, and deceptions it has promoted. The chapter on the domination and elimination of Native Americans by people of European origins is one of the most ugly in the annals of world history.

The other traditional approach is to idealize Native Americans as noble savages. This idealization, while more sensitive than the first, leads to confusion about native care of the land, the moral superiority of native peoples, the ease and comfort of nomadic life in a harsh climate, and the appropriateness of native religions in modern technological society and in the environmental movement.

The Gwich'in have a different, not a superior or inferior way of life. They are a shrewd and politically interested community of people who have learned how to negotiate from strength. They know of the potential monetary rewards of oil production in ANWR. They know that the Porcupine Caribou Herd is resilient and that the environmental consequences of oil production at Prudhoe Bay are not yet clear. They know they have political support in the rest of North America and how to use it. They know as sub-Arctic people that they have different political interests than the Inupiat on the north slope. They know that northeastern Alaska is no Eden.

How then should North Americans view the Gwich'in? Most appropriate is a perspective that begins with respect and exhibits a concern for their social integrity. Included should be a frank recognition that a conflict continues between two cultures, the one closely linked to a subsistence way of life on the land, the other, more powerful, linked to modern technology and capitalistic economic organization.

Traditionally, the Gwich'in were hunter-gatherers who long ago migrated from Asia and settled in the sub-Arctic south of the Brooks Range in Alaska and the Yukon and Northwest Territories in Canada. They subsisted directly off the land, primarily on the Porcupine Caribou Herd, which they harvested in sustainable numbers. Life was difficult, but the people were resourceful. They relied on sharing, the extended family, and respect for the wisdom of others, especially elders.

Necessarily, they had a special relation to the land and to its flora and fauna. To the Gwich'in, the land is sacred. It is inalienable. It can not be bought or sold, but is held in common as the basis of subsistence. Subsistence is much more than a way of securing food. It is a productive system that entails living directly off the land and demands the organized labor of practically everyone in the community. There are countless tasks in a subsistence economy, each requiring specialized skills. Subsistence is also a system of distribution and exchange that operates according to long-established rules. It links the generations and knits the community into a common culture. It is the material basis for Gwich'in values and underlies the relation of the Gwich'in to the land.

Modern industrial society is obviously different, perhaps most obviously in how it relates to the land. Those in modern society are not as close to the land. They do not see it as sacred. They buy and sell it and encumber it as private property. They view it through the eyes of the economist as a factor of production and obtain its produce by selling their labor and purchasing the means of subsistence in markets far removed from the land.

The traditional Gwich'in way of life persists in spite of deep inroads from modern industrial society. Cultures are never static, of course, but the rapidity of the changes, many of which have been imposed, not chosen, have the Gwich'in worried about their future. Imported goods and food;

movement into villages under the influence of Christian missionaries; the introduction of schools, welfare payments, and wage labor; and the acceptance of labor-saving and recreational technologies have brought unprecedented and swift changes. With them have come values and methods of social organization quite foreign to native peoples and a sense of inferiority and powerlessness.

That identity and alcoholism are problems is not surprising. The imports from modern society form a barrier walling off Native Americans from their traditional cultures. The words of Inupiat Polly Koutchak express this sense of being walled off that also seems to characterize the lives of many Gwich'in.

> I always feel deep within myself the urge to live a traditional way of life—the way of my ancestors. I feel I could speak my Native tongue, but I was raised speaking the adopted tongue of my people, English. I feel I could dance the songs of my people, but they were abolished when the white man came to our land. I feel I could heal a sick one the way it was done by my ancestors, but the White man not only came with their medicine—they came with diseases. What I'm trying to emphasize is I am one in modern day attempting to live a double life—and, from that my life is filled with confusion. I have a wanting deep within myself to live the life of my ancestors, but the modernized world I was raised in is restricting me from doing so. (Quoted in Thomas R. Berger. *Village Journey.* New York: Hill and Wang, 1985, p. 13.)

The future of the Gwich'in's subsistence way of life is in jeopardy. Ron Blanchard's account, however, reveals considerable evidence of continuing social integrity. The Gwich'in have organized themselves to defend their interests. A spirit of resistance is expressed in the refusal by some to speak English and in opposition to oil production in ANWR. The Gwich'in recognize shortcomings in their school system and the importance of language to cultural identity. Younger people are returning to the villages to raise their families. Many seem determined to overcome the ravages of alcoholism. Skeptics might view this evidence as staged by the Gwich'in to impress unsophisticated observers or as a failure to assimilate to a superior culture. In contrast, eyes of respect will interpret this evidence as a triumph of the human spirit.

Nor should the Gwich'in's subsistence way of life be dismissed. Granted the Gwich'in have purchased the tools to make that way of life easier and as a result must resort to wage labor. Granted also, they have supplemented their diets with food from the outside, thereby improving nutrition. These actions are not decisive, however. Their subsistence way of life will continue as long as they choose to live in rural Alaska, for the simple reason that a market economy will never produce a sufficient economic base to support them in this setting. Except for the oil, which is not on Gwich'in lands, there are not enough commercially valuable resources in rural Alaska.

Respect for the Gwich'in in their subsistence way of life is important in this case. From the outside it is a matter of justice and recognizing the legitimacy of Gwich'in concern about identity, the land, and the caribou. From the inside it is a matter of economic sufficiency and the maintenance of a common culture.

The Porcupine Caribou Herd is central to Gwich'in integrity. The caribou are the means of continued subsistence. Cultural identity is bound up with the land and the herd. Oil exploration is viewed as a threat to the herd and as another one of those barriers that wall the Gwich'in off from their identity. Respect in this case means listening to what these people are saying.

NATURE'S INTEGRITY

When anthropocentrism dominated discussions such as this, a commentary would have ended with the preceding section or with a short statement of the value of the Porcupine Caribou Herd as a resource for Gwich'in subsistence. Utilitarian considerations dominated analysis. The intrinsic value of landscapes, species, and ecosystems was left out or separated off into the realms of philosophy or theology. This is no longer the case. Analysis needs to be fully integrated and nature's systems viewed as having value of their own.

The issue for the integrity of nature in this case is the sustainability of the Porcupine Caribou Herd, whose survival depends on the preservation of summer habitat on the north slope of the Brooks Range in ANWR. On the one hand, the need to preserve this habitat is symbolic of a more general problem: the worldwide degradation of land and ecosystems that causes the extinction of species and the reduction of biodiversity.

The causes of this wider degradation are complex, but certainly an increased human population that consumes more and uses more powerful technologies is principal among them. Oil exploration and development in ANWR on fragile Arctic tundra is simply another example of behavior that degrades the natural environment, Glen Stone and his safeguards not withstanding. In some cases, and this may be one, any intrusion whatsoever can be destructive, and humans should probably stay out.

On the other hand, the issue is quite specific: the impact of oil exploration and development on the herd and other species that inhabit the Arctic ecosystem. Exploration itself may be innocent enough if all it means is looking around, overturning a few rocks, probing the ground here and there, and then leaving. Who could object? Producing oil is another matter.

The case itself offers important information about the herd, not all of which bears repeating. The herd numbers about 180,000 animals and has been increasing in size at a rate of 4 to 5 percent since 1979. Critical to the herd is its summer calving and feeding in areas believed to have the greatest potential for oil discovery. If the herd is displaced from its richest feeding grounds to others where the vegetation is less nutritious and predators are more numerous, the herd may suffer. Less nutrition means less weight gain. Weight gain is critical for the females and is directly related to calf survival and birth rates the following summer. Predators are found in greater numbers to the south in the foothills of the Brooks Range. Presumably the herd would move in that direction with displacement, since this is what occurs in years of heavy snowfall in the prime feeding areas. In good weather years, displacement might have little effect, but scientists are concerned about other years where displacement would add to already bad conditions and put the herd under stress.

The more than twenty years of experience with the Central Arctic Herd at Prudhoe Bay is the only evidence that scientists have to predict effects on the Porcupine Herd in ANWR. The Central Arctic Herd numbers about 12,000 animals. It appeared to grow rapidly in the late 1970s and early 1980s. After 1985 the ratio of calves per one hundred cows dropped, more so in areas in the herd's western range near oil production at Prudhoe Bay. Scientists are cautious about these data, however. There is no long-range information on numbers or calf/cow ratios. The estimates of herd size are based on aerial surveys. Natural fluctuations in ratios and size are to be expected, and without base-line data, causes of short-range fluctuations are difficult to determine. The data suggest negative impacts but are not conclusive. Until more data are gathered, scientists are reluctant to make predictions on the basis of trends in the Central Arctic Herd.

Scientists have arrived at several significant conclusions, however. The Central Arctic Herd avoids humans, roads, and production facilities at Prudhoe Bay, the females more than the males. In other words, production facilities displace the herd. Also, the herd as measured by calf density is in worse shape the closer its animals are to production facilities. This is the evidence that worries scientists and the Gwich'in, for displacement in ANWR would drive females to less favorable calving and feeding grounds.

PERSONAL INTEGRITY

Mary Peters's reluctance to speak English in public gatherings is probably difficult for most North Americans to understand. English is, after all, the main language of international communication, not to mention the language of common culture in the United States. If Mary's first priority is to get the Gwich'in's message out to observers such as Ron, it would behoove her to communicate directly instead of through an interpreter.

Mary is, however, speaking to her own community as well, and it is probably more important for her to establish her own integrity within the community before she speaks to outsiders. Whatever else, her reluctance to speak English should not be viewed by outsiders as a snub or as culturally backward. To expect Mary to give up what is central to her culture and her own identity is the epitome of cultural imperialism. Mary's act is in keeping with her intention to reinvigorate Gwich'in culture.

As for Ron Blanchard, he must decide how to word his report and what to recommend concerning oil exploration and production in ANWR. Personal integrity depends on receiving God's power of integrity. Ron's first act should be a prayer for openness and discernment.

Ron might next reconsider his intentions. The case makes clear that he is troubled by the threats to Gwich'in social integrity. The disintegration of the Porcupine Caribou Herd would threaten their subsistence way of life and arrest efforts to reinvigorate old traditions. Ron is no doubt aware of the tortured history of Native Americans in post-Columbian North and South America. Under the norm of justice with its concern for the poor and oppressed, he might well give the Gwich'in the benefit of his doubts about their motivations, their reading of the scientific evidence, and the political nature of their appeal. He should be careful not to cloud his judgment with patronizing illusions about Gwich'in nobility, however.

The case also reveals that Ron has convictions about excess energy consumption. He listens carefully to Glen Stone, who is convinced that energy sufficiency for North Americans is at stake, but does not appear to be swayed.

The evidence on the threat of oil production to the integrity of the caribou herd should also be a consideration. If he is perceptive, Ron will pick up the doubts and cautions of scientists who have studied the possible consequences. The lack of conclusive evidence should lead him to be cautious himself. No longer, he might conclude, can an ethic that only considers human integrity control outcomes. He should also remember that the Porcupine Caribou Herd has intrinsic value as part of God's good creation.

Finally, Ron will want to bring a special awareness to his decision, an awareness that applies to any visitor to a different culture. Ron is not alone in his lack of understanding of Gwich'in ways or training in methods of observation. In such situations humility about one's own capacities and respect for the integrity of others are paramount virtues. He should be careful to qualify his recommendations with an admission of his own limitations. He should also be prepared to do more study and listening and to look at his own consumption of energy.

What Ron decides to do with his observations is finally his responsibility, as it is the responsibility of every visitor to other cultures. Ethical analysis can pave the way to good decisions, but good character and personal integrity are needed to translate analysis into good actions.

CONCLUSION

The case against exploration and production in ANWR is strong. It rests on three pillars: (1) respect for Gwich'in social integrity, (2) respect for nature's integrity, and (3) the failure of North Americans to curb their energy appetites. The case may not be as strong as it seems, however. ANWR is not on Gwich'in lands or even in the same ecosystem. The main link of the Gwich'in to ANWR is the Porcupine Caribou Herd. If it can be demonstrated beyond a reasonable doubt that oil production represents little or no threat to the herd, then Gwich'in integrity is not threatened and the first two pillars fall. Should North Americans curb their demand for energy and thereafter use the oil in ANWR to fuel the transition to sustainable energy consumption, then the third pillar crumbles.

For the moment, however, the pillars stand. The effects on the herd are not clear, the herd is central to Gwich'in integrity, and North Americans have yet to make a determined effort to change their habits. The oil should be left in the ground. It will not go away.

ADDITIONAL RESOURCES

Berger, Thomas R. *Village Journey.* New York: Hill and Wang, 1985.

Brown, Joseph Epes. *The Spiritual Legacy of the American Indian.* New York: Crossroad, 1993.

Childers, Robert, and Mary Kancewick. "The Gwich'in (Kutchin): Conservation and Cultural Protection in the Arctic Borderlands." Gwich'in Steering Committee, P.O. Box 202768, Anchorage, AK 99520.

Cobb, John. *Sustainability.* Maryknoll, NY: Orbis Books, 1992.

McCabe, T. R., et al. "Research on the Potential Effects of Petroleum Development on Wildlife and their Habitat, Arctic National Wildlife Refuge: Interim Report 1988-1990." Alaska Fish and Wildlife Research Center and Arctic National Wildlife Refuge, 1990.

McKennan, Robert A. *The Chandalar Kutchin.* Arctic Institute of North America, Technical Paper No. 17, September 1965.

Nash, James A. *Loving Nature.* Nashville: Abingdon Press, 1991.

Nash, Roderick. *Wilderness and the American Mind.* New Haven, CT: Yale University Press. 3rd ed., 1982.

Osgood, Cornelius. *Contributions to the Ethnography of the Kutchin.* Yale University Publications in Anthropology, No. 14. New Haven, CT: Human Relations Area Files Press, 1970.

PART V

BUSINESS

Case

Big Business and the Boys' Club

Pastor Dave Hopkins stepped off the elevator and through the carved mahogany door into the quiet elegance of the Chicago Men's Club. He was struck by the contrast between this environment and the recent images of the Jamaican slums which prompted his request for this luncheon meeting. After giving his name to the club's host, Dave was courteously informed that he was several minutes early; he was welcome to wait in the bar until Mr. Palmer and the rest of his party arrived.

Dave Hopkins's mind sifted through the events of the past four weeks as he considered how he would share his Jamaican experience with Frank Palmer and George Delaney, executives in transnational corporations with interests in the Caribbean as well as members of his affluent North Shore congregation, and Harold Atkins, a management consultant to the travel industry and a good friend of George. The previous month while Dave and his wife, Carol, were vacationing in Jamaica, they unexpectedly ran into Anthony Robinson, a Jamaican pastor who had done his seminary "field education" in the United States under Dave's direction. When Dave and Carol saw Tony for the first time in four years, he was playing the piano in their hotel's cocktail lounge. They spoke briefly during Tony's break; he invited them to come with him the following morning to his new "parish."

After serving as associate pastor—in Tony's terms "unsuccessfully"—in a large Jamaican congregation, Tony had requested and been granted by his conference an unsalaried, three-year leave from regular pastoral duties to work in the slums of Montego Bay. Tony worked primarily with a boys' club during the day and supported himself and his ministry by playing the piano at night in the lounge of a fashionable tourist hotel.

Dave remembered vividly the events of the next morning as they drove through Montego in the Hopkinses' rented car. At the time Dave expressed his astonishment at the contrast between the extreme poverty of the great mass of people in the area and the plush tourist zone and the homes of affluent business and government leaders. In Tony's "parish" Dave and Carol saw hundreds of crude palm shanties, many with seven and eight occupants. There were no plumbing facilities, and the only available water, as much as a half mile away from some huts, came from a single faucet put in by the city. Tony explained that most of the adult population was uneducated with little or no hope for employment in an increasingly urban-oriented nation.

In his words, Tony was convinced that "the very presence of the concentrated wealth—the fruits of an economy largely based on the tourist industry, where those fruits are not shared with the nation although they are primarily the products of the natural tropical setting of our island—is essentially destructive and explosive." Tony continued, "The young people with whom I work have virtually no public education available. They see the contrast between the haves and have-nots and are understandably bitter and frustrated. My boys turn to gangs, drugs, and stealing out of desperation and a lack of self-worth. The human tragedy in this slum is a crime against God's good creation and is contrary to Christ's mandate to love our neighbors as ourselves. In Luke 4:18 Jesus declares his mission as 'good news to the poor and liberty for the oppressed.' We are called by Christ to be in solidarity with the poor and oppressed of our world. This is not only my parish, but as a Christian it is also yours."

In his spare time while with his former congregation and now full time, Tony worked with a gang of young boys. He used his gifts as a musician to teach them to play the few instruments he could gather. They had slowly formed a band. Now Tony felt there was real competition among the boys to belong to the band. "For most of these boys playing an instrument gives them the first feeling of accomplishment they have ever experienced. It is only with a concept of pride and self-worth that these young men can even begin to hope for a different life."

Tony's plea to Dave Hopkins still rang in his ears. "Reverend Hopkins, I've got over a hundred boys and twelve instruments. My church is struggling in Jamaica; it simply has no funds to work in the slums, and most of the church members place no priority on this kind of ministry. Through your congregation and your contacts in the U.S., can you get support for my club? God has empowered these boys to fight for human dignity. Join us in this struggle for liberation. I know from my time with your congregation that you have influential and powerful businessmen who could help us.

"Bauxite, exported to the U.S., is Jamaica's primary source of foreign exchange. But the U.S.-based tourist industry is second and more directly affects our economy. Tourism annually grosses millions of dollars through the exploitation of our beaches and the cheap labor of our people. Yet virtually no Jamaicans are in management positions. Day laborers, with visions of North American dollars, come from coastal villages and small farms up in the mountains to work in the hotels. With limited skills and no job security, they are at the mercy of fluctuating tourism trends and more often than not end up homeless and unemployed. Whole families try to survive by begging tourists to buy shells, fruit, or straw hats. These factors directly contribute to the growth of the slums. Tourism has also corrupted our culture by its presence, producing assembly line handicrafts and phony festivals. Don't your Christian executives who benefit from the social structures which have been created by their businesses here have some real responsibility for their brothers and sisters in Jamaica who are negatively affected by those structures?"

Dave Hopkins snapped back to the present as Frank Palmer put his hand on Dave's shoulder and said, "Welcome to the club again. Our table is waiting." After the men had ordered lunch, Dave sketched the essence of his morning in Kingston and put Anthony Robinson's questions to his friends.

Frank Palmer, now sixty-six, recently retired from the vice-presidency of Consolidated International Beverage Company, turned to Dave with a grin. "When the church urged you and Carol to take that vacation, I should have known you couldn't just go and escape for a week! Well, to deal with the issues Tony put to us, we may first need to sort out why we have any responsibility. I personally believe that I *am* my brother's keeper. As a Christian, I find it impossible to observe conditions such as you describe and not seek a responsible way to help. Revolting conditions of hunger and health address not only company executives but boards of directors and stockholders. There is a minimal but increasing sense of corporate responsibility in many companies. Tony is right. We get a profit—we must give in return. As the Bible says, 'Those to whom much has been given, much will be required.' The issue then goes from rationale to strategy."

At this point George Delaney cut in, "Frank, as corporations we do give already in terms of salaries for individuals, opportunities for small local businesses, and taxes to the government which provide funds that country had no access to prior to our arrival. As you know, I am in the hotel business and Tony has got to face some realities. He speaks of U.S. companies grossing millions in the Caribbean. This is true, but he has a superficial view of gross operating profit. The return on investment is frequently very poor. The initial risk of building a hotel is increased by political instability and even the danger of eventual expropriation of property. For weeks following recent political unrest, the Jamaican tourist industry lost revenue of over a million dollars a day from cancelled reservations. After the tremendous expense of building in a developing country, the management then has to continue to import at great expense the luxuries our customers expect. Most tourists really want to feel at home with familiar cuisine, in the air-conditioned comfort of their hotel which provides a secure base for a controlled exposure to an alien culture in the streets and markets.

"To provide that U.S.-like retreat center in another culture is expensive. In fact the percentage of operating profit in the Caribbean is the lowest of any major overseas operation as reflected in the studies for Worldwide Hotel Operations which I brought along for your reference. In addition Horwath and Horwath's statistics show the Caribbean to have some of the highest employee salaries and benefits. We return a tremendous amount of income to those people. Good Calvinists like us acknowledge we're all sinners, but a significant number of Jamaicans benefit from U.S. corporate presence.

"Look, Frank, for me to say I'm against helping the less fortunate is like saying I'm against motherhood. But as you have said in the past, you don't sell a moral attitude on its own merits. You've got to convince a company that it's in its own self-interest to create a good working environment in order for its business to prosper. That's not only good business, it's sound policy based on human nature. Frank, while we may disagree on the rationale, we seem to agree on the conclusion. The long-term view of stability and profitability call for a controlled, careful strategy for corporate involvement in international issues."

"But George," Dave Hopkins responded, "aren't we called as Christians to 'serve the world' and not to attempt first to maximize our own benefits? I've seen you personally take a strong stand in the community on issues you felt were morally correct, even when this might jeopardize your image or result in a personal loss in the view of some people. Why must the assuming of social responsibility for a corporation always be based on self-interest in contrast to the individual's responsibility? And as Tony has indicated, what about the self-interest of the vast majority of Jamaicans who don't benefit from those statistically high employee salaries? While acknowledging our own sin, don't we also have to see the sin of an elite group of Jamaicans who link their self-interest to U.S. corporate profit?"

Harold Atkins, thirty-eight, who headed one of the largest consultant firms in the Midwest, had been silent up to this point. Harold now spoke clearly and firmly. "Self-interest or not, I frankly don't think there is *any* premise for a business to become involved in the social concerns of a host country. Just as our country is based on a clear separation of church and state, so should our economic institutions function independently. Our Lutheran friends got it right when they speak of two realms, one secular and one religious.

"A corporation is not an individual. A business has one responsibility— to create customers. If it does this well, there's profit which benefits host and guest. If not, both are out of business. An individual can afford to act responsibly in relation to his or her moral commitments. There is no corporate moral commitment in a business. Corporations do not have the luxury of being responsible in the same way. I may personally give money or time to some world social agency, but I'm not about to counsel my client to do the same thing. My client's primary responsibility is to his or her stockholders who have invested in a business, not in a philanthropic organization."

Frank Palmer slowly turned to Harold. "I used to operate with a similar logic in executive decisions, although I don't think I was ever asked to articulate it. Now, I am less persuaded. That logic appears, so my children argue, to divide one's life into neat compartments that don't correlate with one another. Why should a company be released from moral responsibility simply because it's a corporate institution? A business has several levels of obligation, only one of which is to its stockholders. True, you can't sell being a 'do-gooder,' but I am accountable for my employees because they are my employees, and I am accountable for those in need because they are in need. Somehow I must assume responsibility for my influence in my private and corporate life—even for my sins. This is at the heart of any sense of stewardship for the natural and human resources of the world. I'm not thinking simply about myself; I'm worried about the world my grandchildren and Jamaicans' grandchildren will be living in."

As the lunch arrived, Dave Hopkins joked that judging by the intensity of the conversation, he certainly didn't need to encourage his friends to express their opinions. Dave indicated that he was struck by the genuine ambiguity and complexity of the problem and needed to focus the concern he felt. "If we all agree that *some* moral responsibility exists—be that personal or corporate—how, for example, could an influential individual or hotel chain in the Caribbean go about effecting change for those in need? How can we respond, if at all, to Tony's request for help?"

"I've learned from experience," responded George Delaney, "that it is a mistake to sidestep the established channels. Governments, even of developing nations, tend to thrive on the status quo. We must convince them that economic stability depends on a solid middle class. It's in both our best interests to establish technical training programs. We should also seek to support, through supervised grants which use the resources of our money and our people, health and education projects as well as indigenous crafts and music. This helps maintain the original culture; it also protects the reasons the tourists go to places like Jamaica. Mutual self-interest is the key."

Harold Atkins retorted, "But how do you justify any immediate return to your stockholders? The hotels I advise pay fair wages by local standards; this is income for people who wouldn't otherwise have jobs. These people appear content with their lives. You're making paternalistic assumptions that it is in the best self-interest of Jamaicans for their country to become a copy of our society. My hotels pay high taxes. It's the local government's responsibility to channel the taxes into social programs if they see fit. But the ultimate use of taxes is not my client's business. Personally, however, I would be willing to give Dave, here, money to be sent to Tony's boys' club."

"Now here's where I have to back off," interposed George. "Tony is not working through channels. It is my understanding that he was given that leave of absence from the church after a dispute with his conference over priorities. Lack of local support for his program also seems to indicate alienation from his former congregation. I remember Tony as a responsible young man, but to give him money without some form of control is another matter. To ask a hotel or corporation to sponsor such a charitable project could jeopardize their relationship to the established middle class and possibly to the government. If these boys reach a point of 'self-realization' in which they put on pressure to evict my hotels, or worse, expropriate the investment, a project without supervision would be self-destructive. We must face the realization that our businesses are parasites on another culture. We need to work for the most symbiotic relationship possible between a parasite and its host. We don't seek the death of the host or the extermination of the parasite. Both organisms can survive and flourish through negotiated mutual interest and respect."

Frank Palmer shook his head. "Our lives, our corporations are involved in risks every day. We must respond in a way which is not demeaning. We can't offer assistance to Tony and then show him we have no confidence in his vision for his own people. A semi-paternalistic attitude is perhaps inevitable, but the over-paternalistic style of the 'company mill' will corrupt our humanity and theirs. We need more than bigger mission gifts—strings or no strings attached. The request from Tony, our former pastor and student, is to assume some responsibility for those who are in need based on Christian concern. I'm reminded of Christ's repeated call to Peter to 'feed my sheep.' Tony points us to children who are hungry for human dignity. A strategy for development ought to involve business, government, and church interests in Kingston and Chicago. Our church never touched me in this area, or perhaps I never listened. I feel called—I just don't know where."

George Delaney responded, "Frank, this is the vision of a retired corporation executive who has leisure and security. I wish you luck. Project-oriented, mutual-interest programs are what Tony really needs and if my competition will concur, we could make some headway here. A low-profit region like the Caribbean may be a place to try out such an approach. We have less to lose by the risk."

Harold Atkins countered, "As a consultant I don't think you have weighed properly the pressures of profit and growth at home or of instability and corruption in Jamaica. Are you willing to make the necessary payoffs? A corporation advisor would counsel, 'Don't exceed your corporate responsibilities for involvement.' However, as an individual I will make a pledge and write a check to Tony for his work. I always wanted to play a flute; this way I can at least buy one."

"The meal is almost over," Dave said. "We seem to have gone in so many different directions I'm wondering if there is any way we can consolidate our efforts in response to Tony."

Commentary

Big Business and the Boys' Club

Jesus Christ ministered to the poor and the politically powerless and lived within their midst. For centuries this man and his ministry have confronted his rich and powerful followers with the scandal of relating poverty and powerlessness to the wealth, might, and indifference of Caesar in his various ecclesiastical, political, and military configurations. In this case the destitution and muted desperation of Jamaican youth joined in a boys' club confront the confidence born of power of businessmen gathered in the quiet elegance of the Chicago Men's Club. Are these two all-male clubs destined to remain alienated from each other and the women of the world until the Lord returns in glory? Or has the power of Jesus Christ trickled down to all the clubs of this world?

This is a case first about corporate responsibility and second about poor countries and the place of transnational corporations (TNCs) within them. Since the latter is more appropriately the subject of the case "Prophets from Brazil," this commentary will focus on corporate responsibility.

The surface questions in the case are whether and how to assist Tony Robinson and the boys in his club. The deeper question is whether corporations have social responsibility beyond their economic responsibilities to produce goods and services, hire workers, and realize a profit.

This is a complex case. The characters may at first glance seem easy to understand, but their positions are a maze of assumptions, strategies, and theological understandings. Exploring this maze is the primary order of business. Four routes through the maze are offered by Tony Robinson, Frank Palmer, George Delaney, and Harold Atkins. Each route provides a way to assist Tony and thereby to exercise corporate responsibility. Each has theological foundations. And each is open to criticism.

TONY ROBINSON

Tony is the first of the four to make an appearance. Dave Hopkins and his wife run into him in the cocktail lounge of their Jamaican hotel where Tony is playing the piano at night to support his work in a Montego Bay slum during the day. Tony recounts the ups and downs of his ministry in the four years since their last meeting. The term "unsuccessful" is used to describe his service in a large Jamaican congregation. Later George Delaney reveals that Tony was given a leave of absence from the congregation after a dispute over priorities. George adds that Tony does not work through channels. Almost unnoticed is the further information that Tony worked with a gang of young boys in his spare time at this former congregation. Apparently this gang and its slum environment are Tony's new parish.

From this sketchy information and his obvious sympathies, it is safe to assume that Tony feels squeezed between rich and poor worlds inside Jamaica, and North and South global perspectives outside. He is not playing the game according to the "rules" and as a result finds himself isolated and without resources except for his music.

Tony is outraged at the conditions in the slums of Montego Bay and blames the tourist industry and its confederates in the Jamaican government, whose generosity has meant the slum has all of one water spigot. Tony clearly takes the liberation perspective developed at some length in other cases in this volume, for example, "Vietnam's Children" and "Prophets from Brazil." His approach to relief of the poor is to jump into the thick of the fray and to empower the poor to provide their own relief. Specifically he is using the vehicle of a band to drive the boys to a new and liberated consciousness based on an awareness of their own self-worth. He seeks the support of TNCs in order to empower the boys. This is explosive stuff, and George Delaney is correct to recognize it as such.

Tony seems ambivalent about TNCs. He lays at their feet the ills of Jamaican society. The conclusion would seem to follow that they should get out and take along their "phony festivals" and "controlled exposure to an alien culture." But Tony does not follow through to this conclusion. Furthermore, he draws pay from his adversaries and even asks them through Dave to support his work with the boys. He apparently believes that corporations have a responsibility to help pick up the pieces of the shattered Jamaican culture.

Liberation theology is the foundation of Tony's perspective. He cites Luke 4:18, a favorite text of liberationists. He makes use of liberation themes and methods as he tries to create a new awareness among the boys. His criticism of TNCs echoes liberation theologians. He explicitly urges Dave Hopkins to join the struggle for liberation.

George Delaney insinuates that Tony is a dangerous radical. This is understandable, for however much Tony actually deserves this label, his ideas and actions are clear threats to TNCs and to George as an executive in the tourist business. "Who knows," George must be thinking, "those kids might rise up and burn the hotels. And if they stop short of that and just cause local riots, Jamaica will be dead to tourism overnight." To the supporters of TNCs and the form of development they bring to poor countries, George's insinuation and thoughts will be well founded. To supporters of liberation they will seem self-serving.

FRANK PALMER

On the surface of things Frank seems to be the good guy in the discussion at the men's club. He is so willing to help. A retired executive of a beverage company, Frank leads off the discussion with his versions of helping the poor and corporate responsibility.

According to Frank the way to help the poor is to involve business, government, and church interests in a coordinated development effort. He seems to assume that such a coordinated development plan is on the drawing boards and that the interests he mentions can be harmoniously drawn into such an effort on behalf of the poor. Unfortunately, there is no plan, harmony is nonexistent, and he admits a lack of direction.

On the matter of corporate responsibility, however, Frank is clearer and more direct. The wretched conditions of Montego's poor cry out for correction. TNCs have been among the forces which have generated these conditions and profited from them. TNCs have a social responsibility beyond making a profit which in no way differs from that of an individual. They are called to respond to Tony's request.

Theologically Frank anchors his position in the biblical concern for the poor, repentance, stewardship, and the integration of all life under the lordship of Jesus Christ. He cites Jesus' summons to "feed my sheep." He mentions Cain's response, "Am I my brother's keeper?" to God's query regarding the whereabouts of Abel, Cain's slain brother, and thus Frank emphatically rejects Cain's implication that he is not responsible for his neighbor. Frank insists that a corporation is responsible on several levels for its acts, and especially for its sins, suggesting that TNCs have been short-sighted in poor countries and need to change their ways. He links this responsibility to the grand theme of stewardship. Individuals and corporations are God's stewards and are responsible for passing on to future generations what they have inherited in no worse—and preferably in better—shape than they received it. Finally, he rejects Harold Atkins's separation of reality into individual and social spheres with different moralities. For Frank there is one world in Christ. Corporations cannot claim release from social responsibility just because they have characteristics and functions which distinguish them from individuals.

Several criticisms are directed at Frank's position. George calls him paternalistic, a charge which has some foundation. Frank advocates corporate responsibility but links it neither to substantive social change nor to the participation of the poor. His coordinated development effort is not coordinated with the poor he would coordinate! Business, government, and church leaders will presumably do all the work, then descend on the poor with their grand schemes. He also appears satisfied with responding to the symptoms of poverty with repentance and charity.

Harold Atkins refuses to budge from his distinction between individual and social realms and its implied rejection of Frank's argument for corporate social responsibility. In so doing he follows a long and honorable tradition in Christianity which makes this distinction. This tradition holds that groups have different functions and less moral resources than individuals and sometimes must act in ways which cannot be justified on ideal grounds. Violence and the justifiable war response to it is only one instance of this.

Left unmentioned is Frank's optimism that responsibility can be exercised easily, and a harmony of interests established. His sense of sin is almost nonexistent or at least not explicit.

GEORGE DELANEY

George is engaging because of his hard-headed realism. An executive in a TNC with interests in the Caribbean, he looks at corporate responsibility in dollars and cents terms and with a careful calculation of interests. His position may not be as hard-boiled as it at first seems, however. He does not subscribe to an unvarnished version of Adam Smith's "invisible hand," which guides the pursuit of self-interest toward the social good. He does not agree with Harold Atkins that corporations discharge all their social responsibilities in making a profit. His dogged pursuit of mutual self-interest is hard-headed in its understanding of sin, but leaves the door open for TNCs to do more than just pursue profit.

For obvious reasons George is very cautious about helping the poor. He argues that Dave and Frank are overlooking the many ways in which TNCs already assist the poor through salaries, purchases in local markets, and taxes to governments. He assumes that these expenditures represent new money for Jamaica, an assumption which may be true in the case of his firm, but which is not generally true in poor countries, where TNC investment funds often come from local sources.

George goes on to give details about the Caribbean region and its travel industry, which he depicts as being on the brink of disaster. The purpose of all his realism about social unrest and costs is probably to persuade his colleagues that the travel industry can afford neither social change nor social responsibility.

To Jamaicans of Tony Robinson's persuasion, however, George's other details about luxury, familiar cuisine, air-conditioned comfort, controlled exposure, and alien cultures send a different message. These Jamaicans will automatically compare these details to their experience of poverty and conclude that George is arrogant and insensitive. Dave Hopkins softens this conclusion a bit when he points out George's involvement on moral issues in his own community.

The essence of George's position on assistance to the poor and the role of TNCs can be summarized in the words "mutual self-interest through established channels." What he appears to be advocating is a TNC-led model of development which stresses rapid economic growth. Eventually, or so the logic of this perspective goes, the poor will be best served by a careful strategy of corporate involvement with local governments which slowly lets the gains of economic growth trickle down to the poor. Stability and a solid middle class are essential ingredients.

George understands self-interest to be the motivating force in economic decisions and reasons from this to an accommodation of interests in mutually beneficial projects. He is not naive about harmonious accommodation, however. He recognizes that Tony's view cannot be included. Negotiations should go on between established powers with radicals such as Tony excluded.

Theologically, George's perspective rests on his view of sin. More precisely, it rests on the good which results from containing sin, especially the sin of those who threaten the established order. He refers to the tradition of Protestant reformer John Calvin and its heavy stress on sin. He returns again and again to self-interest as the primary motivator. He speaks of a "sound policy based on human nature." Finally, his anxiety about instability and revolution suggests a strong fear of anarchy. Order must be maintained even if it means a measure of repression.

George has historical evidence to support his case. The tortured course of human history offers ample grounds for realism. But for his colleagues Frank Palmer and Dave Hopkins, George's realism must be too thoroughgoing. For them, mutual accommodation of self-interest, particularly when it refuses to accommodate a majority of the population, cannot be the limit of human creativity and morality. Dave even protests George's realism by citing his involvement in the community. Still George makes reference to no positive norms. Jesus Christ does not seem to make a difference for him in social affairs. Corporate social responsibility for its own sake is apparently too much to expect.

For all his consistency on sin, George is not particularly consistent in apportioning it. While he assumes corporations are motivated by self-interest, he is not nearly as worried about their sin as about Tony's. He overlooks entirely the well-documented evidence of TNC contributions to oppressive conditions in the poor world. He is oblivious to the failure of TNC-led development to decrease poverty. He ignores altogether the sin of the "solid middle class," which partially controls most governments. Indeed, in most poor countries the middle class George refers to is a small, wealthy elite protecting its own interests. Witness the one water spigot in the Montego Bay slum. In short, George's prescription is to protect the rich and constrain the poor.

HAROLD ATKINS

Harold is the youngest of the trio of businessmen and head of the largest travel consulting firm in the Midwest. The strength of his conviction that corporations have no place in the social welfare business or interfering in Jamaican internal politics may suggest an uncaring attitude. Such a suggestion would be wide of the mark, for Harold makes quite clear his willingness to give as an individual.

The division of individuals and corporations into separate spheres is the driving conception in Harold's scheme of things. Harold, unlike George Delaney, expresses no reluctance to assist Tony. He almost writes a check on the spot out of his personal account. He would not, however, approve a request from the treasurer of his company to issue a check on the corporate account. Individuals may give, but corporations may not.

This division of things into separate spheres is deeply ingrained in Western ways of thinking. It stems among other places from ancient Greek thought with its dualisms of light and dark, mind and body, and good and evil. It informs the U.S. Constitution with its separation of powers and its distinction between church and state. In religious terms it is expressed in the "two-realms" understanding to which Harold himself refers.

Harold argues that corporations have one and only one social responsibility, to make a profit. Profits are the lifeblood of any business enterprise. Without them a business must shut its doors, and when it does, it fails in its ancillary responsibilities to shareholders, employees, customers, and even the public through its incapacity to pay taxes. Profits are also an important signaling device. They tell investors where to put their money so that resources will be efficiently allocated. Harold is certainly correct in one respect. There is little room for romanticism about profits and their link to the production of goods and services. Profits are the first priority of any business in a market economy.

The question, however, is not really about the priority of profits. No one at the lunch table would disagree. Even the absent Tony would probably concur. The question is whether corporations have other social responsibilities. Harold seems to think not.

His full argument, were he to make it, would probably go something like this. The moral responsibility of corporate executives is to produce goods and services and in so doing to serve the interests of the owners. Investors entrust their funds to executives and become owners or shareholders with the expectation of a return. Executives are stewards of these funds and break trust with the owners when they use corporate profits for their own self-selected causes. In effect they levy a tax on the shareholders without giving them representation in the decision. Morally, executives must respect the wishes of shareholders and abstain from trying to do good for them. It is the owners who should be the ones to exercise moral responsibility as they allocate their corporate dividends among competing claims.

Harold might also argue on pragmatic grounds. Using hard-won earnings on extraneous social concerns not only reduces profits directly and makes a company less attractive as an investment, but also can indirectly necessitate higher prices to cover higher costs, as with a company taking solitary action to clean up its pollution while competitors continue to pass pollution costs on to the public in dirty air and water. Either way a competitive disadvantage results and with it inefficiency.

On pragmatic grounds Harold might also question Frank Palmer's knee-jerk advocacy of corporate social responsibility. Would Frank really want powerful corporations paternalistically mucking around in the affairs of nations and individuals? The days of the company town are over. Corporations are not well situated to set priorities for governments or to decide complex moral and social issues. More than likely they will set directions in their own narrow self-interest and bungle tasks they have assigned themselves.

Thus for a host of philosophical, moral, and pragmatic reasons Harold would urge corporations to stick to production and money making and let individuals and governments set social priorities.

Theologically, Harold bases his perspective on the call to give, which he would answer individually with personal good deeds and socially with government activity. He also cites the "two-realms" understanding first articulated by Augustine and later developed by Luther. This perspective divides reality into sacred and secular spheres which respectively are governed by God's right and left hands. The right hand of God, exercised in the church, is the hand of faith, hope, and love. Grace, forgiveness, charity, and nonviolence abound in this realm. The left hand of God, exercised by governments and other social institutions, is the hand of order, pragmatic calculation, and justice. Punishment, coercion, and even justifiable violence (the so-called "sword" as a symbol of the ordering function) have important roles to play. These two spheres are distinct, if not separate, and should not be confused. They are held together by the two hands of one God and by individuals who are free to live in both spheres while recognizing their differences.

Corporations as economic institutions are part of the secular realm and are governed by different norms than individuals. The function of corporations is not to love people, which it cannot do anyway, but to order economic life so there are sufficient resources for basic necessities. For corporations to get mixed up in charity or noneconomic social concerns is to confuse the way God has ordered human life. This confusion will lead to disorder and in the end accomplish little. Charity is the province of individuals and groups organized to provide it.

This perspective is well established in the tradition. Yet a too rigid separation of realms, which Harold may be guilty of, misses the subtleties of the traditional two-realms formulation. The realms are not separate. To repeat, they are held together by God and by individuals who carry motives of love and intentions to serve ethically from their personal faith into the social realm. Faith, hope, love, grace, forgiveness, charity, and nonviolence are not irrelevant to the primary economic function of corporations. At the very least corporations can act justly, obey the law, and refrain from causing injury.

Frank Palmer counters Harold's tendency to separate by distinguishing levels of responsibility. He makes a good point. Corporations have different functions and priorities, but God's realm of love, though distinct, is relevant to every level of Harold's work and to the business of his firm. The thorny issue is discerning relevance from distinction and deciding what is the appropriate exercise of corporate social responsibility.

CORPORATE RESPONSIBILITY

Actually a number of mediating possibilities stand between Frank's "either" of full social responsibility and Harold's "or" of limited responsibility. George Delaney articulates one position in spite of its problems. He advocates social responsibility as long as it is consistent with the overall interests of the company, with long-term profit presumably high on his list of interests. Another position would allow for social responsibility if it enhances profitability and would give managerial discretion if it does not.

Harold Atkins's perspective shorn of its theological wraps is usually associated with economist Milton Friedman. In a now classic essay, "The Social Responsibility of Business Is To Increase Its Profits" (*The New York Times Sunday Magazine,* September 13, 1970), Friedman set the case for profits as the exclusive responsibility of corporations. Friedman made many of the same arguments as Harold Atkins. Corporations are not persons. Managers have a moral responsibility to serve stockholders with profits. Individuals and social institutions other than corporations are better situated to set and carry out social priorities.

But even Friedman stepped back from an extreme interpretation of this view. In a little-noticed sentence of his essay, Friedman spoke of profit seeking "while conforming to the basic rules of society, both those embodied in law and those embodied in social custom." Conforming to the law does not substantially change his position, but his openness to social custom certainly makes a difference.

The fact is that most North Americans expect corporations to be ethical. The best run and most profitable firms, as ethicist Charles McCoy points out, are often ones in which values and social responsibility are woven deeply into the corporate fabric. In other words, there is such a thing as corporate character, and ethics flow out of character.

McCoy and others go on to observe that corporations cannot avoid social responsibility. They are so large and powerful that their activities inevitably spill over into noneconomic realms. It is really not so much a matter of "yes" or "no" to social responsibility as it is of being responsible or irresponsible.

Corporations being responsible does not mean they should become flag-waving social activists out front on each and every social cause. Profits are primary in a market system. Corporations cannot meet all the claims placed on them and certainly should not fool themselves about moral purity. Harold Atkins is correct about the exercise of corporate social responsibility. It can cause competitive disadvantage and injustice and lead to the setting of wrong priorities and to poor execution. All these are considerations which constrain the capacity, if not the imperative, to be moral.

How managers should act in pursuing corporate responsibility is open to debate. At very least there are two moral minimums: to act according to the law and to avoid and correct injury. To follow the law is self-explanatory, however ambiguous it may be at times. To avoid causing injury and to rectify past injuries caused may be as simple as adequate on-the-job safety precautions or as complex as pulling investments out of places where human rights are abused. Included in this second minimum is certainly the just treatment of employees and customers.

Beyond this minimum the debate begins. The call to charity and the obligation to lend assistance are strong parts of the Christian tradition, more so when there is a critical need, proximity, capability, and no one present who is better able. The distinctions encountered in the two-realms understanding give pause and to a degree constrain, but do not finally limit this obligation. Jesus Christ is the lord of both realms, and the Christian is called to live ethically as an individual and as a member of social institutions. Life is of a piece, not separated into exclusive spheres.

The forms that corporate responsibility can take are infinite, but four general categories stand out:

1. Self-regulation to avoid or to correct injury.
2. Affirmative action to correct internal corporate abuses and to improve conditions internal and external to the corporation.
3. Leadership in moral causes.
4. Developing corporate character and managing values so that morality permeates the corporation.

In particular the fourth should receive greater attention than it has.

Should Tony then be assisted? It would be a small matter and generous for the three businessmen to open their pockets and give individually. As for a corporate gift, that would also be in order, easily accomplished, and a matter for objection only to those purists who deny any social responsibility for corporations.

In the larger context, however, this apparently simple question raises fundamental and perplexing dilemmas. In terms of the Christian tradition the dilemma is how to connect the poverty and powerlessness of Jesus and his followers to the wealth and might of the modern corporation. In terms of poor countries the dilemma is how to bring poor peasants and urban slum dwellers into a just relationship with TNCs and local elites. The three solutions proposed in the men's club in typical power-broker fashion all rely on charity, although Frank talks vaguely about a coordinated development effort and George about mutual assistance projects. None includes a shift of power and privilege. Tony's overall orientation has seeds for fundamental change, but little is said about power.

Is charity all rich Christians can do to link the worlds of poor and rich? Perhaps corporate responsibility means something more daring: either to take the poor as the point of departure or get out. To take the world's poor as a point of departure would be difficult for TNCs. They have little expertise in meeting the needs of the poor, and, with self-interest as a given, little inclination. The poor have no money to buy their products, and TNCs make high profits with things as they are.

To pull out of poor countries might then be the responsible path. Jamaica might be better off without the tourist industry. But try to tell Jamaicans that. A few might listen, but whatever else they do, TNCs provide jobs and thereby infuse or at least generate income. They may not be the right kind of jobs, and taking them may mean serving the status quo, but Jamaicans have few alternatives. No institutions are waiting in the wings to infuse large amounts of capital while taking the poor as their point of departure.

This more daring either/or of corporate responsibility is an indictment of TNCs. It is not, however, an indictment of TNC executives as mean-spirited and uncharitable. They are part of a system which has been tremendously productive and meets the material needs of many people. They must be self-interested. The problems they face are systemic. At present, TNC-led market capitalism is not adequately meeting the needs of the world's poor. Sensitive executives feel squeezed between the forces at work. Perhaps one thing they could do is to pay Tony a visit and learn firsthand about conditions in Jamaica and the view from the vantage point of the poor.

For the time being, anyway, the two worlds of poor and rich remain alienated and apart. The power of Jesus Christ has not been allowed to trickle down. This leaves Christians themselves squeezed between conflicting perspectives and wondering which alternative is the best to act on in an imperfect world.

ADDITIONAL RESOURCES

Beauchamp, Thomas L., and Norman E. Bowie, eds. *Ethical Theory and Business.* 2nd ed. Englewood Cliffs: Prentice-Hall, 1983.

Copeland, Warren. *Economic Justice: The Social Ethics of U.S. Economic Policies.* Nashville: Abingdon, 1988.

Friedman, Milton. *Capitalism and Freedom.* Chicago: University of Chicago Press, 1962.

————. "The Social Responsibility of Business Is To Increase Its Profits." *The New York Times Sunday Magazine* (September 13, 1970).

Green, Ronald M. *The Ethical Manager: A New Method for Business Ethics.* New York: Macmillan Publishing Co., 1994.

McCoy, Charles S. *Management of Values*. Boston: Pitman, 1985.

Niebuhr, Reinhold. *Moral Man and Immoral Society*. New York: Charles Scribner's Sons, 1932.

Simon, John G., Charles W. Powers, and Jon P. Gunneman. *The Ethical Investor*. New Haven, CT: Yale University Press, 1972.

Case

The Healthy Christian Life

Jan Overbroek stared across the broad oak table at the pastor, then quickly over at his wife Ellie looking for some clue on how to respond. Ellie looked exhausted. For the past half hour she had been trying to get their two young sons ready for bed. She had slipped quietly into a chair beside him just in time to hear Reverend Wiemer's proposal.

"Jan," the pastor said, "I would like you and Ellie to talk to the church study group next week about your approach to farming and how it reflects your faith in God and your beliefs about the healthy Christian life."

The healthy Christian life? Caught by surprise, Jan turned the phrase quickly over in his mind. How could he pretend to share with others when he had plenty of doubts about what that meant himself? From the look in her eyes Jan sensed that Ellie was puzzled too.

In fact, telling others about their method of farming was nothing new for either Jan or Ellie. Over the past five years the nearby state university regularly sent out teams of extension agents and even other farmers to study the way the Overbroeks were transforming a traditional farm into a chemical-free dairy operation. What the Overbroeks were doing was not easy, but Jan and Ellie were making it work, technically as well as financially.

Although Jan always loved the out-of-doors, he never intended to choose such a life's work. From a suburban background, he planned to finish his soils major at the university, then work for the field staff of a large agricultural products company back in his home state. Much of his training focused on the technology and high-input techniques available to modern farmers to promote weed and pest control and to maximize production on large scale acreages.

This case was prepared by Mary Agria and L. Shannon Jung, Center for Theology and Land, Dubuque, Iowa. Copyright © The Case Study Institute. All names have been changed to protect the privacy of the individuals involved.

Then during a supposedly routine internship in his senior year Jan was placed with Ellie's father whose low-input approach to farming was founded on basic biological principles, the antithesis of high-tech corporate farming. Through skilled management, even modest acreage farms could be financially viable, or sustainable, as some farmers referred to the concept.

The more he studied what Ellie's father was doing, the more he came to appreciate it. Large-scale farming depends on the extensive use of pesticides and chemical weed suppressants that can endanger farmers' health and that of their families. Environmentalists worry about the long term effects on the land and ground water. Even consumers have begun to express concern about the quality of their food supply.

As important as those concerns were, many of Jan's instructors at the university pointed out that the bottom line was still economics. To keep labor costs down, agro-business specialists insisted, chemical farming was a necessity. During his internship, however, Jan saw living proof that there might be another way. People like Ellie's father were turning back the clock, so to speak, to move forward, using and improving low-input techniques abandoned by most farmers over the past generation.

"This isn't some nostalgia thing," Ellie's father had explained, "simply good business. Instead of high chemical costs, you've got to be willing to substitute passes across the field with the cultivator. You put your money in labor. Insect control is a bit trickier. Either customers need to be educated to buy a slightly less perfect looking product or the crops need to be sold to processors for produce where appearance doesn't matter. If you do use any chemicals, it is just on individual rows or small areas of the field where it may be impossible to cultivate."

"Economics again," Jan had responded skeptically. "Every time processing is involved, it costs the farmer more profits."

But for all his doubts, Jan's plans had undergone a dramatic transformation. He had found his life's work. When he completed his degree, he and Ellie had decided to marry, and using loans from family, friends, and the local bank, they had leased farmland near her childhood home. Their dream was to operate a dairy farm using environmentally friendly methods. Both were convinced that farming in a more traditional way would be better for the land, better for the customer, and better for them as a farm family.

Working closely with state university agriculturists, the Overbroeks began to rotate crops and utilize supposedly old-fashioned tilling methods. Their goal was to move to intensive grazing. Trained as a textbook farmer, it hurt Jan especially to hear the reactions of some of their neighbors.

"Haven't seen a field look like that since my grandfather's day," Jan overheard a farmer in his fifties comment at the feed store one afternoon when he did not know Jan was in earshot. "Stubble from the last season right up there among the new crop."

The man's companion shook his head. "August Treves worked all his life to get those fields weed-free. He'd turn over in his grave to see them like this."

Going to the bank was a humiliating business for Jan. Every "innovation" needed to be justified painstakingly to skeptical bank officers. Without the help of the state university in monitoring the operation, it would have been hard to get the needed financial backing. The paperwork was mountainous.

"We put a lot of emphasis on farmers running a modern, efficient operation," their loan officer, Cy Morton, reminded them on a regular basis. "What you're doing is pretty risky."

More distant external forces like governmental regulations and the market itself seemed to conspire against them. Certification as an "organic" farm was complicated. Even if Jan and Ellie were to comply with all the paperwork, the meager dollar premium for selling chemical-free products did not make it worth the effort.

"Customers worry about food quality," one of the distributors commiserated when the Overbroeks explored marketing their milk through a health-food cooperative. "They worry, but not enough to pay for it. Government subsidies that keep the price of food artificially low don't help any."

Still Jan and Ellie persisted. When their first son, Josh, was born, Ellie could no longer take turns with Jan operating the tractor. They were forced to add a hired hand to share some of the heavier work, shaving their meager profit margin a little bit more.

"Sometimes I feel like all we do is work," Ellie sighed as she finished the latest round of reports. It was midnight, and by six both she and Jan needed to be out in the barn again. On top of everything else, Ellie had been doing taxes this year part-time for one of the accounting firms in town. The money certainly came in handy, but both Jan and Ellie worried that their boys were not getting the attention they needed.

"Maybe it would help to start thinking about seasonal calving for the herd," Jan suggested, "so that in the no-crop months we could take a vacation as a family. The hired hand could watch after things. We could probably borrow my brother's camper and get away from here for a few weeks. Take the kids to Orlando over Easter or something."

Scarce as their time was to enjoy life together as a family, money was even scarcer. The Overbroeks could not buy and enjoy many of the things that their urban visitors from the university took for granted.

"I envy you two," the director of the agricultural research office, Harold Blum, offered wistfully on one of his recent inspection visits. He gestured in the direction of Ellie's tidy garden, the clothes billowing on the line, and the well-kept red barns and outbuildings. "This is as close to the good life as it gets!"

Jan wondered what Harold would think if he knew how long they had agonized over whether they could afford a decent quality "boom box." Even going out to dinner these days was a major event.

Visits from Jan's family were especially stressful. Ellie did not say anything when her sister-in-law talked enthusiastically about the new wicker sectional she and her husband had purchased last winter, but Jan knew what she was thinking. Their own sofa, left over from Jan's college days, was faded and threadbare.

"Farming may seem harder this way," Jan tried to explain when his parents protested the hard physical labor he and Ellie put in during the summer months. "But it is also less expensive and probably the reason why we're still in operation when many young couples who use conventional petrochemical farming methods have gone under. We may not have much of a financial cushion, but at least we're still here!"

It was hard sometimes not to sound defensive or to admit that ultimately the finances of low-input farming were merely secondary issues to both Jan and Ellie. "It's the right way to go," Jan said when pressed on the subject. "It's the right way to treat the land. It's what makes the land rich and beautiful."

Right or wrong, Jan and Ellie did not control the weather, however. Just when things were looking up, nature went on the rampage. After two years of drought, the rains came for three months straight, and farmers all around them were struggling just to hang on. For the Overbroeks, it was harder than ever to fight disease and insects without resorting to chemicals. Their yields per acre were disastrously low.

"Is what we're doing really worth it?" Jan could not bear to articulate his worst fears even to Ellie. At the tiny crossroads church amid rolling meadows and cornfields, Pastor Wiemer, himself a product of an urban seminary, prayed for the weather, the land, and the people on it every Sunday now. There was a lot to pray about. Four of their neighbors, all running conventional petrochemical farming operations, were undergoing treatment for cancer. The sheriff had been out twice in the past month to a neighboring farm. "Domestic dispute," the weekly newspaper summed it up tersely.

Jan and Ellie were fairly regular churchgoers, even if their style of farming made it hard to attend during the growing season. They enrolled both boys in Sunday school, but had not taken active roles in adult-oriented congregational activities themselves. So when Pastor Wiemer showed up at their home that June evening, his proposal was the last thing the Overbroeks expected.

"We'll be talking about the healthy Christian life all next month," the pastor told Jan, "and I can't think of anyone in the congregation who has thought about that more than you and Ellie."

Jan did not hold back his reservations. "I really believe that this is the way God wants me to farm, and I care a lot about how my family lives—the food we put on the table and the time we have together. But I don't feel comfortable talking about it that way. For starters my neighbors believe in taking care of their land too, and I don't want them to think they're right and I'm wrong."

"Around here people don't say much about what they're thinking and feeling, especially when it comes to their work and finances," Ellie added. "That's pretty much left to God and the bank. Besides, I'm not sure anybody would see us as models of anything."

Jan could guess where she was coming from. How would anything they say about the healthy Christian life make sense to the Hansons down the road whose farm was sold at auction six months ago? Or to Elise Ortiz who was struggling to feed her five children on a waitress' salary since her husband had been killed in an accident at the canning plant last year?

Pastor Wiemer stood up and took one last look around the modestly furnished kitchen. "I wish you'd think about it," he persisted. "You can let me know after church on Sunday."

Commentary

The Healthy Christian Life

To Ellie and Jan Overbroek, the healthy Christian life is far more than chemical-free farming. It is also a way of life that includes hard work, modest consumption, and values that prize the land and the human communities sustained by the land. Ellie and Jan have been asked to share their motivations and methods with their local church study group. Clear on their methods and already a powerful witness in their small community, they are probably more anxious about how they will be understood within their community. Their qualms about putting their values into words must be seen in the context of the rural culture in which they are living.

They are not alone with their qualms. Many of the cases in this volume testify to an uneasiness with the way Americans are treating the land, the values foundational to modern society, and the emphasis on powerful technologies. The questions Pastor Wiemer raises about the healthy Christian life are addressed to everyone, although social settings may differ markedly. Translating faith into action and faithful stewardship are as relevant to the urban consumer as they are to the policy maker in Washington, D.C.; to the corporate executive facing unemployment, as to the farmer down the road from the Overbroeks.

STEWARDSHIP

Scripture and theology offer a vision of the just community and the healthy Christian life that details the relationship between persons and the land. The Mosaic law offered a vision of human community structured around a number of concerns that were echoed in Jesus' words and actions and in Christian theology.

First, the land was understood to belong to God who entrusted it to Israel "to keep and till" (Genesis 2:15) for the good of all its people. This understanding of the Israelites as stewards of God's land was remembered in practical ways, and this recognition of land as under God's ownership and human stewardship was basic to Jesus' ministry. When Rome conquered Israel and Judah, Caesar claimed to own the land by conquest and ordered Jews to pay taxes to Caesar to use it. Jews understood their first-fruits offerings to the Temple as the legitimate form of taxation to the real owner, God. During Jesus' boyhood the Romans had first held a census and then instituted taxation based on the census rolls, despite Jewish opposition and periodic rebellion. When Jesus was asked whether Jews should pay taxes to Caesar, he was faced with the most dangerous politico-religious question of his day. He first disarmed his hearers by asking his questioner for a Roman coin, demonstrating that he did not carry such coins and therefore was not a part of Caesar's economy. His ultimate answer, to give to Caesar what was Caesar's and to God what was God's, was not simply clever. For Jewish farmers whose taxes were to be paid in the fruit of the land, his answer confirmed their religious belief that if the land were God's, paying the fruit of the land to Caesar in taxes was idolatrous.

In this case study the Overbroeks express something of an understanding of stewardship. They express it most powerfully in their actions. Jan makes it more explicit for both of them when he says: "It is the right way to go. . . . It's the right way to treat the land." They even see farming in a religious sense as a vocation, as their choice of a way to devote themselves to the activity of God in the world. The text says that Jan had found his life's work, and that their dream was to operate a dairy farm using environmentally friendly methods.

A second concern of the scriptural vision is for the just community. Justice is more than merely obeying law; it is to participate in God's intentions. Justice therefore encompasses not only equity between individuals, but also compassion for the needy and a concern for the quality of communal life. The law demanded a basic equity: the courts and officials were to treat the rich and poor alike, and merchants were to use the same scales for everyone, not robbing the weak. The oath of a poor person was to be respected as that of a rich person. And yet there were special protections for the poor and the weak. God's law for Israelite society insisted that there was to be no permanent underclass. Not only was enslavement for debt limited to seven years regardless of the size of the debt, but the law provided that every fifty years, in the Jubilee year, debts were to be canceled, slaves were to be freed, and land was to be returned to the original owners. If the Jubilee law were carried out, no single family or group of families would ever control vast holdings to the detriment of the rest.

On farms the entire crop was never to be harvested, so that the poor could glean from the edges of the fields and the last of the vineyards lest they go hungry in winter. The law gave hope for surviving misfortune on a day-to-day basis, as well as hope for a new start free of slavery and debt. The law implemented this vision not only by demanding that individuals treat each other with justice and compassion, but also by demanding that social institutions and the authorities that controlled them enforce these provisions. Were the spirit of these demands taken seriously, perhaps fewer couples using the petrochemical farming methods that Jan refers to would have gone under, and the "domestic disputes" on neighboring farms could have been avoided.

A third concern of the Mosaic law was with the cultivation and conservation of resources. The law enjoined farmers to let fields lie fallow every seven years so that the land would regain its fertility. Fruit trees and vineyards were not to be harvested until they were mature, lest their strength be sapped. According to the law, land is the basis of community prosperity; it must be treated with respect, not used up and drained of its life-giving power. Land is a gift for all generations. Jan exclaims, "It's what makes the land rich and beautiful."

Theological reflection in the Jewish and Christian traditions has often joined the understanding of stewardship with that of land conservation. This is especially true in the modern treatment of private property, where private property is understood as a provisional right only, a right that can be revoked if the land is not used to meet serious needs of the community now and in the future.

Together these concerns make for a rich land ethic. In present day terms the land is to be used to meet basic human needs of all people and to contribute to the nutritional needs of communities. It has utilitarian value and its produce may be consumed. But it also has intrinsic value as part of God's good creation and should be conserved and enhanced, appreciated and even revered. This land ethic seems to be the spiritual basis for the Overbroeks' farming practices. Since the healthy Christian life presupposes a healthy land, it may also serve as the basis for a more encompassing personal and community ethic.

THE FARM CRISIS

To understand fully what Jan and Ellie's commitment to chemical-free farming means, the decision needs to be put into the context of social forces at work well beyond their two hundred forty acres. Farming as a profession in the United States in the past several decades has been a risky business.

The Overbroeks were only children and do not personally remember the halcyon days of the 1970s when American agriculture was experiencing a growth spurt. In part to combat the worsening U.S. trade balance, governmental policies and agencies encouraged farmers to increase their production and exports to global markets. Markets in poor countries were booming thanks in part to the weakened dollar and investment by oil-rich Middle Eastern countries. Even the Soviet Union was beginning to buy American wheat.

Farmers around the U.S. were encouraged to respond to the demand by accumulating heavy debt to purchase more land, equipment, and livestock. Not only the government, but banks contributed to the expansionist mood, loaning money liberally based on ever-escalating real estate values. Even farmers who owned their land outright were assured by agribusiness specialists that indebtedness for the sake of expansion and modernization was sound business practice. Farming was becoming big business.

When the crash came, it was quick and painful. To combat inflation, the government tightened monetary policy, which had the effects of increasing the value of the dollar overseas, slowing the inflation of land prices, and raising interest rates. As the dollar gained value, American agricultural products became more expensive to foreign buyers. Reduced rates of inflation brought the devaluation of land. Farmers needing to purchase equipment faced higher interest rates at the same time their collateral, the land itself, was rapidly losing value.

Government food policies and the related decline in market prices in the 1980s compounded the problem. As was the case in many industrialized countries, The U.S. government set agricultural policies designed to maximize consumer dollars that could be spent on industrial products. Dumping agricultural reserves onto the market and establishing low prices on farm products had the effect of holding food prices artificially low. Earnings did not reflect actual production costs, and farmers had trouble meeting debt payments.

Although agricultural prices rallied in the mid-1980s, small farmers in particular had accumulated so much debt that it became increasingly difficult to pay taxes or to respond to increasing production costs. In desperation some sold off equipment, and spouses moonlighted at paid jobs off the farm.

The resulting farm crisis was not only an economic but also a social tragedy. When the land and everything on it was repossessed, farmers lost not only their livelihood but their homes and heritage as well. Many of the farms lost during the crisis had been in the same family for generations.

Today family farms that are lost to unpaid debt are seldom bought by other families breaking into farming, but by corporations or wealthy individuals who hire managers to run large farms on which the owners do not live. Such ownership patterns undermine local communities. Town businesses, such as grocery and hardware stores, insurance agencies, drugstores, and local newspapers, suffer from the lower number of farmers who patronize them, and absentee owners have little interest in supporting local communities.

Land conservation practices also suffer under corporate farming whether in poor nations or rich ones. The corporate motivation for farming is profit. The owners are not committed to a particular farm or local community; they do not intend to live there, raise their children there, make local friends, or pass on the farm as a legacy to their children. Because the farm unit, however large, is usually only one small part of the corporation's holdings, the emphasis is often on short-term profit. When the farm unit loses money, the losses can be used to lower taxes on profits elsewhere, and ultimately the land is sold, with the capital transferred to some other high-profit enterprise. Land conservation limits high short-term profit and is seldom a concern to business people who are accustomed to dealing with nonrenewable resources that are replaced when they wear out.

Today farming is thought to require huge capital investment, tremendous acreage, and high levels of mechanization. Family farmers seem to lack economy of scale. Many people believe that corporate farming patterns are inevitable because family farms are not as efficient. In this view the displacement of farmers is regrettable but necessary for the progress from which all will benefit. If one accepts this view, then the real issues are how to minimize the suffering of those caught in the transition between these patterns of agriculture.

Before reaching such a conclusion, however, the role of government must be considered. The government has been a major player in this drama through its power to influence the conditions farmers face. Upon examination is does not appear that governmental decisions were undertaken with adequate understanding of their effects on small farmers or the land.

Americans need to decide as a society whether the small- or medium-scale family farm or large-scale agribusiness is more compatible with long-term interests. There are many other areas of long-range planning that will impact farming in the years to come. Some cities, especially in the Southwest, worried about water availability, are buying large tracts of farmland with a view to siphoning off their water resources in the future. Food processing and retail sales are increasingly monopolized by large firms, as are agricultural supply businesses. What dangers for consumers lie in the prospect of food production also moving into the hands of a few powerful corporations? Are there ways of preventing such monopolies or of controlling their power? What is the size limit between medium and large farms? Is it measured in the number or nature of owners, number of acres or square miles, or number of farm workers on a farm?

In short, Jan and Ellie's case is not merely a matter of making ends meet. It is part of a complex, global economic, political, and environmental crisis affecting both farmers and consumers. Although farmers are increasingly aware of the environmental problems associated with large-scale, chemical-based agriculture, cheap food policies and attitudes of consumers remain powerful impediments to change. The number of farms employing small-scale, environmentally friendly techniques has not increased substantially in recent years.

SUSTAINABLE AGRICULTURE

Advocates of high-input corporate farming tend to dismiss alternative low-input or so-called sustainable agriculture methods as a new form of idealism with little relevance to farming in the U.S. and to the need of feeding a rapidly increasing world population. They point out that the heavy use of chemical fertilizers, weed suppressants, pesticides, and animal food supplements, when combined with biogenetic research and modern farm machinery, leads to the increased productivity needed to feed the world. The so-called "green revolution," they say, is proof positive of their perspective.

American farmers, in general, are conditioned to feel pride in their low-cost, high-yield food production. In recent years, however, there has been growing concern that the focus on large corporate farms and sophisticated technologies has been carried beyond the point of viability. Heavy reliance on chemical inputs has been linked to environmental pollution, health problems, safety of the food supply, and loss of topsoil.

To solve these problems, some agricultural and economic specialists argue that farmers need to go back in order to move forward. With a change in governmental policies to encourage smaller farms and training in crop rotation, use of high-yield plant and livestock strains, and efficient management, farmers using alternative, labor-intensive practices can compete economically with less degradation of the land. This case seems particularly strong in specialty agriculture and livestock operations.

Consider, for example, the use of nitrogen, phosphorus, and potassium fertilizers over the past thirty years. In 1960 use of these chemicals stood at approximately 7.3 million combined tons. In 1981, the peak of such synthetic fertilizer use, that total had grown to 22.3 million tons. Currently total fertilizer use stands at 19 million tons annually. The reduction is traceable mainly to the large acreage held out of production because of governmental programs. On a per acre basis fertilizer use continues to remain steady for most crops.

Environmentalists argue that such intensive chemical use cannot help but lead to disastrous long-term effects on both the land itself and ground water supplies. Witness the flooding along the Mississippi in the summer of 1993 that, among other things, resulted in an enormous outpouring of farm chemicals into the Gulf of Mexico with predictable effects on marine life along the coast. Or consider the $15 million study underway in Iowa and North Carolina by the Department of Agriculture aimed at pinpointing why farmers have high cancer rates and tendencies toward certain kidney and reproductive diseases that some researchers attribute to sustained exposure to farm chemicals. When long-term costs to health and the environment are factored in, the economic argument for what the Overbroeks are doing becomes even more powerful.

The Overbroeks share these concerns. Although operating from deeply held religious and ethical beliefs, they are also convinced that low-input farming is a matter of good economics. They are not alone. In the face of mounting debt and inability to get bank loans for chemical supplies and machinery, a number of the Overbroek's neighbors who had clung to expensive inputs at every stage of their operations are beginning to second-guess their decisions. But so many are operating on the verge of bankruptcy that they are afraid to risk any change that would reduce the productivity that those chemical-intensive practices ensure.

State universities, such as the one studying the Overbroek farm, are beginning to pursue research that helps support farmers who desire to convert their operations to low-input methods. It is important in this regard to remember that the concept of low-input farming is not a recent development. Farmers like Ellie's father represent an agricultural counterculture that has been struggling against the bigger-is-better farm movement ever since the emphasis on expensive technology began in the 19th century. Even though he and others like him ran successful "biodynamic" farms for decades, most farmers considered such colleagues to be well-meaning eccentrics.

To counter such stereotypes, both the terminology and techniques associated with low-input farming have been undergoing transformations in recent years. The once popular term "organic agriculture" has fallen out of favor in part because it smacks of an idealistic, zealot-like militancy. Books such as *Alternative Agriculture* (Washington, D.C.: Academy Press) by the National Research Council are invaluable studies of the economic and technical underpinnings to sustainable approaches. Such studies are careful not to single out one approach as universally applicable to every farm or farmer.

Increasingly the term "sustainable agriculture" has come to be used. Sustainable agriculture is an umbrella term for low-input farming based on an understanding of ecological systems and emphasizing alternative, low-input, regenerative, and organic practices. Rectifying problems of ground water contamination, soil erosion, and risks to human health are part of what is considered stewardship of the land.

Those who practice sustainable agriculture have several goals. First, they seek to promote biological diversity. Second, they attempt to protect and restore natural resources while recycling nutrients and waste products. Third, they try to account for all costs, including social and environmental costs. Finally, they work politically to implement policies to support their work.

Advocates of sustainable agriculture face the combined forces of accepted practice and thinking, the financial interests of indebted farmers and lenders, the inertia of agricultural schools, an entrenched bureaucracy, and unresponsive consumers. As for consumers, they need to put their food dollars on the line if farmers are to receive reasonable compensation for their work and priority to be given to a safe food supply.

THE HEALTHY CHRISTIAN LIFE

Amid the complexities of present day agriculture, what is the healthy Christian life? Jan and Ellie Overbroek have every right to question and wonder. If pressed, Jan and Ellie would probably indicate that the healthy Christian life is much more than sustainable agricultural practices.

First, they might indicate how much it is a communal activity. Farmers and their families are active members of their communities, participating in cooperatives and farm organizations, attending schools and churches, and supporting local banks and hospitals. They cannot experience the endless series of births, growing seasons, harvests, and weather changes without developing a fundamental philosophy of life that promotes the spirit of community living. This is the reason that a countryside dotted with family farms is so healthy. It might not even be too strong to say that the well being of agriculture depends on such farms and the communities they support.

Churches are very much a part of healthy rural settings. They act as a gathering place for farmers to exchange information and discuss the elements of good farming practice. They provide support to farm families and farmers who run risks by changing their practices. Grounded in an understanding of stewardship, churches have a responsibility to support regenerative, healthier methods of farming.

Second, the Overbroeks might speak in religious terms, informed as they seem to be by a deep love of creation and a sense of accountability to God. With this foundation they might go on to share their belief about work and family. They would probably articulate a fairly traditional work ethic, seeing farming as a vocation in which one serves God and neighbor. This sense of vocation would also be extended to their roles as business people, marriage partners, parents, church leaders, and members of their community. They would also share their conviction that money and time are means, not ends, and set their priorities accordingly. Couches, for example, are not as important as the experiences they share within the family and with others. Both Ellie and Jan would be reluctant, however, to codify their way of life, because they would see it as a holistic process.

Third, the Overbroeks might speak in spiritual terms about the land. This would probably be the most difficult to articulate, for the sensual experience of the land is not readily translated into words. What is it about the land around "home" that has an almost magnetic attraction? The Overbroeks might describe the birth of a calf, a field of ripened grain, black earth sifting through fingers in spring just before planting, the smell after a summer thunderstorm, the view out the kitchen window toward the barn, and the experience of orienting spatially to the grid of midwestern farmland. These common place experiences add up so that the land becomes deeply personal and calls individuals into relationships that find expression in work and community life.

Finally, the healthy Christian life would include a sense of humility. Ellie and Jan's hesitation to impose their beliefs on others shows a respect for their neighbors. Are the neighboring farmers less right in their approach to the land and their farming practices? As Jan points out, most of them also believe that they are being faithful stewards of the earth and the environment. Are Harold Blum and Jan's sister-in-law less right because their lives include comforts the Overbroeks may never have? Is Elise Ortiz to be criticized as she tries to bring up her children as a single parent?

Many will not fully appreciate the extent to which the cultural norms of the Overbroeks' rural community make it difficult for Ellie and Jan to share their doubts and hopes overtly with others. Jan is looked on as an outsider in the community. Having grown up in that congregation, Ellie must have been aware that some parishioners considered her father a bit odd for his approach to farming. Now Ellie and Jan are pursuing those same goals, perhaps opening old wounds and personal doubts.

Ellie and Jan's qualms about sharing their beliefs are a matter of being sensitive to their neighbor, not a lack of conviction and courage. Especially in tough times, many Christians would find it equally hard to put forward their personal vision in ways that might be misunderstood or that could hurt those who are grappling with formidable problems in their personal or professional lives. Failure and doubt also are hard to discuss in a secular culture that is success oriented.

If pressed on the subject, the Overbroeks might argue that for them to believe is to act ethically in a way that sees their lives as part of a larger whole. They would not see a separation between the practice of religion and the practice of life.

These last two aspects of the healthy Christian life, humility and the land, are a fitting place to end. The present course of industrial society including its farming sector may not be sustainable. Part of the ideology of growth that informs this course is that the land is something to be dominated. In extreme terms the ethic of domination has led to atrocities, such as the slaughter of the buffalo. In more subtle terms it has led to the slow degradation of agricultural land. Perhaps a new found sense of humility that rejects domination for an ethic of careful stewardship will make the Overbroek's healthy Christian life seem more plausible.

ADDITIONAL RESOURCES

Browne, William P., et al. *Sacred Cows and Hot Potatoes: Agrarian Myths and Agricultural Policy*. Boulder, CO: The Westview Press, 1992.

Edwards, Clive A., ed. *Sustainable Agriculture Systems*. Ankeny, IA: Soil and Conservation Society, 1990.

Hess, Charles E., et al. *Agricultural Biotechnology: Strategies for National Competitiveness*. Washington, DC: National Academy Press, 1987.

Jung, L. Shannon. *We Are Home: A Spirituality of the Environment*. Mahwah, NJ: Paulist Press, 1993.

Krebs, A.V. *The Corporate Reapers: The Book of Agribusiness*. Washington, DC: Essential Books, 1992.

National Research Council. *Alternative Agriculture*. Washington, DC: National Academy Press, 1989.

Platt, Lavonne Godwin, ed. *Hope for the Family Farm: Trust God and Care for the Land*. Newton, KS: Faith and Life Press, 1987.

Poincelot, Raymond P. *Toward a More Sustainable Agriculture*. Westport, CT: AVI Publishing Co. Inc., 1986.

Slattery, Patrick. *Caretakers of Creation: Farmers Reflect on Their Faith and Work*. Minneapolis, MN: Augsburg Press, 1991.

PART VI

MEDICINE

Case

Baby Boy Hernandez

Mary Flemming closed her office door, trying to shut out any more interruptions to her morning. She had a difficult staff meeting in thirty minutes and wanted to finish the outline for a paper she was presenting as an incoming officer of the State Hospital Administrators Association.

As the Associate Administrator for Medical Care at Oglethorpe Memorial Hospital, Mary was responsible for oversight of one of the five regional neonatal intensive care units in the state. In light of increasing fiscal problems, Mary had been asked to address issues of funding for neonatal care.

Mary glanced through her notes, aware of the dramatic changes in care for newborns after the hospital had been designated as a regional prenatal center. As a matter of fact, the excellent neonatal program at Memorial had been a significant factor in luring Mary from her previous position. The State Department of Human Resources, in collaboration with the Council on Maternal and Infant Health, had identified and awarded federal funds to select hospitals for renovations, equipment, staff, and newborn transport vehicles. Mary was convinced that under the direction of Dr. Sam McBride, Memorial had one of the best neonatal units in the South.

The effects of the program had been dramatic. Although it was still the state's number-one health problem, infant mortality had dropped 25 percent after the system was established. There was a parallel drop in the number of premature infants with permanent mental and physical handicaps. When Mary had first come to Memorial, it was a thrill for her to see those little babies survive. The whole unit rejoiced with the families, and Mary remembered the heartwarming letters she and members of the staff

This case was prepared by William P. Bristol and Alice Frazer Evans. Copyright © The Case Study Institute and distributed by The Case Clearing House, Yale Divinity School Library, 409 Prospect Street, New Haven, CT 06511. Revised 1993. The names of all places and persons have been disguised to protect the privacy of the individuals involved in this situation.

199

had received from grateful parents. Memorial was saving an average of seventy-five babies a year who would have died without specialized care.

But in the past few years Mary felt that problems with the unit had begun to outweigh the benefits. As the technology had improved, smaller and smaller babies began to survive. However, as the birth weight went down, the incidence of long-term complications and the cost of care went up. Mary checked back over her files for the previous year. During that year Memorial had admitted over fifty infants weighing less than seven hundred grams (less than a pound and a half). The cost of care for some ran as high as $500,000 per infant, with an average cost of $150,000. The real squeeze came because a disproportionate number of mothers with SGA (small for gestational age) babies sent to Memorial from Comstock and other county hospitals were indigent, with no medical insurance whatever. In the early years of the program, the $5,000 per infant state subsidy for these babies was significant; today it hardly seemed to make a dent. On top of that, the state funds available to Memorial ran out completely a little more than halfway into the fiscal year. With the present state budget squeeze, Mary had little hope that additional funds would be allotted to neonatal care. With the skyrocketing cost per infant, the end result was a cut in state funds.

In the past Mary could have charged some indigent cases off to the Department of Children Services. She knew her predecessor had even charged some to the old migrant worker program that the state ran during the seventies. When she had first come to Memorial, Mary had been able to elevate costs in some areas to absorb the losses, but both federal and insurance programs designed regulations to prevent cost shifts. Increasingly, patients of independent means were going to the smaller, private hospitals for maternal care. Last year, counting overhead costs, Memorial's Neonatal Intensive Care Unit lost over a million dollars. Mary knew the hospital, specifically her department, was faced with some serious decisions. And, she ruefully realized, she had been dumb enough to agree to address the issue before her colleagues at next week's association meeting. They were all aware of the problem; she had to come up with some answers.

Mary glanced at her watch and realized she was due at the neonatology staff meeting. Twice a week various members of the staff gathered for what was called "the patient planning meeting." More often, Mary mused, it could be described as a battle royal. Baby Boy Hernandez was today's topic. Mary muttered to herself as she hurried down the hall, silently swearing at Comstock County Hospital for dumping another non-paying obstetric case on Memorial. This Hernandez baby alone had run up a bill approaching $125,000, and Sam McBride still didn't have the kid off the respirator. Migrant workers such as Anita Hernandez had always been a problem in this part of the state. They had no money, no insurance, and rarely spoke English.

Most of the staff showed up on time, although two nurse representatives had just been called away to a "code." As they gathered around the coffee table in the small lounge next to the nursery, Mary nodded to Sam McBride, young Corey Blake, Mrs. Darden—the chief ward clerk of the neonatal unit—and several house staff Mary was sure Sam had dragged along to the meeting. Mary watched Sam as he joked with the pediatric interns he was supervising. Corey sat alone at the edge of the group.

Corey Blake was the midwifery student who had delivered Baby Hernandez in the ambulance on the way from Community Hospital. She spoke Spanish fluently. Blake had pulled some minor miracle in just getting the baby from Comstock to the unit. A Furman graduate, she had earned her RN and then spent time as a nurse in the Southwest with a missionary group. Her parents lived in Atlanta, and she had returned to Emory to enter the two-year midwifery program which was now receiving state funding. Mary knew Corey had originally intended to return to New Mexico, but her field supervisor at Memorial was encouraging her to stay. In a private personnel review with her supervisor, Mary remembered her saying that there were certainly enough poor, pregnant women in the surrounding counties to keep Blake happy for all of her days. Everybody in the county seemed poor since the recession hit and the textile mill closed in Comstock.

When Mary had encouraged the hospital board to accept the midwife supervision program at Memorial, she wasn't averse to the income or the promise of more if additional state funding came through. She also saw the logic of programs directed to low-cost preventative medicine that the midwives were being trained to deliver. The 80 to 90 percent increase in survivability of low birthweight babies was because of improvement in medical care, not because of prevention of low birthweight babies. Mary recalled a major Institute of Medicine study. Low birthweight babies (2500 grams or less) were forty times more likely to die than normal weight babies and had increased risk of long-term handicaps. Inadequate prenatal care appeared to be directly linked to low birth weight. Corey's program focused on this kind of care, especially for poor, nonwhite women. Studies indicated there were as many as two thousand indigent, high-risk pregnant women in the six counties surrounding Memorial. Mary saw the long-term logic of putting state funds here. But she wasn't sure yet that midwives were the answer.

Mary knew that in spite of her skill, Corey Blake had a hard time being accepted by the medical staff. Mary recalled a conversation she had over-heard between two interns about "those damn midwives." It wasn't that they disliked Corey—"she was pretty enough"—but all she preached was "feeding the poor" and "vitamins." And in spite of her license, she would never be able to handle any "real emergencies."

Mary shifted her attention to Sam McBride as Sam called the group together. In Mary's estimation, Sam was a fine doctor. An Emory graduate, he had taken his pediatric training in Pennsylvania before returning to the state university as a fellow in neonatology. He had been hired by Memorial nine years ago to head the neonatology staff. Late one night over coffee Sam had shared with Mary some "war stories" of his first years at the hospital. Those were the heydays in the development of neonatal care. New techniques were coming out every day, survival rates of the mid-weight babies were excellent, and the neonatologists were a fun, swashbuckling group. No one complained that the annual meetings were held at Aspen; they were all good skiers. Mary knew that underneath that jovial exterior Sam had not only the skill but a driving passion for saving the babies.

Sam opened the meeting with a frank discussion of the Hernandez baby's current and future problems. The infant, barely twenty-five weeks, weighed only 500 grams, less than one pound. He had developed a refractory hypoglycemia and respiratory distress syndrome (RDS) necessitating a respirator. Then as the baby's RDS got better, he went into heart failure. Sam suspected intraventricular hemorrhaging due to a combination of prematurity and possibly lack of closure of the ductus arteriosis. He was considering calling in a cardiac surgeon. Sam added that even five years ago most kids this small didn't live long enough to be troubled with hemorrhaging. As of this morning, the baby's hypoglycemia and jaundice were under control and the RDS was getting better. But the boy was not weaning well from the respirator. In addition, Sam was convinced that because the baby had required long-term supplemental oxygen, retinopathy (blindness) was a strong possibility. He also noted that thirty percent of the babies with intraventricular hemorrhaging had residual neurological impairment, and many developed cerebral palsy. In addition, the baby's nutrition was lousy and the only weight he seemed to be gaining was water weight. Hyperalimentation was plagued with complications, but it seemed the only reasonable route to get the child through this nutritional crisis. Sam wished the baby's mother had eaten better.

During this long discourse, Mary Flemming had become increasingly upset. She struggled to keep her voice under control. "Dr. McBride, do you have any idea what this gift from the county is costing us—not only in terms of dollars, but staff time and energy? We've got to consider the broad picture. Many more cases like this one and you ultimately threaten the very survival of the hospital. Is there any possibility you can transfer him back to Comstock Community Hospital?"

Sam McBride did not respond to Mary's question. Instead, he turned to Corey and asked her to tell the staff what she knew about Anita Hernandez. Corey glanced quickly at both Mary and Sam McBride. Her initial hesitancy soon turned to confidence as she began to share her observations. Ms. Hernandez should have gone home long ago, wherever home would be for her now, but she had not done well following her delivery. Although Anita told Corey that she was twenty-two, she looked more like sixteen and was really very frail and underweight. She also smoked constantly, a habit that Corey said was obviously not going to change since the woman had no reason to trust her judgment.

Corey continued: "As you all know, following delivery, Anita developed a pelvic infection; it was pretty rough for a few days until we brought the sepsis under control. But this did give me a chance to talk to Anita about her life. She had been born down around Harlingen, Texas, and had been making the trek north and east following the sun. She ended up here weeding peanuts and processing peaches. This was her second pregnancy. Her first baby, a girl, lives with her grandmother just south of Harlingen. The baby was very pretty in the picture, a chubby three-year-old with gorgeous eyes. Quite a contrast to Anita right now."

Corey paused a minute and then added that there was one thing that particularly bothered her. Anita didn't go down to the nursery to see her son very often, and she hadn't named him yet. Corey paused again briefly and then continued: "I guess I need to say too that I don't know where she'll go when she leaves the hospital. She won't be strong enough to work for several weeks. There's a good possibility this baby will be physically handicapped as long as he lives. This will be a tremendous burden for Anita." Corey's voice became stronger. "I know you all realize that in our surrounding counties there are hundreds of women in worse shape than Anita. I spend most of my days in the county clinics and in the shacks where our rural poor people live. Between the mill closings and the crop failures, there are people out there starving to death."

Before Mary or other members of the staff could respond, a nurse hurried into the lounge to call Dr. McBride. In the nursery, the cardiac arrest alert sounded shrill in contrast to the monotonous beeps of the other monitors. There was a flurry of surgical green as the nurses went to work on Baby Boy Hernandez.

The staff meeting was postponed until further notice. Mary Flemming walked slowly back to her office.

Commentary

Baby Boy Hernandez

From Mary Flemming's perspective there are two questions posed in this case. One is what kind of care Baby Boy Hernandez should receive. The other is how to make the neonatal unit financially secure. In Flemming's mind, these two questions are closely connected. Both of these questions in turn provoke other questions. Who should decide the fate of this child and others like him? On what criteria should the decision be based? Should the financial security of the neonatal unit, and perhaps the hospital, be secured by limiting access to the unit to those who can pay? These latter questions raise an issue that Flemming does not consider, but which underlies all the others: Is the overall health care delivery system, of which this neonatal unit forms a small part, one which is just and equitable?

SCRIPTURAL AND THEOLOGICAL RESOURCES

Scripture can be a powerful source of Christian values relevant to this case. Though it does not directly address issues in medical technology, scripture has a great deal to say about the value of life and the place of death in life. For scripture, life is more than existence alone. When Deuteronomy 30:19 says "choose life," it explains the choice of life over death as a choice for goodness, for loving God, for keeping God's laws, for community, for prosperity and achieving fullness of life. Physical life is not the ultimate value. Stories in the Old Testament make clear that individual life, while valuable, can be sacrificed in the interest of the quality of life of the community; war and capital punishment are taken for granted in the stories of the patriarchs, the Exodus, and in the Mosaic law. Within Israel the Mosaic law was to ensure that the life of the poor and powerless was respected by the rich and powerful. This included provisions such as one that stated that the poor be allowed to glean the edges of the fields of the rich (Lev. 19:9-10) and one that declared that the cloak of the poor man not be taken overnight as security for loans (Deut. 24:10-13). David's killing of Uriah in order to hide his adultery with Bathsheba was a scandal not merely because he shed blood, but because he abused the power entrusted in him by Yahweh by killing another in his charge (2 Sam. 11-12).

Many of Israel's laws were based in prohibitions on idolatry. One such command was that the Israelites not sacrifice children (Deut. 18:10), as their pagan neighbors did in the dedication of their public buildings in order to appease the gods who threatened earthquake, winds, and lightning. If we interpret this prohibition literally, as merely forbidding the killing of children on altars to pagan gods, we fail to understand scripture as relevant to our lives. The purpose of the prohibition was to remind us that social institutions are not to be secured by the sacrifice of innocent life. Rather, for the law, the purpose of social institutions was to safeguard the life of persons and community.

According to the Gospels, Jesus, too, understood life in broader terms than mere individual existence, or he would never have risked—deliberately and repeatedly—his own death in order to carry out his mission of announcing the reign of God (Mark 9:30-32; Luke 9:43-45; Matt. 17:22-23, 20:17-19). Furthermore, he clearly calls his apostles, in the name of fullness of life, to risk death (Luke 21:12-18; Matt. 10:34-39; Mark 13:9-13). Though each of us is also called to discipleship, we can only make the decision to risk ourselves. Thus, while life is not for the follower of Jesus the ultimate value, Jesus gives no support for deciding to end the life of another person in the name of a higher value. The decision that one should die in the interests of the many was that of Caiaphas, the high priest responsible for the death of Jesus (John 18:14).

Though the Gospels detail Jesus' many warnings of the judgment to come for groups who exploit or mislead the poor and weak (such as the scribes and Pharisees, or the moneychangers in the Temple), he himself refused to judge and condemn individuals. He not only refused to condemn the adulterous woman, but he intervened to stop the crowd from stoning her as the law prescribed (John 8:11). He refrained from condemning his own betrayer (John 13:18-30), and promised salvation to the thief crucified beside him (Luke 23:43). If Jesus was not willing to condemn the guilty, can it be legitimate to condemn the innocent?

The theological traditions of Christianity reflect scriptural traditions concerning the value of life and the need to protect the life and welfare of the weak. From early times Christianity condemned infanticide. Furthermore, in the development of the just war teaching, the church placed both women and children in the protected category of noncombatants who were to have total immunity from war. The theological and moral teachings most directly relevant to this case are twentieth-century teachings in medical ethics. Among Roman Catholics, the 1952 distinction made by Pope Pius XII between ordinary and extraordinary means of preserving life gave what seemed to be helpful criteria to the debate about euthanasia. Pius maintained that there are extraordinary measures of preserving life which are not morally required. For many in medical ethics even outside of Catholicism there followed two decades where this was the standard often used— that ordinary means of preserving life, such as food, water, oxygen, and common medications could not be denied to the sick/dying, but that extraordinary measures, such as mechanical respirators, food tubes, radiation, and surgery, or experimental techniques in general, were not required.

This teaching was easily applied at both ends of the treatment spectrum. It supported standard medical practice, which insisted that the poor, the retarded, and the otherwise defenseless had moral rights to ordinary medical care which could not be denied. On the other hand, for seriously ill patients who wanted to be allowed to die without painful or intrusive interventions which could only possibly or minimally extend their lives, the teaching made clear to what extent families and medical personnel could accommodate their wishes. The teaching was understood as objective, as concentrated on means of preserving life, rather than on complicated subjective judgments of quality and length of life.

There were always problems with this teaching. One which became obvious in succeeding decades is that advances in medical science tremendously alter what medical personnel understand as ordinary and extraordinary measures of preserving life. What was extraordinary a decade ago is standard today. At any given time, it may be difficult to judge whether a particular treatment is ordinary or not. Innumerable surgeries and mechanical techniques which used to be experimental are now routine.

Some analysts of our health care system point out that another problem with the ordinary/extraordinary teaching is that it functions to justify the provision of a higher quality of health care to the rich than to the poor. Everyone is to have access to ordinary measures of preserving life, but within a capitalist society, the voluntary nature of extraordinary measures serves to make them dependent upon the ability to pay. This is certainly the case with Baby Boy Hernandez. The infant unit is understood to provide extraordinary measures of care, far above the standard care of other hospitals. The child whose right to the care is questioned is the one who cannot pay.

Recognition of both these problems with the ordinary/extraordinary teaching has led to an unwillingness on the part of the medical profession in the last twenty years to decide treatment on the basis of means alone. Instead, there has been a shift toward joining the means issue with an evaluation of the possible benefits of treatments weighed against the counter-indications for the treatment. Sometimes this consequential evaluation is done on medical grounds alone; more recently medical ethics has moved toward incorporating more perspectives in this evaluation, as we see by the varied personnel involved in the conference described in our case. Chancy or experimental treatments are more likely to be morally required when they offer the possibility of restoring full life and health with minimum pain and risk.

RIGHT TO DECIDE

Also of great interest in the theological/moral literature on preserving threatened life is the question of who makes the decision. Cases where patients are not competent to choose for themselves are the most difficult. In such cases, treatment is usually decided by the parents or close relatives in conjunction with the medical staff. In this case Anita Hernandez, the mother and natural guardian, may be either uninterested in or incapable of representing the best interests of the child. The decision may have been shifted to the hospital team by default. This is a difficult position for medical personnel, for the presumption in their training is that they deal with a competent patient or relative whom they can expect to represent the psychological, relational, and personal values of the patient, while the medical staff represents the medical interests of the patient. Only relatively recently has it been recognized that medical personnel also inevitably represent their own interests and the interests of the institution as well as the medical interests of the patient. These interests can sometimes conflict.

In this case Corey Blake, a member of the hospital staff, is the spokesperson for the relational situation of the child. As she presents the situation, the mother does not seem interested in the child and is hard-pressed to care for herself. The child will probably have serious long-term medical problems. It would be easy to be swayed by the fact that the person who presents this grim analysis is the member of the staff who has dedicated herself to medical care for the poor and who was earliest involved with the mother and child. There is temptation to see Corey as the natural advocate of the child. If even she cannot make a good case for continuing care, then who could? But Corey also represents a midwife program, a primary care health program which is here appended to a major institution devoted to emergency medical intervention. From the perspective of primary health care, priority funding should be aimed at ensuring that all have basic nutrition, vitamins, vaccinations, sanitation, and health monitoring, so that the need for emergency intervention is greatly reduced. In this case, Corey's program is now funded largely by the university and the state, with hope for additional state funding. Midwifery is understood by the staff as unequal in the real work of emergency intervention, and more or less peripherally valuable. Corey, more than anyone else, may feel threatened by the financial burden this baby poses, since hers may be one of the programs most vulnerable to state financial cuts.

Even if Corey were to become an advocate for the child, there are other factors undermining such advocacy. By reason of both her sex and her professional credentials Corey is not accepted as the equal of some of the other members of the professional staff. Even if she were strongly to advocate prolonging the life of the child, the description of her relationship with male medical personnel—who describe her as "pretty enough"—suggests that she might not be taken seriously unless she were to resort to stereotypical feminine attempts at persuasion, i.e., flirtation or seduction. While such an attempt may or may not be effective in the short run, it would threaten not only her dignity and self-respect, but make it impossible for her to earn professional respect from the male staff in the future.

Is there an advocate for this child? And if there were, on what criteria should advocacy be based? On an absolute right to life, whatever the social and medical conditions? On an equal right to the quality of care given children who can pay? Or only on a strictly medical evaluation that this child has a good chance to live and grow in a normal life?

SOCIAL ANALYSIS

If we apply social analysis to this case the issue which immediately emerges is that the question of whether to allow this child to die would not have arisen if the parents were able to pay for his care. Within a health care system designed, as ours is, around centers which specialize in emergency intervention, treatment is both therapeutic and experimental. That is, the treatment of newborns is designed not only to save this particular child but to thereby develop new techniques which save future newborns. Specialized units such as this one have greater success than ordinary hospitals precisely because they can call on greater experience in experimenting with technique. Such experimental systems, however, have no internal brake. They are inherently inflationary, as the number of possible interventions is exponentially increased over time, and it becomes difficult to discover medical reasons not to expand treatment constantly. The only brakes are financial, so that treatment expands until there is no more money to support its maintenance or expansion. Preservation of such units is often understood to be essential because of their proven success in saving babies, so financial limits often press administrators to see the problem in terms of limiting access. Since the threat is financial, the most obvious criterion for limiting access is ability to pay.

Critics maintain that such a system ensures that public monies support centers from which the disadvantaged end up being excluded, thus perpetuating their disadvantaged status. Our health care system, because it is organized around such specialized intervention centers, tends to neglect basic health care and to support high levels of care for only part of the population. This is why we have the ironic situation of being the nation which represents the apex of sophisticated techniques for saving newborns at the same time that we have one of the highest infant mortality rates in the developed world; sixteen nations have lower rates than ours. If the purpose of our system were to save as many lives as possible and to ensure the health of the greatest numbers, the available funds would be spent on relatively inexpensive diagnosis and treatment of the most common health problems, rather than on high technology interventions for the few.

When we understand that present medical personnel are trained and employed in the high-tech system, which also supports employment in high-tech equipment industries and the construction and insurance industries, we can see a large interest group supporting the present system. In our case, the medical conferences held in skiing resorts across the country illustrate this point. Those elements which are best rewarded by the present system—doctors, administrators, and industrial and insurance executives—are those who are best organized to wield political power and are recognized by media and government as the experts in the field of medicine. But support for the present system is not merely a matter of self-interest on the part of those employed within it.

The present system is also the one geared to produce astounding breakthroughs in medical science. The quest for new knowledge and techniques which will save lives is a major attraction of the present system for researchers and inventors, as Mary Flemming makes clear in speaking of Sam McBride, the head of the neonatal unit. Such people are willing to work long hours, expend great energy, and often dedicate themselves to their work. The work is exciting, it is fast evolving, and the gratification that comes from saving frail underweight babies is both immense and immediate. The system is set up to support this scientific quest, which has far outstripped the ability of the system to distribute the products of the quest to the entire population.

REACHING A DECISION

What seems to be happening in this case is that the question of how to treat the Hernandez baby is being conflated with the question of how to balance the neonatal unit's budget. This seems to be a mistake. What kind of treatment the Hernandez baby should receive should not be determined on the basis of the financial health of the neonatal unit. Treatment should be decided using the same criteria which are used for all the other infants in the neonatal unit. The criteria which should be applied to all the infants will certainly be influenced by the financial resources of the neonatal unit. This seems necessary and appropriate.

Furthermore, the resources available to the neonatal unit should not represent the sum of the funds available for maternal and infant care. The basic needs of some should not be neglected in favor of the extraordinary needs of others. This is not a matter of equalizing spending for all infants; the most threatened have a primary claim on our care and resources. But among those infants who are threatened, spending should be allocated so as to save the largest possible number in the fullest manner possible.

It is not possible to completely equalize medical care for the poor and the non-poor, just as it is impossible to equalize education or housing for the poor and the non-poor, for none of these services exists in a vacuum; they are all interrelated. Even if the neonatal unit is able to keep this child alive in the short term, because it is so underweight and underdeveloped for its age its long-term recovery will depend upon the level of food and housing, not to mention health monitoring, that Ms. Hernandez provides.

A major issue for Christian ethics is whether in such situations we apply the norm of equity to the means or to the end. Do we give the same care to the poor and the non-poor, or do we give to the poor whatever is necessary to allow them future equity with the non-poor? If the Hernandez baby were continued at levels of extraordinary care, should he be released at the weight at which middle-class babies are released, or should he be allowed an extra margin due to the fact that his food and housing and overall care will likely be less than theirs after his release? If we insist on the same degree of care for the same medical condition regardless of class, then in marginal cases the extraordinary care will have been wasted on the poor child, for the resources to sustain long-term recovery are lacking. And yet while we attempt to reform the very structures of our nation in the direction of greater justice, we must also work to see that existing structures do not exacerbate or reinforce existing discrimination and injustice by excluding the poor from basic opportunities such as life-saving medical care.

ADDITIONAL RESOURCES

Fletcher, John. "Abortion, Euthanasia and Care of Defective Newborns." In Thomas A. Shannon, ed., *Bioethics*. 3rd ed. Mahwah, NJ: Paulist, 1987.

Maguire, Daniel C. *Death by Choice*. Garden City, NY: Doubleday, 1974.

Nelson, James B. *Rediscovering the Person in Medical Care*. Minneapolis, MN: Augsburg, 1976. Chapters 5-6.

Outka, Gene. "Social Justice and Equal Access to Health Care." In Shannon, ed., *Bioethics*.

Ramsey, Paul. *The Patient as Person*. New Haven, CT: Yale University Press, 1970.

Shannon, Thomas A., ed. *Bioethics*. 4th ed. Mahwah, NJ: Paulist Press, 1993.

Thurow, Lester C. "Medicine Versus Economics." In Shannon, ed., *Bioethics*.

Case

Dan's Little Bomb

"The Governor will get crucified in the press! I can see the headline now: 'Governor Burns OK's Prison Sex, Orders Prisons to Distribute Condoms!' We'll get accused of advocating homosexuality and gang rape." Keith Patterson, Governor Burns's aide, was clearly appalled at the request Dan had brought to the meeting.

Dan Rinks, the state commissioner of corrections, had known that his proposal was a political bomb that no one would want to touch, but he had felt obliged to request this meeting with the governor's staff. As patiently as he could, Dan repeated the reasons he was suggesting that all state prisons for men make condoms available to inmates as one part of a larger reform that would segregate from the general population both incoming first-offender prisoners and prisoners judged to need protection due to prior victimization or threats. "There are two basic sexual problems in prisons now," Dan explained. "First, due to its higher rate of prior IV drug use, the prison population has a much higher incidence of AIDS than the general population. Second, despite policies to the contrary, both voluntary and coercive sexual activity regularly occur in prisons. No official believes that either type can be prevented altogether."

"Why not?" demanded the state attorney general, Ben Wiseman.

"Because to prevent sexual activity we would have to keep all the prisoners in isolation. Not only do we not have the facilities for that," Dan explained, "but we know from the history of penology that isolating prisoners is severe and inhumane treatment that can drive normal persons to severe mental instability. The courts would never allow it. Even if it were humane and allowed, think of what it would cost! We are already 61 percent over capacity in the state prisons. The maximum security prison is 72

This case was prepared by Christine E. Gudorf. Copyright © The Case Study Institute. All names have been disguised to protect the privacy of the individuals involved.

percent over capacity, despite our building program. We're going to have the courts breathing down our necks again about overcrowding if we don't build more facilities. As I see it, we not only have to continue the prison building program to take care of the increase in the size of the prison population, but we should also invest about a million and a half to remodel the facilities for segregated 'safe' wings, and about half a million a year for the extra staffing it would require."

Keith Patterson interjected, "Dan, your budgets have gone up by over 25 percent every year for five years. If I understand this, you not only want to continue with the $18 million for prison construction already earmarked in the budget for next year, but you want the construction budget raised to $19.5 million at the same time you want the operating budget increased by half a million—so that you can distribute condoms to prisoners!"

Keith ran his hand through his hair in a weary gesture. "The legislature has already earmarked the corrections budget as the place to find the money for pay raises in the state university system. The faculty union is threatening a strike next September if the new budget doesn't end the three-year wage freeze and restore a wage scale comparable to surrounding states. The presidents of the universities gripe that they are losing their best faculty and administrators and can't hire competitively due to funding constraints. Senator Fedderman, the chair of the House Budget Committee, pressed the governor to see the lobbyist for Corrections, Inc., who claims that by contracting prison administration to private companies we can save over 10 percent of the operating budget for corrections. The lobbyist claims the present cost of $41.38 per day per inmate is unnecessarily high."

Dan lightly pounded the table for emphasis. "The budget for corrections has gone up every year for eleven years because the number of inmates has gone sky high, not because we spend more per inmate. You know that, Keith. Our $41.38 is slightly under the national average for state prisons, and has actually dropped steadily over the last decade when corrected for inflation. I know other states are privatizing parts of the corrections system. But those companies are in it for profit, not for prisoner welfare, much less AIDS prevention. Is that what you want? What is corrections supposed to do? The courts keep sending us more and more prisoners. Then periodically the courts slap us with injunctions against accepting more inmates. Corrections takes hell from the press every time overcrowding results in paroling an inmate who guns down a convenience store clerk or rapes and kills some kid. Then you ask why we don't have prisons with single person cells, where the number of inmates to guards in the showers, dining halls, workplaces and exercise yards is so low that the guards can watch every inmate every minute?

"It's impossible," Dan insisted. "Inmates aren't isolated individuals. They form gangs that cooperate, things like staging a fight to distract a guard so nobody notices a guy getting carried off to a dark corner. And it's tough to get victims to report sexual attacks. Not only are men ashamed to admit they've been raped, but they also fear that reporting will expose them to retaliation without punishing the offender. The rapist always has witnesses proclaiming his innocence."

At that point Judy Davids, the head of the state's department of health and welfare, asked, "Is the danger of AIDS infection really so high? I know that the chances of contracting AIDS in anal intercourse is much higher than in vaginal sex. But I thought prisoners practice not only anal sex, but oral sex, where the rates of transmission are much lower than even vaginal sex. Unless the number of infected prisoners is very high, we can't be talking about a high risk."

"Well, Judy, our HIV+ rate was lower than the 17.4 percent rate of the New York City prisons in 1992, but higher than the 4.25 percent rate of the national sample of jails and prisons in 1992," said Dan. "The last time we tested the whole population was 1989, and then we were at 8.9 percent. Since then only incoming prisoners have been tested. Now, taking into account the comings and goings of inmates, we have at least a 10.6 percent rate. Think about it. More than one in ten are confirmed as infected, but there are undoubtedly more, since that figure does not include any spread of HIV within the prisons since 1989."

At that point Harlan White, another of Governor Burns's aides, interrupted, "I don't understand. Aren't most of the infected men IV drug users and not homosexuals?"

"Yes, they contracted the virus through shared needles, but they can still pass it on sexually," responded Dan.

"But," Harlan persisted, "aren't they heterosexuals?"

Suddenly realizing that Harlan presumed that only homosexuals were sexually active in an all male population, Dan replied, "That's true, Harlan, but homosexual and heterosexual refer to their predominant orientation, and not to their behavior in a specific act. Most of our male prison population has a heterosexual orientation: they are primarily attracted to women. But in prison, without access to women, some of those heterosexuals engage in homosexual acts. Most of them still regard themselves as heterosexuals, especially if they take the dominant role."

"But if they are heterosexual, why engage in homosexual acts?" Harlan demanded.

"For a lot of different reasons," replied Dan, "just like reasons for sex outside of prison. Some want sex, even with another man, because it satisfies needs for physical touch, for affection, for sexual release, for intimacy. Some use sex to assert power and control over others, or to compensate for the lack of control over their own lives in prison. Sex is also instrumental in defining the prisoner hierarchy."

Keith Patterson jumped back into the discussion. "So far, we've only heard about possible dangers of AIDS spread. What evidence do you have that sexual activity in the prisons is actually spreading AIDS, and if so, how much?"

Dan replied, "I can't gather evidence without funds to do regular testing, and even then, because of the way AIDS works, the evidence wouldn't be conclusive. As a doctor, Judy can probably answer that question better than I."

Judy hesitated, then stated, "There's no way to get the evidence you want, Keith. All our tests for AIDS—the Elisa, the Western Blot, and the new SUDS test—all test for the presence of the antibodies and not the presence of the virus. Until the antibodies appear, no testing will pick up the early stage, which usually lasts one to three months. We know from a California study, now confirmed, that some persons can test negative for up to thirty-six months after exposure. During this period when the tests are negative, the person is nonetheless HIV+ and can transmit the virus. It usually takes from eight to ten years for the disease to develop, but even if a prisoner who tests clean at entry comes down with full-blown AIDS by his fourth year, you still won't necessarily know that he contracted the virus before he came to prison. African statistics, for example, show an average span from initial contact with the virus to death that is less than half the U.S. average. Variables include the individual's basic health, the quality of care he receives, as well as differences in environmental dangers."

Dan added, "We simply can't afford regular blood tests on the whole population. It's bankrupting us to take care of the prisoners with symptomatic HIV and full-blown AIDS infections."

"All right," Keith Patterson impatiently insisted, "so we don't know— and maybe can't know—how much AIDS is being spread within the prisons. We don't have many prisoners complaining of rape, and we don't have many prisoners caught violating the ban on consensual sex. Why is it necessary to do anything? I can't imagine that prison rapists are going to worry enough about passing or receiving AIDS that they start using condoms anyway. And consensual sex is forbidden—so why should we make it safer for inmates to disobey the rules? Won't distributing condoms actually encourage more consensual and coercive sex?"

Dan didn't answer for a minute. Then he leaned back in his chair, and folded his hands on the table. Very slowly and deliberately, he began. "When I was in charge of the maximum security penitentiary in Portsmouth a few years ago, there was an eighteen-year-old sent up for two years on drug charges. He'd been passing out amphetamines—diet pills—he swiped from his doctor father's office to his buddies in the college dorm during exam week. He'd never been arrested before and normally would have gotten probation. He had a lot of the pills, however, and both the D.A. and the judge were running for re-election on anti-drug programs. When the minimum security prison got slapped with a court order to redress overcrowding, the kid was sent to Portsmouth. I got a call in the middle of his second night. The guard found him unconscious in a pool of blood in the showers. He spent a couple of months in the hospital having a series of operations to repair his anus and colon. He said over fifteen guys raped him. If any one of those inmates was HIV+, then that rape could easily be fatal.

"You may be right that nothing can persuade those fifteen rapists to use condoms," Dan added, "but shouldn't we offer a kid like that condoms so that when he comes back from the hospital and bargains with one of the bigger, tougher inmates for protection from others in return for sex—and if he's smart that's what he does—he can bargain for condom use, too?"

"But then," Attorney General Wiseman protested, "you're really saying that the condoms are for consensual sex! I'm sorry, I can't accept condoning homosexual sex under any circumstances."

Dan and Judy began speaking at the same time. Dan waved his hand for Judy to speak first. Judy leaned forward and forcefully insisted, "No! That's simply not accurate, Ben. Don't you think that a violent gang rape qualifies as coercion? I look at this in terms of women's experience of coercion. There are circumstances when it is simply too dangerous to continue to resist. Nobody should repeatedly have to risk being killed in order to be judged a victim of coercion. Once should be enough. When a rapist has a knife at one's throat, or when a husband who has previously beaten and raped his wife comes home and demands sex, those women are not fully consenting when they cooperate. I don't think you can easily distinguish consensual and coercive sex in a violent context like prison."

"Okay, okay," Ben Wiseman responded impatiently, "far be it from me to oppose the mighty women's movement. But isn't it going to make it harder to enforce rules against sex between prisoners if we hand out condoms?"

Omar Jenkins, another of Governor Burns's aides, and the only African-American in the group, interjected, "I'm very uncomfortable with the shape this discussion is taking. I know, Dan, that the story about the kid is effective when you are trying to get white, middle-class groups like this one to take the welfare of prisoners seriously. But I am uncomfortable with the implication that this middle-class white kid was some kind of innocent lamb thrown to the guilty black and brown wolves. This kid was at least guilty. We all know that a few of the inmates are not even guilty of the crimes for which they were convicted. People get released on wrongful conviction judgments every year, and we know that the disproportionately high number of black, hispanic, and poor white inmates has as much to do with the inadequate legal representation their overworked and underfunded court-assigned lawyers can provide as it does with the poverty that breeds crime. Look at the study released last week on juvenile offenders. Black juveniles in this state were five times more likely to be tried as adults than white juveniles charged with the same offense, and white juveniles were five times more likely than blacks convicted of the same crime to be released to their families rather than sentenced to incarceration. The fact is, the justice system is *more* likely to break down in the case of minorities and the poor than for rich white kids."

Dan replied, "I didn't mean to imply that this kid was the only, or the typical, victim in our prisons, Omar. My point was that the criminal justice system breaks down for even the most privileged social groups, so they need to care about the prisons, too. I want to institute a prisoner protection policy for all the prisoners threatened with coercive sex. Prisoners who have been sexually coerced or threatened with coercion could report it and be transferred to a segregated unit. All incoming first-offense inmates would go into this unit and remain there unless they attacked or threatened another inmate. If we can protect victims, they will be more willing to come forward. This plan may not work, but I think we have to try it."

"Why do you think it won't work?" Judy asked.

"Because," Dan replied, "there are so many factions in a prison population. There are antagonisms between the various racial groups and between religious groups. In some of the prisons there are class and regional groupings as well, not to mention organized criminal gangs. There's always the possibility that an inmate reports an attack, gets transferred to the segregated unit, but gets knifed to death by some group that staged an attack to get one of their own transferred to the segregated unit to get revenge. False accusations against an inmate who reports are almost impossible to prevent. Inmate hierarchies use the rules to manipulate the system. Even when we know what's going on, we generally can't prove it. But," he concluded, "segregated units are the best alternative. We have to crack down on coercive sex by protecting victims who bring charges and make both AIDS education and condoms available to all."

There was a moment of tired silence. Keith Patterson reminded everyone that it was after 5:30, thanked everyone for coming, and before adjourning the meeting reminded them that he would report to the governor, and depending upon the governor's response, possibly schedule a meeting for them with Governor Burns.

As he walked back to his office in the governor's mansion, Keith tried to decide what he should advise. Governor Burns was not going to be pleased with Dan's little bomb. He faced a tough re-election campaign and was under a lot of pressure on education issues. To win in November, he probably had to not only prevent a strike in the universities, but also defuse the issue of low scores on the state achievement tests now required for high school graduation. It was not easy to be the "Education Governor" when 20 percent of seniors could not pass the tests. Some kind of remedial programs had to be funded. The legislature already wanted to fund the university raises by cutting the corrections budget; would they want to fund remedial programs from the corrections budget as well? What would be the political costs to the governor of not only preventing cuts, but actually raising the corrections operating budget so Dan could implement the segregated units? Just making condoms available, without the segregated unit, would be cheaper; but if distribution got reported in the media, it would undoubtedly raise charges of supporting homosexuality and violent sex. The public *might* buy a program to punish sexual predators and protect victims in prisons even if it involved distributing condoms. But could the governor afford to find out, especially if funding the program meant fighting the legislature on how to fund education relief?

On the other hand, Dan's story of the young college kid raped in prison—whatever his race—reminded Keith that the son of one of the governor's aides, a long-time friend, had just been arrested on charges of possessing marijuana in a national park, and the family was terrified he might receive a prison term. Dan's story might give the governor pause.

Keith remembered back to his own high school and college days when he had decided to go into politics and law in order to contribute to his society. Those days felt very remote and naive now. It wasn't as simple as he had thought. Those things that needed to be done could usually be discerned. The problem was how to do them, and in what priority. What should he advise the governor?

Commentary

Dan's Little Bomb

The incarceration rate in the United States (455/100,000 persons) is the highest in the world, followed by South Africa (311/100,0000) and Venezuela (177/100,000). In addition to these three, only three other nations in the world (Hungary, Canada, and China) have incarceration rates of over 80/100,000. The present U.S. rate has increased over 250 percent since 1980, and about 5,000 percent since 1972, when it was 9/100,000.

The 1980s and 1990s in the United States have been periods of prison building. In 1992, for example, $4.9 billion was spent on new prison construction alone. In 1993, state and federal governments constructed 113 new prisons at an average cost of $54,200 per inmate bed in state prisons and $78,000 per inmate bed in federal prisons. Department of Justice statistics reveal that operating budgets for prisons in the U.S. totaled $12.6 billion in 1980 and rose to $20.6 billion in 1992. Prison personnel increased 73 percent during the 1980s.

The increase in the prison population correlates with rising rates of poverty and joblessness during the 1980s. At the same time, the rate of violent felonies rose 23 percent between 1980 and 1990, and the rate of drug-related arrests rose 126 percent. The average state prison operates at 131 percent of the population capacity it was built to house. The federal system operates at 142 percent of capacity, 171 percent on the one-to-a-cell standard which prevailed in the past. Prison overcrowding is so extreme that 80 percent of the states are under strict federal court orders to reduce overcrowding. Mandatory minimum sentences for drug and firearm offenses, which were introduced into federal law in 1986 and copied by many states, are one of the major causes of overcrowding. They are also a major cause of violent criminals being released early in order to free beds for criminals convicted of minor drug offenses. The proportion of inmates in federal prisons convicted on drug-related offenses rose from 22 percent in 1981 to 62 percent in 1993, and is expected to rise to 70 percent by 1995, though there is a general agreement that the vast majority of the drug offenders in the system are petty criminals, not the organizers and controllers of the drug trade. With the rise in drug offenders has also come a rise in the incidence of HIV+ within the prisons, since many of these petty drug offenders are also drug users who have shared needles.

Use of intravenous (IV) drugs is the principal method by which prison inmates became HIV infected before entering prison. Many of these inmates were not aware of their HIV+ status until testing within the prison system informed them. Physical symptoms of AIDS are not present during the incubation period in which the virus is destroying the helper T cells of the immune system. It is not until the immune system has become very fragile, usually eight to ten years after infection, that the HIV infected person becomes increasingly aware of a series of opportunistic health problems. The weakened immune system can no longer stave off such problems because the number of helper T cells has dropped from a normal of 800-900 to below 200 per cubic milliliter of blood.

PLACING RESPONSIBILITY

Keith Patterson raises an important question when he asks why it is necessary to do anything, since it is impossible to prove that any inmate contracted AIDS in prison. Since the average sentence for drug-related offenses, now six and one-half years, is more than the average time served for manslaughter, armed assault, and all sexual offenses, only a relatively small proportion of inmates serve more than the eight- to ten-year AIDS incubation period. AIDS developed by an inmate serving less than eight years was probably contracted before prison.

There are a variety of answers as to why the state should accept responsibility for prison AIDS. A legal approach might well focus on the legal and constitutional implications of incarceration. Prisoners have been incarcerated to pay a debt to society and lose a number of their personal freedoms as punishment. But law and the constitution, influenced by religious and philosophical thought, dictate that some degree of personal autonomy is inalienable and that the most basic forms of bodyright—right to control one's own body—endure even in incarceration. Complete denial of bodyright undermines the self-respect upon which respect for others in society must be built. Thus violation of bodyright not only serves as an obstacle to rehabilitation, where that may be a goal of incarceration, but also more broadly serves to encourage the prisoner, once released into society, to ignore bodyright in others. Respect for bodyright is the reason why courts have insisted that prisoners cannot be used as subjects in medical or other research without their consent and have forbidden cruel and unusual punishments, including extended solitary confinement and denial of basic physical needs. (Many Christians also consider capital punishment as a formidable denial of bodyright.)

From the perspective of Christian scriptures and theology, there are additional reasons why the state should accept responsibility for prison AIDS. Both the Old Testament and the New Testament assume that violations of the law should be punished. The Mosaic Law includes sections that recount the specific punishments to be inflicted on transgressors (examples: Dt. 17:1-7; 19:1-13; 21:18-21; 22:13-22; 24:7; Nu. 35; Lev. 24:13-21; 26:14-33). In the New Testament, Jesus not only lays out a method for correcting and punishing various degrees of transgression within the community (Mt. 18:15-20), but describes a variety of punishments in store for wrongdoers come the Judgment (Mt. 5-6). At the same time, both testaments teach in a variety of ways that ultimate judgment belongs to the Lord, not to humans. While humans do have to take responsibility for maintaining justice in their communities, their judgment is fallible and provisional. "Do not judge," said Jesus, "lest you be judged" (Mt. 7:1); he went on to urge his followers to trust their father in heaven. God, he says, makes "the sun rise on the evil and the good, and sends rain on the righteous and the unrighteous" (Mt. 5:45). Ultimate judgment is the Lord's, and it is still in the future, on Judgment Day (Mt. 10:12-15). Furthermore, both testaments ring with avowals of God's forgiveness and undeserved mercy for human beings, both of which remind humans not to usurp God's prerogatives in judgment.

Christian theology has frequently capitulated to temptations to legalism, despite the scriptural evidence that Jesus combated legalism in the Judaism of his own day. Legalism in Christianity has encouraged Christians to understand those who violate the laws/rules of the church as damned. But despite temptations to claim to know and impose God's judgment on other persons, Christian tradition has also insisted that because God is loving and merciful, because God has a preferential option for the poor, the weak, and the suffering that is not based on their merit but on their need, even the greatest sinner may hope for the gift of salvation. If God can forgive and save the worst sinners in the world, there can be no excuse for humans deciding that any convicted prisoner has thereby forfeited his or her right to dignity and concern. From the perspective of Christian tradition, the reason that the state is obliged to do something about AIDS in prison despite the lack of complaints from prisoners is that the state acts for society. Society lives under the command to love and not to judge each and every neighbor, especially those who are weak and marginalized, unable to protect themselves.

What does love of neighbor mean in the context of U.S. prisons? One troubling issue is that of HIV testing after arrival in prison. The case is unclear as to whether there is no HIV testing at all after arrival or if there is no *mandatory* testing after arrival. Because Dan cites cost as the inhibitor, it is possible that testing is not available to inmates. It is questionable whether the absence of testing upon request can be defended in the state's prisons. Free AIDS testing is provided by health departments in all states; denial of such testing to prisoners may constitute cruel and unusual punishment in that it prevents the infected from pursuing treatment.

Testing is now sufficiently advanced to provide early detection; early treatment to slow the deterioration of the immune system can significantly extend life. Testing upon request and full information on AIDS, including information on how it is contracted, the rates of infection within the prison, and the prognosis for HIV infected persons, should be provided to all prisoners as a minimum requirement of love of neighbor.

There are, however, serious questions as to the morality of mandatory testing. Dan speaks as if the only bar to universal testing in the prisons is economic. Despite the facts that the AIDS disease has been 100 percent fatal to date and that there is no cure in sight, arguments for violating personal bodyright of prisoners through mandatory testing are not generally persuasive because personal knowledge of HIV+ status has not been shown to reduce behaviors with high risk of transmission. U.S. media have publicized a number of cases of individuals who responded to knowledge of their own HIV+ status by deliberately attempting to infect other persons. Until there is reliable statistical evidence as to what proportion of the population responds to knowledge of HIV+ status by reducing high-risk behaviors and what proportion responds by increasing the likelihood of infectious contact with others, defense of mandatory testing as in the common good must also include the intention to either make public the HIV+ status of persons without their consent or to subject HIV+ persons to mandatory isolation, neither of which U.S. society, unlike some others, has been willing to do.

Any effective AIDS education program must involve the active participation of inmates. Inmates should be a part of any planning for both the proposed segregated unit and the AIDS prevention program. Peer education has proved better able to garner the attention and interest of affected populations, better able to convey the necessary information, and better able to influence behavior. Within the homosexual community in the U.S., peer education and counseling regarding AIDS and peer ministry to PWAs (Persons with AIDS) have not only significantly reduced the transmission rate of AIDS within that community but have become models for many other communities in how to deal more effectively and compassionately with the massive tragedy of AIDS. Prisoners cut off by incarceration from families and other sources of personal support are in critical need of peer support. Medical and chaplaincy services cannot offer sufficient individual support to the sick and dying, to those fearfully waiting sickness and death, and to the cell mates and friends of those affected. Inmates should be trained to minister to each other. Such ministry could be an important aspect of restoring to individual inmates purpose and self-esteem through community service.

MISCONCEPTIONS ABOUT AIDS

Full information about AIDS is necessary for prisoners for the same reason it is necessary for the entire population: so that persons may make responsible choices. There are many misconceptions about AIDS. The World Health Organization estimates that by the year 2000 over 40 million men, women, and children will be HIV+ and over 10 million adults and 5 million children will have developed full-blown AIDS. Over 150,000 persons in the U.S. died of AIDS by 1993. To date 80 percent of HIV transmission worldwide is heterosexual, and by 2000 over 90 percent of HIV transmission will be heterosexual. While initial HIV transmission in the developed world occurred between homosexuals and IV drug users, transmission in the developing world occurred within heterosexual sex. As the epidemic matures in the developed world, its transmission pattern shifts toward transmission through heterosexual sex and IV drugs.

Though the HIV virus has been isolated in the semen, blood, vaginal secretions, saliva, tears and breast milk of infected individuals, blood and semen are the two body fluids that consistently contain the highest concentrations of the virus. Sexual transmission in semen occurs when semen from an infected person is ejaculated into a vagina, anus, or mouth which has some tear or sore that allows the virus to pass into the bloodstream. Though all sex with an infected partner is dangerous, receptive anal sex, which normally involves some small tears in the lining of the colon, is an especially dangerous practice for both men and women. Just as the risk of female to male transmission of HIV in coitus is considerably lower than that for male to female, there is considerably less risk of transmission from the receptor in anal sex to the insertor, and from the receptor in fellatio to the fellated. This normally means that when coercive prison sex occurs, the victim of the sexual assault sustains much higher risk of infection than the rapist.

Many people consider condoms the answer to the threat of AIDS. The use of latex condoms, especially those treated with the spermicide Nonoxynol-9, does greatly reduce the risk. (Condoms made from animal tissues are permeable by the HIV virus.) Only abstaining from sex altogether is a more effective method than latex condoms for avoiding HIV infection. But condom use by no means eliminates risk, because of the frequency of both ruptures in the condom surface and spillage during withdrawal. Studies to date in the U.S. show 10 to 30 percent failure rates of condoms; in some developing nations the failure rates are 30 to 60 percent, due to inferior manufacturing standards and poor storage and transport. Condom failure rates should be a part of the information furnished to prisoners and to the general public.

CHRISTIAN REVELATION AND CONSCIENCE FORMATION

Given all this information, what should the governor decide? To a certain extent, his decision will depend upon his understanding of how he serves his constituents. Is he obligated to decide according to the preference of the majority as disclosed, for example, by opinion polls, or was he elected by the majority to gather the relevant data and use his own best judgment in making choices? Many politicians feel pressured to abide by the preference of the majority of their constituents in order to protect their chances of re-election. Even some of these same politicians, however, have come across single issues on which they feel obliged to disregard the preference of their constituents in order to follow the demands of individual conscience.

If the governor is swayed by public opinion, Dan probably has little chance of implementing his program, so widespread are fears and misconceptions about AIDS, about homosexual sex, and about prisoners. Prisoners at risk of AIDS from either voluntary or coerced homosexual sex do not stack up well in popular opinion against children and teachers. Much of society would prefer to forget about prisons, AIDS, and homosexual sex.

Elected officials who feel obliged to follow public opinion often ignore their responsibility to educate the public and the obligation to follow their conscience. Public officials have an obligation to educate the public so that the voting public can make informed choices, even when that education might not be popular.

The media have a parallel obligation to inform the public of all the relevant facts and all the available analysis of social reality. The obligation of media to inform the public should take precedence over public entertainment. That obligation to inform the public is not exhausted by informing the public of the preference of the majority which may have been influenced by ignorance, prejudice, or exploitative manipulation of facts or emotions.

We have no clues in this case as to the disposition of Governor Burns's conscience. Most humans have developed their consciences only in certain limited areas of their lives and remain insensitive to sin and evil in other areas. Christian ethical teaching has insisted that individuals should regard the stance of informed, mature conscience as obligatory.

A well-formed and informed Christian conscience will consider that Yahweh's covenant with the Israelites and Jesus' ministry both illustrate a preferential option for the poor which becomes binding upon those who would call themselves Christian and follow the way of the Christ. Jesus characterized his own mission in the words of Isaiah: "The Spirit of the Lord is upon me because he has anointed me to bring good news to the poor. He has sent me to proclaim release to the captives and recovery of sight to the blind, and let the oppressed go free, to proclaim the year of the Lord's favor" (Lk. 4: 18-19). There is nothing in the preferential option for the poor which indicates that prisoners must always be preferred over children and teachers, but the preferential option would prohibit dismissing the claims of the prisoners as if they had no status at all.

The preferential option for the poor would dictate that the governor opt to protect the group with the greatest need, the most vulnerable group. Just as God rescued the Hebrews from slavery in Egypt because of their suffering, and not their virtue, so Jesus promised that God is a loving Parent who responds to each of us according to our needs, not our desserts (Mt. 7:7-11). Jesus of the Gospels lived out this same loving commitment to others and called his audience to respond—through love of both God and neighbor—to God's love as it had been expressed within creation, within salvation history, and within the mission of Jesus himself.

In the Christian theological tradition as well, all human persons are children of God and deserve equal respect. Not only is each person important as a child of God, but each Christian is connected to all others to make up the Body of Christ, the church (1 Cor. 12). Because of these integral connections between the members of a society, there are not only many separate individual goods to be achieved in society, but there is also a common good. The governor needs to pursue a choice that contributes to the common good and gives a preference to the most needy. The common good may benefit more from attempts to lower the prison HIV rate. Such a lowering would affect the rates in the society at large, since released prisoners would not be infecting wives and girlfriends and children with HIV. As the rate of prisoner AIDS lowered over time, so would the costs to the state of treating prison AIDS.

Accepting that the state has an obligation to impede increases in the HIV transmission rate in prison leaves open the question of means. Allowing Dan to exercise his own judgment about whether the prison hospitals pass out condoms and provide testing to prisoners who request them would involve minimal expense and minimal political risk for the governor. Combining provision of testing and condoms upon request with an AIDS education program for all the state prison workers and inmates would involve more expense and more political risk for the governor. Funding provision of testing, condoms, and education as well as Dan's request for segregated units in order to reduce coercive prison sex would involve the most expense and the most risk, but may be more likely to significantly lower AIDS transmissions than simply supplying condoms or condoms and education, and more likely to protect prisoners from brutal sexual assault.

Alternatively, it is possible that the common good might be more benefited by aiding education, which more directly affects the majority of the population. We do not have sufficient information to analyze the benefits from funding professorial raises and remedial programs in education. If, for example, low educational levels in the state were responsible for the reluctance of major employers to locate there, remedial programs might over time lower the unemployment rate, and thus many other social indices of poverty and deprivation.

ADDITIONAL RESOURCES

Edna McConnell Clark Foundation. "Americans Behind Bars." New York: 1993.

Gostin, Larry, and William J. Curran. "The Limits of Compulsion in Controlling AIDS." In Arthur Zucker, Donald Borchert, and David Stewart, eds. *Medical Ethics: A Reader.* Englewood Cliffs, NJ: Prentice-Hall, 1992.

Jung, Patricia Beattie, and Ralph F. Smith. *Heterosexism: An Ethical Challenge.* Albany, NY: SUNY Press, 1993.

Maguire, Daniel C. *The Moral Core of Judaism and Christianity.* Minneapolis, MN: Fortress, 1993.

Mann, Jonathan, Daniel J. M. Tarantola, and Thomas W. Netter, eds. *AIDS in the World: A Global Report.* Cambridge, MA: Harvard University Press, 1992.

Price, Monroe E. *Shattered Mirrors: Our Search for Identity and Community in the AIDS Era.* Cambridge, MA: Harvard University Press, 1989.

PART VII

SEXUALITY

Case

Getting Away from It All

"I wish you would have died in that fire and not my father!" The apartment door slammed as Alicia stormed out. Helen Edwards grimaced as another piece of plaster fell in the narrow hallway. She walked to the front window and peered out to see Alicia emerge from the stairwell and run across the littered cement courtyard to the next housing block where her friend Mae lived. Would it do any good to drag her fourteen-year-old daughter back to the Mid-Town Teen Clinic?

Rock music blared from Alicia's portable radio. As Helen went to turn it off, she looked at the clock and hurried to get her handbag. She could not stop now to find Alicia or she would be late to work again. Helen did not cry very often. It was not her way. But she was as close to tears as she had been in a long time.

She tried to imagine what Alicia was feeling, to remember what it was like to be so young. Helen's hands felt cold as she maneuvered her old car through the heavy morning traffic. Helen felt like she had never been young. Her eldest, Joe, had been born when she was fifteen. Then Sam came along a year later. When Alicia was born, Helen swore she would never let her become a teenage mother and fall into the same trap she had gotten herself into. Daniel Moore, Alicia's father, had had some problems, but he was a good man. They had struggled to raise their three children, but then their life together had ended when Daniel died in a fire at the factory where he had worked.

Six months after Daniel died, Helen married Jim Edwards. She remembered the arguments with Jim about a baby. Helen had said there was no way they could afford another child. Jim was employed temporarily with odd jobs. Hers was the only steady salary. Jim was insistent and eventually

---

won out. Jackie, their baby, was now nearly a year old and looked just like Jim.

It had not worked out too badly. Jackie was a good baby and everybody loved her, especially Jim. Helen clenched the wheel when she remembered that Jim had spent nearly a week's salary, over $180, on baby clothes that Jackie outgrew in less than a month.

Helen had worked for the Andersons for about six years. Although she started as a domestic, she increasingly took over the care of their four children. Mrs. Anderson had said that Helen should think about going to the vocational school and getting her child care certificate. She could even start her own center. But there were too many nights she stayed late, sometimes overnight. Helen remembered feeling proud that Alicia, even at ten, could put together a supper for her brothers.

The Andersons had given Helen a month's leave to have Jackie and welcomed her back afterwards. Some days she could even bring Jackie to work. Usually she left the baby with Mrs. Morris, an older neighbor in their apartment block. Alicia was supposed to pick her up after school. That was happening less and less.

Helen's mind went back over the past few months trying to piece together the changes she saw in Alicia. Even though Jim had been with them for nearly two years, Alicia still did not get along with him. Close friends did not help much when they kept commenting on how much Alicia looked like her father. Then when Jim was drunk, sometimes on weekends, he would shout at Alicia. Alicia would stay away from the apartment for hours at a time. Helen learned she was running around with a much older group of teens in the project. Some of them were dropouts. Several had police records. Helen's oldest boy told her it was a rough crowd. A lot of them were into drugs.

Helen became determined to move her family out of the project. She spent hours reading newspaper ads, looking for anything they could afford. Because Mrs. Anderson did not make her fool with social security, Helen's take-home, including overtime, was sometimes over $800 per month. They needed at least three bedrooms, and most rents started at $600 per month. Helen had found a two bedroom she thought they could afford, but the manager refused to show it to her when he found out she had four children.

Several weeks later in September Helen learned that Alicia, then thirteen, had a boyfriend who was seventeen. Not long after he gave Alicia two tapes and a bracelet. Helen made an appointment for Alicia at the Mid-Town Teen Clinic. Helen tried to talk to her about not getting pregnant. She was still a little girl. For her own sake as well as that of a child she might have, she needed to wait until she was older. Helen hoped Alicia would listen to someone at the clinic.

When Alicia came out of the interview with Ms. Wilson, she showed Helen a six-month supply of birth control pills and promised her mother she would take them. Alicia made an appointment to come back again in six months. Helen continued to search for a new place to live. Less than three months after the visit to the teen clinic, Alicia told her mother she thought she was pregnant. Helen talked to Mrs. Anderson the next afternoon. Mrs. Anderson made arrangements for Alicia to see her own gynecologist. Helen would have to pay $80 for the visit. Helen took the day off to take Alicia to the doctor's office. She sat and waited for over an hour in the lounge while Alicia saw the nurses and then the doctor. Alicia was very quiet when she came out. She cried on the way home. She told her mother the doctor had been very straight about the options, and that if the tests were positive, she had to decide what to do. She said that she wanted to talk to her boyfriend first.

The doctor's office called Helen at the Anderson's the next day. The blood test was negative. They were sure Alicia was not pregnant. That night Alicia said she would go back to the clinic. She had thrown the pills away when she thought she was pregnant. Helen took another afternoon off to drive Alicia back to the teen clinic. Alicia promised again she would be careful.

Over the next two months Alicia drew further and further away from the family. She began spending every afternoon with her friend Mae. Helen learned from her oldest boy that Mae was eighteen and had dropped out of school when she had a baby. She lived with her mother and got $135 a month from welfare.

Helen had not worried too much about her boys. Joe and Sam seemed to manage all right in high school. They tried odd jobs when they could. Helen remembered seeing on television that unemployment for teens in the city was over 75 percent. But just keeping Alicia in school was a problem. Her truancy had gotten so bad that Helen had taken to driving Alicia to school to make sure she got there. Then pressure at work made this impossible. If Helen could not make it to the Andersons by 8:30, they would have to get someone else.

Things at home seemed to get worse. It was a bitter cold winter and the heat bills were high. By the end of January Helen hardly had enough money to buy groceries. The phone company had come and taken out the phones again. Jim still had not found anything steady. He was going on weekend binges more often. One night after he hit Helen and swore at Alicia, Helen decided that Alicia needed to go and live with her cousin in Atlanta. Alicia was back home in three weeks. Her aunt refused to keep her. Helen never found out what happened.

Jim left the first week in March. A week later Alicia's school counselor called Helen at the Andersons. Alicia was being suspended for fighting with another girl in school. Helen told the Andersons she needed to quit work and stay at home with her daughter. She made arrangements for a good friend at church who was unemployed to work temporarily for her.

Two weeks later Helen went back to work for the Andersons. She had hoped staying at home with Alicia would help, but Helen found Alicia almost impossible to handle. Several days she did not come home at all. Helen remembered one night she was so mad at Alicia that she told her she would turn her over to the juvenile court. When the period of suspension was over, there were days when Alicia left school soon after she got there. The school counselor told Helen she had a case load of over four hundred children. She did not know what to suggest for Alicia. Had Helen tried taking her to the Mid-Town Teen Clinic?

For the month Helen had been back at the Andersons, Alicia seemed a bit more responsible and was coming more regularly to pick up Jackie from Mrs. Morris. Helen knew that Alicia had another boyfriend, but she had refused to talk about him.

Then this morning when she was taking off the bed sheets to do laundry, Helen found Alicia's unused container of birth control pills under her mattress. Helen shooed the boys off to school early and told Alicia to stay. "What do you think you are up to, girl? Why aren't you taking these things? I know your cycle. You still have time to start this month. Has this fancy new boyfriend of yours put ideas into your head? There's no way I'll believe that boy is using any protection." Helen tried to keep her voice under control, but knew she was shouting at Alicia.

Alicia glared back at her mother. "My boyfriend gave me that blouse you wouldn't buy me for my birthday. He treats me like a woman. He thinks it would be cool to have a baby. You can't make me take those things. I'm old enough to make my own decisions. Besides, my boyfriend doesn't want me to take them. You're always picking on me. I wish you had died in that fire. . . . "

As Helen pulled her car into the Andersons' long driveway, she saw Mrs. Anderson waiting with the two-year-old. She smiled as Helen got out of the car. "Helen, I have a wonderful surprise. This next week when the children's private school has spring break, Mr. Anderson and I plan to take the family to St. Simon's Island. We learned yesterday we can have one of the larger houses, and there would be just enough room for you and Jackie. I've heard you say you have never been on a trip and that you have never seen the ocean. With so much for them to do, the children should be easy for you to watch on the beach. And Mr. Anderson and I would be around most evenings. Helen, you really look tired and need to get away from it all. Why not come along with us?"

Commentary

Getting Away from It All

It is important to note at the outset that the case does not state the ethnic background of the Edwards. As 70 to 80 percent of the population of most urban housing projects are black or Hispanic, it would be understandable if one assumed the Edwards are members of an ethnic minority. However, using statistics as an entry point for this case may be a trap into stereotypic responses that could obscure deeper issues. In order to understand better the ethical decisions that Helen and Alicia face, one might attempt to enter the case, at least imaginatively, through the subculture of the urban housing project in which the Edwards live and through their personal perspectives. In this case conditions of poverty are far more relevant than issues of race.

CHARACTERS: THE PERSONAL DILEMMA

Alicia

"Getting away from it all" may be a temptation for Alicia as well as Helen. Alicia is experiencing pressure from several directions. She is faced with the persistent love of a mother trying to protect her at a stage in life when independence is particularly important. She also cares for a baby sister and has responsibility for meal preparation for two brothers, which began when she was only ten. These tasks are made more burdensome since the baby, Jackie, is the favorite of Alicia's stepfather, while Alicia is rejected. When Jim is drunk, he alternately ignores and yells at her. Alicia may have had no time or way to grieve after the death of her own father.

Alicia is probably also experiencing the physical withdrawal of affection by her mother. Traditionally, when children reach adolescence and parents become aware of their sexuality, there is an unconscious withdrawal of parental touch. Though Alicia hears her mother express concern, she experiences her as demanding and, because of Helen's work schedule in a distant suburb, as absent.

If this is a typical low-income urban area, then school provides more pressure. Alicia's mother wants performance in an urban school system which probably is predominantly segregated and likely has high dropout rates and overburdened teachers. Alicia knows the score and so does Helen: There are no jobs, even if one finishes school. The big money is in drugs.

Alicia knows from experience how hard it is to get advice and help. She recalls how embarrassing it was to have her mother drive her to the teen clinic. The counselors were so busy they could only spend a few minutes with her, and nobody is that quick with good advice. Then when Alicia was both scared and happy she might be pregnant, she had to go to Mrs. Anderson's doctor. Alicia may resent the Andersons as the cause of her mother's absence and react with anger to their privileges and access to a private physician in contrast to the public clinic. It would not be surprising that Alicia finds neither dignity nor meaning at home or in school.

Through her sexuality, Alicia finds the intimacy, affection, and attention she craves, as well as a possible means of getting away from the trapped feeling of the project. The normal hormonal changes in her body and increasing sexual energy offer a viable outlet for her frustration. Her boyfriend wants a baby, and Alicia wants to please the only person in her life who makes her feel special. Alicia knows her mother was pregnant at fifteen. Perhaps she and her boyfriend could make it too on Aid for Dependent Children (AFDC). Then she could be free and on her own. However, Alicia realizes that some of the women who have been in the project for two or three generations, like Mae's mother, weren't all that happy. Husbands who last more than two years are in short supply. Alicia must wonder whether she has any real choice or any real hope.

Alicia is a remarkable young woman. She has homemaking and survival skills at age fifteen that would surpass most of her peers in the affluent suburbs. Refusing to be dominated by her mother or her aunt, she appears determined to make her own decisions and create some kind of a meaningful future.

Helen

As the mother of a teenage daughter on the verge of perpetuating the cycle of children bearing children, Helen recalls swearing at Alicia's birth that this would not happen to her daughter. She may feel terrible guilt that she is unable to control the situation. Helen is offered a way, at least temporarily, of getting away from it all. Would a trip to the ocean that she had so longed to see be the break she needs? She knows the Andersons gain the most by her going. They are good people, even if paternalistic. Helen tries not to think about the power they have to shape her situation. Helen must be angry and lonely with Daniel, her first husband, dead and Jim now gone. But if she goes away at this critical time, is this surrender to a system that will swallow up her daughter as well? They will both be victims when that boy disappears and leaves her with a daughter and a grandchild to care for.

Helen also may wonder whether it really makes any difference if she goes or stays. Although the unfolding story seems already out of her hands, she still feels responsible. Helen may dream of the child care certificate and the independence it promises. However, the price is high in precious time, money, and energy with the possibility of only disappointment at the end.

Helen Edwards is a woman of loving instincts with an extraordinary capacity to care for others while still sustaining her own family. She is resourceful with medical options for Alicia, vocational possibilities for herself, and in seeking housing alternatives for the family. Helen is a woman of determination and commitment.

Jim Edwards

For many middle-class readers Jim may be the most difficult of the characters to understand. There are four women to every marriageable man in many poor ethnic communities. Many males in poor urban communities have been killed or disabled through gang or neighborhood clashes and police confrontations. Others are in prison or institutionalized for drug or alcohol abuse. They are caught in a system where inner city unemployment is ten times higher than in most suburban communities. Unemployed men are viewed by the dominant society as redundant or disposable. There must be some place to show your manhood, and fathering children has an honored tradition. Alcohol and drugs are a means of getting away from it all that few would condone, but certainly most who are knowledgeable would also understand.

Jim has the right to seek a loving relationship, including the pleasure of a baby in his house. However, if he is unable to find work, Jim's very presence in the household reduces the social welfare benefits the family would be eligible to receive. He may be taking, in his judgment, the most responsible, caring, and painful decision as he distances himself from the family. Whether his absence is a sign of abandonment or commitment may be a question of perspective.

The Andersons

Helen's employers are clearly middle-class or upper-middle-class, whether they are white, black, or Hispanic. As concerned employers, they have granted maternity leave, offered medical assistance, and encouraged Helen's vocational advancement. Yet the schedule of evenings and over-nights does not suggest the job is designed with the need of a parent employee in mind. Whether adequate salary and vacation with pay are part of the package for Helen, we do not know. However, these benefits would be contrary to the accepted pattern for most domestic workers. The decision not to withhold social security payments from Helen's salary, which also eliminates payment of a matching employer contribution, is illegal. Though

Helen states she needs the extra cash now, this decision may not be to her benefit in the long run.

The Andersons should be asking themselves several personal and moral questions. How can the welfare of their children be compared to the welfare of Helen's children? Does their access to wealth, at least compared to the Edwards, provide rights of time and attention not equally owed to Alicia, Jackie, and their brothers? The case gives no details about Helen's employee benefits such as medical care or retirement. However, traditionally benefits are rare for domestic help and child care providers, despite the value of these services if measured by their impact on the quality of an employer's family life.

The Andersons appear genuinely concerned about Helen and her family in terms of immediate personal problems. They have provided understanding, some work flexibility, and special resources such as access to their family physician. A major question which arises concerns the degree of the Andersons' responsibility for or even acknowledgment of the structural injustices which burden families such as the Edwards. The gap between poverty and privilege widens when social injustice is reduced to a private concern for a single individual.

Questions of structural justice may be more complicated than the personal issues. What responsibility do the Andersons, or any member of a privileged segment of society, have for the inadequate housing, education, employment, and medical facilities for the poor? Where are the limits of responsibility for the welfare of employees, who are also children of God, with special needs for their families? A critical moral issue in this case may be what the famous twelfth-century rabbi Maimonides called the eighth and most meritorious step of charity—"to anticipate charity, by preventing poverty."

THE SITUATION: A NATIONAL TRAGEDY

A double-edged national tragedy that this case reveals is the growing level of poverty concentrated among children and youth and the higher levels of teenage pregnancy which are a consequence of and contributor to that poverty. The United States is progressively being divided into two nations or two worlds. The communities are as distinct as the separation of rich and poor worlds at the global level. The gap runs along lines of race, economics, and sex.

Senator Daniel Patrick Moynihan in his response to the President's 1988 State of the Union address declared, "there are more poor Americans today than a quarter of a century ago, and . . . the poorest group in our population are children." For the citizens of the wealthiest nation in the world the newest census figures should be profoundly shocking. In the United States: one child in four is born into poverty. One child in five lives through adolescence in poverty. For black and Hispanic families the reality is even harsher. One in two black children is poor as are two of five Hispanic children. One of the most disturbing indices of poverty in the United States is a higher infant mortality rate than in eleven other nations in the industrialized world. This national tragedy challenges our self-perception as a humane, prosperous, and progressive people.

Poverty hits children and young mothers hardest. From 1975 to 1985 female-headed, single-parent households such as the Edwards increased from 2.4 million to 3.4 million, with 40 percent of those households living in poverty even with the mother employed. The United States has the highest adolescent birthrate of any industrialized nation. It is the Alicias of our society who become children bearing children. A recent report from the Education Commission of the States notes that at least 15 percent of all Americans between the ages of sixteen and nineteen are unlikely to become productive adults because they are already "disconnected" from society as a result of drug abuse, delinquency, pregnancy, unemployment, and/or dropping out of school—all signs of "alienation and disconnection." The report acknowledges an unconscionably disproportionate representation of poor, black, and Hispanic teens in the statistics. These statistics have not changed significantly since these reports.

Over one million teens become pregnant each year. These pregnancies will result in: staggering rates of infant mortality; increased dropout rates; drug, alcohol, and child abuse; divorce; unemployment; and even suicide. Teenage pregnancy of this magnitude is a national as well as a personal tragedy. Yet funding and commitment for prevention-focused education and social programs to address the causes of this moral and systemic problem are at best inadequate. Most authorities on sexuality and health judge current efforts to be paltry.

An extremely high percentage of teenage parents' own mothers conceived in their teens, as did Helen Edwards. The disproportionate number of these who are poor, black, and Hispanic exposes the deep roots of gender, race, and class patterns in our culture. The greatest pressure on those who are extremely poor is often not for stronger ethical norms but simply for survival. The Christian norm for sexual relations within marriage presupposes a loving relationship. Yet the realities of poverty easily threaten the fulfillment of a sustained, loving relationship between sexual partners. The ethical crisis in this case is not simply Helen's parental decision for more supervision or Alicia's decision about childbearing. It is, in many ways, a class-action case that challenges the morality of a society which perpetuates the dehumanizing conditions in which some people live and fails to address the causes of teenage pregnancy.

RELATIONAL NORMS

At the heart of the Christian tradition is a relational norm, the love of God and neighbor. The Christian is called first to love God—"with all your heart, and with all your soul, and with all your mind," and, second, to "love your neighbor as yourself" (Mark 12:30-31). Theologian H. Richard Niebuhr described the principal purpose of the community of faith called the church to be "the increase of the love of God and neighbor." He also suggested that the basic guideline for making an ethical choice is to ask, "What is the loving thing to do?" The biblical standard is a quality of relationship called love that nurtures both freedom and responsibility. This is the freedom for human beings to realize their full potential and for individuals and societies to care for one another. Christians are called to a loving relationship with God, neighbors, and even with enemies. This is the basis for the concept of justice.

Christians consider sexual relationships from the context of the norm of love. Genesis shows God creating partners to be the closest neighbors in this relational norm of love. The New Testament adds to this image, declaring that as God "from the beginning made them male and female . . . a man shall leave his father and mother and be joined to his wife, and the two shall become one" (Matt. 19:4-5). This relationship is sometimes described as a great mystery and compared to the relationship between God and Israel or Christ and the church. Marriage has become so cherished by some Christian churches that it is understood as a sacrament.

It is within this special relational norm of love and marriage that Christianity has traditionally seen the gift of sexuality. Though sexual union produces children, the function of the gift was seldom seen as procreation alone, but was also to enhance the relationship, that quality of loving between the partners. Related to the original biblical accounts, a series of guidelines have emerged from the Christian church, most of which have restricted sexual relations to married partners. Different religious communities at various points in history have employed different standards, but sexual relations within marriage have become normative. These religious traditions have usually been recognized and sanctioned by the secular community as well.

It must be confessed that guidelines for understanding sexual behavior have at times been manipulated, misinterpreted, and used in an oppressive and nonloving manner. Boundaries have been erected by both religious and secular communities with the claim of safeguarding the family or the community. Many who crossed those boundaries were and are treated in ways that violate the very heart of the basic norm of love itself. This is especially true for women who are treated as property not partners, as well as for persons who cross those boundaries in adultery or promiscuity. Those of other sexual preferences are condemned and often ostracized for challenging the interpretation of the norm of married partners and for expressing an alternative understanding of sexuality.

SOME RESPONSES: A SYSTEMATIC AND PERSONAL APPROACH

Having the basic necessities of life to maintain human dignity and a sense of security seem to be essential to sustain loving relationships. Perhaps all the members of the human community must own some responsibility when the support systems for basic needs do not exist or cease to function. In exploring the problems of the ethics of societal structures as well as personal sexual ethics, we should consider which conditions promote and sustain the love of partner, God, and neighbor. Three categories emerge for consideration: education, economics, and emancipation.

Education

While a majority of Americans consider teenage pregnancy a serious national problem, major studies reveal that Americans are also seriously misinformed about the nature and roots of the problem. Better information is especially important for those persons who effect legislation, school policy, and the stated priorities of religious and private institutions. Public forums and seminars must draw on areas of agreement about the data and point to avenues of support and participation.

Myths and stereotypes about teenage pregnancy need to be challenged by comprehensive comparative studies such as those of the Allan Guttmacher Institute. One of the institute's studies compared U.S. statistics with those of six other countries with similar cultural and economic backgrounds, including England and Canada. The results indicate that the United States leads every developed nation in numbers of teenage pregnancies, childbearing adolescents, and in abortion rates. America is the only country in the study where teenage pregnancies have been increasing. Teenage mothers are disproportionately high among poor black and Hispanic families. However, it is misleading to conclude that high U.S. figures are simply a result of an ethnic population that lives in a degree of poverty unknown in most of Western Europe. The rate of teenage pregnancy in the United States for white non-poor adolescents also exceeds that of other countries in the study. Another relevant statistic is that American teenagers are not apt to begin sexual activity earlier or be more sexually active. Finally, welfare does not appear to be the determining incentive for out-of-wedlock births; U.S. welfare benefits are less generous than in other countries in the study.

Developing an approach to teenage pregnancy requires raising awareness of the high cost of failing to invest in solving the problem. The dislocation created by teenage pregnancy takes an incredible emotional, physical, and economic toll on the lives of teenagers, their families, and finally, on society as a whole. The pregnant teenager is "at risk" in terms of being dramatically less likely to complete high school and secure or maintain a job. The same adolescent is significantly more likely to abuse drugs and alcohol, to give birth to a child with physical and mental handicaps, to have children who become teenage parents, to live in poverty, and to attempt suicide. The direct costs to the society in terms of welfare, medicine, and human suffering are staggering.

The key causal factors of teenage pregnancy identified by scientific studies include: (1) lack of available courses on family life; (2) lack of access to birth control information and resources; (3) the depiction of sex by the media; and (4) the breakdown of the family and the loss of support structures for a meaningful future. The first three will be discussed in this section; the last issue will be taken up in the following section on economics.

In regard to sex education the Guttmacher Institute study draws an important overall conclusion. It is not that American culture is sex-obsessed as might be concluded by a sampling of the media, especially television. Rather, the institute concludes that American culture as a whole is prudish and intolerant of premarital sexual activity. These attitudes stem in part from a fear of sexuality which causes many parents not only to be unable to deal openly with sexual activity but to withdraw physical affection from their adolescent children. The church is cited as a factor in this view of sex that also results in a frequent polarization in discussions about mandatory or even voluntary "family life and sex education," to say nothing about the establishment of school-based health clinics which offer contraceptive information. The study concludes, "it is likely that the United States has the lowest level of contraceptive practice among teenagers" of all the industrialized countries studied. Therefore, a critical arena for education is not teenagers but adult Americans who ultimately determine public policy and influence moral values.

Several studies suggest one basic step is to introduce mandatory family and life education courses from kindergarten to grade twelve in as many public and private schools as possible. The fear that such courses will cause earlier or more frequent sexual activity and thus higher pregnancy levels is disputed by most reliable research on the subject. Sex education has been compulsory in Sweden since the 1950s; that country has significantly lower levels of pregnancy and abortion than the United States.

School-based health clinics that are accessible and confidential could also be an important factor in the solution. Some church traditions, however, oppose contraception and abortion on ethical grounds and challenge the use of public tax dollars to support facilities which may dispense information contrary to their teachings. However, in some states pilot school-based clinics have been supported by both prolife and prochoice groups since they have a common interest in preventing teenage pregnancy. Some of these clinics are supervised by parent boards and have restrictions concerning dispensing contraceptives or offering advice on termination of pregnancy. As in Alicia's case, many clinics, even when available, are not near the schools and are often underfunded and understaffed. Given the current polarized climate, enacting necessary legislation for courses and clinics will be a public struggle.

The standard media approach to sex should be countered. Education about responsible attitudes toward sexual behavior must occur in locations where parents and teenagers can be reached effectively. So far the media's impact on people's attitude toward sex has been overwhelmingly negative. Glamorous indiscriminate sexual encounters, usually without a focus on a sustained or loving relationship between partners, are used to sell products and promote ratings. As Planned Parenthood declared in an advertising campaign, "They did it 9,000 times on television last year. How come nobody got pregnant?" A few TV series cautiously discuss contraceptives and condoms, but these are rare. Even fewer series raise the option of abstinence. Fear of AIDS may provide the opportunity to re-evaluate approaches to sexual behavior in the media as well as sex education in the schools.

TV appears to be the most influential media for teenagers and parents. In addition to continuing to pressure the television networks for more responsible broadcasting, concerned citizens need to explore new programs which counter the media's prevailing mode. The most effective programs have focused on community organizations, schools, churches, and clubs. They have employed open and engaging formats such as case studies, videos, and community forums which allow honest discussion of sex and loving relationships. Teenage heroes who speak candidly and confessionally about sex as well as drugs also appear to be getting a hearing.

New educational networks and coalitions are emerging which are taking important steps. Public/private partnership projects are combining the state resources of education, health, and social services with those of corporations, foundations, churches, and civic organizations. One example is The Hartford Action Plan on Infant Health initiated by Connecticut Mutual Life Insurance Company in its concern for a community-integrated project to reduce infant mortality and teen pregnancy in the country's third poorest city. Illinois and Michigan have comprehensive programs, such as Illinois Parents Too Soon, that address the problem through coalitions of the public and private sector. These examples of simultaneous education of policy makers, teens, and parents provide pilot programs for other communities to examine and adapt to their own special circumstances.

Economics

Causal factors of family disintegration and the resulting loss of hope for a meaningful future for both teenagers and parents may be the most critical and also the most complex to address. Without a sense of worth and dignity it is difficult for an individual to utilize the resources made available in schools, clinics, churches, or community organizations. The breakdown of family life in all classes and races, but especially in minority communities, has been linked to economic pressures and the inability to control or even participate in the shaping of one's future in a meaningful way. This breakdown is in part due to racism and the failure of the wider community to provide adequate employment opportunities. Teenage pregnancy is an issue of social justice.

The Census Bureau predicts that 61 percent of the children born in the United States today will live for some time with only one biological parent, usually the mother. Ninety-six percent of all children whose families receive Aid for Dependent Children (AFDC) are from homes with a single head of household; the majority are from minority ethnic groups. Members of the American Public Welfare Association, who often administer such programs, suggest that public aid produces dependency and robs those dependents of dignity. Such programs have produced an "institutional bias against minority children," declares Senator Moynihan. It is revealing that surveys of mothers with dependent children taken prior to the enactment of the program—which was a part of the original 1935 Social Security Act—showed that these mothers opposed the program. These women preferred programs of child care, health insurance, and job training to cope with their economic problems, not welfare payments. A proposal for welfare reform by The National Council of State Human Services Administrators entitled "One in Four" evokes the challenge of children in poverty. It calls for programs to enhance self-support and self-sufficiency for poor families through income security, education, and employment and thus returns to themes articulated by poor mothers in 1935. The report has a special section of recommendations of strategies to help prevent adolescent pregnancy.

There is scant evidence that any nation has significantly addressed the problem of unwanted pregnancies without providing a degree of economic security and hope for a more meaningful life. On a global scale those countries that have combined a guarantee of basic necessities for a life with dignity and reasonable security for senior citizens have achieved significant population reduction. This is true in Western Europe and middle-class North America. This reduction has not occurred in the United States among urban and rural poor who often have little security or hope.

It may startle many North Americans to learn that poor people are not confined to poor countries. U.S. inner city housing projects and rural poverty areas often have a huge number of people who are unemployed and a significant number of temporary workers or migrant laborers. A majority of residents in these communities have inadequate resources and virtually no hope that the cycle of poverty will really change. Unless the systemic issues of poverty—unemployment, scarcity of affordable housing, inadequate education, lack of day care, no health insurance, and limited medical services—are dealt with, the educational strategies to reduce teenage pregnancy will reap minimal results.

The biblical mandate for justice makes it ethically necessary that Christians support systemic changes that assure a basic standard of living for all. In this case study the Andersons and the Edwards both have responsibilities in moving toward this goal. Power within the system rests more with the Andersons. They could respond with adequate salary and health/pension benefits for Helen as well as become advocates in their schools, church, and community on strategies for the prevention of teenage pregnancy. Helen and Alicia have obligations to demand and help develop child care programs, job enhancement opportunities, and a school-based health clinic. Though it will challenge family patterns, Helen's sons need to assume their share of child care and meal preparation. System modification for the sake of justice is a responsibility of all, though what one can do is often in part determined by one's resources.

Emancipation

Freedom and the ability to participate in decisions and structures that shape our lives are what distinguish us as human beings. The shaping of individual and communal ways of being is essential to morality. The idea of being emancipated or liberated from the attitudes or structures that limit one's human potential is central to this volume. Brazilian educator Paulo Freire notes that cultural forms give meaning to the way human beings think, talk, dress, and act. He calls for people to distinguish between the present as given and the present as containing emancipatory possibilities. Emancipation or freedom is as important to the issue of teenage pregnancy as education and economics.

Morality concerns not only what one does but also who one is. The relational norm of love, rooted in the biblical and theological tradition, has to do with a way of being and the formation of character. Ethical issues link together what persons can be as individuals with what they can become as communities. Individuals are shaped by communities and in turn they shape their communities. Emancipation involves freedom and participation. For Alicia, Helen, and the Andersons to be free to live in different ways means the communities in which they function and the structures of society must change. Alicia needs the experience of being loved and affirmed for who she is as a person with a choice about the sexual and parental obligations she wants to assume and at what stage of her life. These value choices are determined to a degree by what Alicia, her family, and her peers believe are real options for the future. Those caught in a life of poverty are seriously limited in the options available to them. Without some trust that the cycle of poverty and dependency can be broken, there is little motivation to risk new ways of being or relating.

While there is a disproportionately high percentage of adolescent mothers who are women of color, the largest numbers are white and from suburban and rural areas. Though the economic issues are more immediate in the urban project and in areas of rural poverty, concerns for meaningfulness and hope are alive and pressing in every part of American culture. Non-poor adolescents from suburbia drift into drugs and loveless sexual experimentation because, they claim, life is "boring" and unfulfilling. The pressing problems in this case are pregnancy and parenting. But the root issue is whether or not individuals can become free enough from the present to live out the possibilities of loving and just relationships.

The symptoms of drug abuse, self-endangering sexual activity, community-alienating behavior, and increasing teenage suicide point to deep problems of motivation. Teams of students and parents, coalitions from the public and private sectors, and studies by religious and secular institutes consistently recommend a renewed concentration on relationships and ethics. More attention, imagination, and funds need to be devoted to "getting with it" rather than "getting away from it all."

ADDITIONAL RESOURCES

Adolescent Pregnancy Prevention: School Community Cooperation. Springfield, IL: Charles C. Thomas, 1981.

Cotter, Jessie. *The Touch Film.* Available from many university film libraries as well as from the distributor, Sterling Films.

Dickmen, Irving. *Winning the Battle for Sex Education.* New York: SIECUS, 1982.

Education Commission of the States. "At Risk Youth" project, 1987. Available from the commission at 300 Lincoln Tower, 1860 Lincoln Street, Denver, CO 80295.

Garfinkel, Irwin, and Sara S. McLanahan. *Single Mothers and Their Children: A New American Dilemma.* Washington, DC: Urban Institute Press, 1986.

Kanerman, Shiela, and Alfred Kahn. *Mothers Alone: Strategies for a Time of Change.* Dover, MA: Auburn House, 1987.

Moynihan, Daniel Patrick. "Our Poorest Citizens—Children." In the *Congressional Record,* 100th Congress, 2nd Session, vol. 134, no. 4 (January 28, 1988), S308.

Rodgers, Harrell, Jr. *Poor Women, Poor Families: The Economic Plight of America's Female Households.* Armonk, NY: M. E. Sharpe, 1986.

Welfare Reform and Poverty. A special issue of *Focus,* vol. 11, no. 1 (Spring 1988). University of Wisconsin—Madison, Institute for Research on Poverty.

Wilson, William Julius. *The Truly Disadvantaged.* Chicago: University of Chicago Press, 1987.

A number of helpful resources are available from the Allan Guttmacher Institute, 11 Fifth Avenue, New York, NY 10003.

Case

More Light

Don Chandler read again the resolution presented by the Social Involvement Committee: "Shepherd Presbyterian Church will not exclude any active member from election or ordination to office on the basis of race, class, gender, marital status, or sexual orientation." He examined the faces of the other members of the church session (governing body) and heard the pastor, Elaine Campbell, saying, "You understand that passing this resolution will declare us to be a 'More Light' congregation, and that is the intent of the motion. Is there any discussion?"

Don thought back to where it all began. Shepherd Presbyterian was a small church of 130 mostly young, well-educated members, with a fair record of social ministry in Tucson. Two years earlier the congregation had elected Morris Wilson, who made no secret of his homosexuality, to an unexpired term on the nine-member session. It had been a contested election. Morris had been nominated from the floor, the election was postponed, and the session and pastor had led the congregation in six weeks of prayer and study on the issue of homosexuality and ordination. A 1978 decision of the denomination's general assembly (national governing body) offered "definitive guidance" that "self-affirmed, practicing homosexual persons" should not be ordained. That complicated the matter, but when it came to a vote at Shepherd Presbyterian, Morris was elected by a two-to-one margin. The pastor, therefore, ordained and installed him on the session. Shepherd's session informed the presbytery (the regional governing body) of their action, and there had been no adverse response.

The debate on Morris's election had been intense, but things seemed to settle down after his ordination. Don remembered how uncomfortable he had felt with the whole subject, opposed at first even to discussing it. But

This case was prepared by J. Shannon Webster. Copyright © The Case Study Institute. The names of all persons and places are disguised to protect the privacy of the persons involved in this situation.

after working with Morris for two years, things had changed. Morris had become a real Christian brother and a partner in the session's ministry. Don still felt uncomfortable about Morris's sexuality, but in talking with the pastor and others he had decided God did not want him to ground his actions in fear and prejudice.

During the second year of Morris's term, a few gay and lesbian people started to come to Shepherd Church, their numbers eventually reaching nine or ten. Three of them went through the New Member Class and joined the church. Don had been concerned, but later discovered when talking with them that several did not know Morris at all. He remembered one comment in particular: "We heard that this was a safe place to worship God."

It seemed to Don that the pastor felt a particular calling to care for the homosexuals attending Shepherd. He remembered a few sermons where Elaine mentioned gays and lesbians specifically as people who needed to be welcomed into the family of faith. The session began to discuss the possibility of declaring Shepherd a "More Light" congregation. In collecting information and ideas, they wrote to all the "More Light" churches in the denomination, receiving answers from most. Two representatives from the session of a Colorado church paid them a personal visit.

Don learned that "More Light" congregations were those which had in some way voted to include homosexuals as members eligible for election and ordination as church leaders, thereby ignoring the denomination's "guidance." During this time the Permanent Judicial Commission of the denomination ruled that the assembly's guidance was binding, and "More Light" decisions were unconstitutional. The ruling had heightened the discomfort and confusion on the part of the Shepherd session. Don learned that the ruling had been a particularly hurtful decision to the gays and lesbians in the congregation. One person in particular, Jake Owens, had been threatened by the ruling. Jake was an intelligent young architect who had come to the point that he would openly share his hurt and loneliness with members of the congregation. Now he shared his fears with Don. Jake had felt attacked and wounded by churches in the past and to Don he seemed vulnerable. A friendship had developed; Don felt paternal toward Jake. Some of Jake's pain had touched Don. He recalled Jake saying to him, "I'd hoped to become a full member of this church, but I've been here before. I'm afraid Campbell has led me out on the dance floor only to leave me there. How much control does the denomination have over our congregation?"

Then the lid blew off. It had come as a surprise to Don. The church had seemed stable until several people suddenly left. The pastor began to look weary, and over lunch one day she shared with Don that she had been making calls every night. The focus was the gay issue. "I know what the people opposed to the gay and lesbian members want," Elaine said, "but I want them to love each other and make room."

Don had received several phone calls from upset church members in recent weeks. Don was an official with the Red Cross and had credibility in the community and frequent contact with members of the church. He was a long-time member of Shepherd Presbyterian and was serving his fourth year on the session. People in the congregation, as well as other members of the session, seemed to give weight to his opinion and often sought him out to talk.

Peter Chapson had called him. "What's going to be next? The church is attacking everything I believe in. First, we can't call God 'Father' anymore. Then I find out that Elaine is working with illegal aliens. Now we're getting this gay business forced on us constantly. When they get up and use those words—gay and lesbian—they're describing sexual acts right in the worship service. How much am I supposed to put up with?"

Patty Becker had called to say she was concerned about her children. "This is not good modeling. The Bible calls homosexuality a sin. I have young children, and I don't want to teach them that it isn't. Look how unhappy those people are. We used to be a family-oriented church. But there's very little emphasis on children or family relationships anymore. Whatever happened to the Ten Commandments: Isn't there anything right or wrong anymore? Have we reached the point where anything you want to do is acceptable?"

Jane Weller told Don how upset she was because her husband was leaving the church. "I don't mind if the gay folks are there," she said. "We've always said we were an inclusive and pluralistic church. I don't want us to turn away anyone who loves Jesus. It's okay if they're there, if they just wouldn't be so vocal. When they become so visible, when you put labels on people like 'gay' and 'lesbian,' all it does is separate us into categories. If we hadn't made such an issue of it, we wouldn't have a problem, and John wouldn't be leaving the church."

Don considered the phone calls as the session turned to the "More Light" resolution. Then he thought about Jake Owens, at home anxious and concerned over the outcome of tonight's meeting. The discussion began in earnest. Morris Wilson sat as restrained and calm as usual.

Alberto Tarver, with occasional nervous glances at Morris, attacked the resolution at once. "We can't condone or accept homosexual activity in any way without flying in the face of biblical anthropology. The model in Genesis for full humanness is a partnership—male and female. In the New Testament the church is the Bride of Christ—same model. Paul classifies homosexuality with idolatry. Will we condone idolatry just to be nice?"

"Why take a position?" said Alice Royal. "Maybe there's another way. I can't agree with Alberto, but we've got a good thing going. Why mess it up by taking a formal vote and making public proclamations? This resolution won't affect our local ministry, and it will only split our congregation. We've reached out to the gay community and fully included them in our church life. The congregation will come around eventually. Meanwhile, we can always take 'no action' on this resolution."

Joan Wall, one of the session's newer members, spoke. "I might favor this," she said, "but first I would need to know how the gays in our congregation feel themselves. May I ask Morris a question? Is this resolution important to the gays? Will they understand it as a sign of care and support, or will it further set them apart and single them out? If we don't pass it, how hurt will they be? Will we lose them?"

Morris sat forward in his chair. "Everyone's different, of course. Yes, it would be affirming, a sign of solidarity. And passing this motion would serve to keep the sexuality issue from coming up every time there is an election. But I doubt anyone would leave if we fail to pass the resolution. Most gays and lesbians are accustomed to rejection and oppression and tend to accept them. In that event I would say most of us would be quite disappointed but not surprised."

"We ought to do the right thing," said Dennis Bench, "whatever the cost. I'm uncomfortable when the denomination asks us to exclude from ordained office one, and only one, group of people. It makes them second-class church members. And the apostle said a lot of different things. In his best moment, he said, 'We are all one in Christ Jesus and heirs of the promise.' Jesus called all kinds of different people to his side and empowered them to serve. If there is any idolatry here, it is thinking sexuality is so all-fired important it could make you unfit for ordination. We've said we are a pluralistic church and we are the Body of Christ. Who is outside God's call? Whom shall we exclude from full participation in Christ's Body?"

"We don't have that choice," Millie Stewart replied. "The General Assembly acted, and our highest court ruled on it. We're still a Presbyterian congregation. We are part of a connectional church. If you disagree with a law, you work to change it. You don't break it. You can always overturn the General Assembly. It's the only thing you can do."

Don felt Elaine Campbell's eyes fall on him. "You've been unusually quiet tonight, Don. Where do you think we should go on this?"

Commentary

More Light

The issue before Don and Shepherd Presbyterian involves choices on three distinct matters. Deciding how to respond to the More Light resolution will require prior decisions about biblically and theologically based moral assessments of homosexuality, about the purpose and shape of Christian ministry, and about the binding character of denominational guidelines. Before taking up each of those issues, it may be helpful first to explore briefly some new information on and perspectives toward homosexuality.

NEW LIGHT

Today most Christian denominations are divided over the issue of homosexuality, largely because the unequivocal condemnation of homosexuality which once characterized the Christian tradition has been challenged by recent social scientific research, by increased openness on the part of homosexuals, and by the resulting increase in knowledge and experience of homosexuals by heterosexuals. Though the social sciences have not by any means answered all the questions about homosexuality, there is a great deal of new light. One conclusion of research is that there is an important distinction between homosexual orientation and homosexual activity. Homosexual orientation refers to a predominate sexual attraction to persons of the same sex. Homosexual orientation for most homosexuals seems to be set at a very early age. It does not seem to be voluntary, often presenting itself to the individual as a fait accompli before the individual begins to reason. It would seem impossible for a homosexual orientation to be sinful if it is not chosen. Homosexual activity is sexual activity with a person of the same sex. To act sexually on the basis of homosexual orientation is a choice, just as to act sexually on the basis of heterosexual orientation is a choice.

There is a great deal of research data, some of it contradictory, on the mental health of sexually active homosexuals and the adequacy of relationships among them. In 1973 the American Psychiatric Association removed homosexuality from the category of mental disorders. The tentative conclusion of most researchers in the last two decades has been that, while social attitudes make it more difficult for an individual to accept a homosexual orientation than a heterosexual one, homosexuals who have fully accepted their orientation match adjusted heterosexuals in mental health and stability. One explanation for earlier classification of homosexuality as a mental disorder is that social attitudes kept gays and lesbians in the closet, thus ensuring that data on homosexuality would be based almost exclusively on those who required psychiatric help—the dysfunctionals.

There is no one clear cause for homosexuality. Some researchers believe there may be a genetic predisposition to homosexuality, a disposition which may be triggered by fetal or infancy experiences. Others assume that unknown environmental factors during early childhood cause homosexuality. Research on the childhoods of homosexuals and heterosexuals reveals no particular phenomenon as especially consequential for either homosexual or heterosexual development. While male homosexuals sometimes show a slightly higher rate of absent fathers, there is some debate about how significant this is, given that it is not the norm. Homosexuals do not differ from heterosexuals in the frequency of heterosexual dating during high school, though they enjoy it less. Despite widespread assumptions to the contrary, homosexuals are less likely than heterosexuals to have been seduced by older or more experienced partners in their initial sexual encounters.

Most therapists agree that exclusive homosexuality is extremely difficult, if not impossible, to change to fully functional heterosexuality, though bisexuals and persons of heterosexual orientation who turned to homosexual encounters due to sexual problems in heterosexual relationships can more often be brought to function fully as heterosexuals.

There is a great deal of variety in homosexual lifestyles. About half of lesbians and one quarter of gays are involved in primary relationships. About 11 percent of lesbians and 16 percent of gays seem little interested in either sexual activity or committed relationships. In between these extremes there are many patterns, and significant differences between lesbians and gay patterns. Lesbians are far more likely to have few partners (the majority have fewer than ten over a lifetime) and to be involved in exclusive relationships.

BIBLICAL AND THEOLOGICAL ASSESSMENTS
OF HOMOSEXUALITY

In general, the attitude of the Bible toward homosexuality is negative. Though it records no teaching of Jesus on homosexuality, the Bible does refer to homosexuality both directly and indirectly. The Mosaic law and St. Paul condemn homosexual practices. The Bible story most often cited in regard to homosexuality is the Genesis story of Sodom and Gomorrah. This story is not a good source because of its indirectness; it is not clear that the immorality for which God punishes the cities is homosexuality, for the event which precipitates the destruction is not homosexual intercourse per se, but the attempt to homosexually gang-rape strangers who should have been protected by hospitality.

The biblical story of David and Jonathan is often cited as one in which homosexuality is approved. Certainly the story suggests a level of intimacy and romance between two men which in our society might suggest a homosexual relationship. But homosexuality is not explicit in the story.

Many biblical scholars insist that condemnation of homosexuality by biblical writers should be understood within the context of those writers' times. Biblical writers did not recognize the existence of homosexual orientation and thus assumed that perpetrators of homosexuality acted out of a heterosexual orientation. Condemnation of homosexuality in Mosaic law probably was based on viewing it in terms of its common practice in pagan temple ritual, and St. Paul's condemnation may have referred to the Greek practice of pederasty, the sexual exploitation of young boys by older men. Since none of the biblical references gives any rationale for its stance on homosexuality, the biblical evidence alone is definitive only for those who view the Bible as a compilation of absolute divine laws.

Those who would not see biblical condemnations of homosexuality as determinative for Christian churches insist that they are not "dismissing the Bible" but merely responding to what they regard as stronger biblical imperatives, especially the command to love one's neighbor. Jesus' own ministry, they maintain, focused special concern on marginalized groups, on persons despised and excluded for aspects of their lives beyond their control.

Further, those who insist homosexuality is not sinful argue that the essence of sin is that it offends God. But this does not mean that the designation of what is sinful and what is not is, or could be, arbitrary on God's part. That which offends God does so because it runs counter to God's intentions for creation, because it destroys or impedes the formation of peaceful, loving, and just relationships within human community. When we forget this, and presume that designations of sin depend totally on the judgments of religious authorities who "represent" God, ignoring the need to test designations of sin by examining their consequences, we allow the concept of sin to be used to exploit.

This was the situation Jesus objected to in his own religious milieu. Priests, scribes, Pharisees, and almost all Jews understood sin as failure to obey the Mosaic law. The common people were understood as sinners by the fact of their ignorance of the law. The Pharisees in particular blamed the poor masses for Israel's status as a conquered, occupied nation; this situation was understood as God's punishment for the masses' failure to obey the many and varied prescriptions of the law.

Jesus strongly objected, and called into question this understanding of sin which characterized his age. He refused to treat those designated as sinners with the prescribed avoidance and disdain. He presented God as loving Father, not as legalistic judge, and lifted concern for persons above concern for law. When he said he had come not for the righteous but for sinners, he was referring to those whom the religious authorities regarded as sinners, those for whom the law offered no hope. Jesus did not prejudicially regard all these persons as unredeemable sinners, as did the purveyors of the law; his chief message to these despised masses was that they should have hope in the saving action of the Father who loved them. The sinful deeds, even of persons such as prostitutes and tax collectors, who were considered the worst of the public sinners, were not the focus of Jesus. For Jesus, the real mark of righteousness was concern for the poorest, weakest, and most despised, and the keynote of sin was turning one's back on those persons and, ultimately, on God. This is what the parable of the Good Samaritan is all about: the good person may be a heretical sinner (a Samaritan), and the priest who obeys every part of the ritual law and worships in the temple may be damned.

Viewed from within this framework, it would seem unreasonable to condemn homosexuality simply on the grounds of proclaiming that "it is sin." We have an obligation to evaluate homosexuality and ask whether and how it separates us from loving, just relationships with God and neighbor. It is not enough to say that "this is sin because St. Paul says so in 1 Corinthians 6:9-10 and 1 Timothy 1:9-10." We must question whether homosexuals per se belong in a list of sinners with idolaters, adulterers, drunkards, slanderers, swindlers, and thieves. Certainly some forms of homosexuality belong in such a list—those which include coercion, the molestation of children, or the use of others as objects—as do similar forms of heterosexuality. We must probe deeper than this. When we fail to probe the concrete reality of a behavior, but decide it is sinful because we are told so by authority we respect, we take the risk of imitating those who condemn the poor as sinners for their ignorance, the risk of wrongfully judging others as sinners.

Theological, as opposed to biblical, treatment of homosexuality has traditionally included two major objections to the practice. The following paragraphs will sketch those two major objections and also briefly present some of the questions and counter-positions that are frequently raised to the tradition's arguments. This would seem fair because these questions and counter-positions can help stir discussion and thought on the issue and because many are quick to accept the traditional assumptions on the matter without giving it deeper thought.

The first of the tradition's major objections to homosexuality is that it is nonprocreative. For those who view procreative possibility as a normative aspect of sexual activity, sometimes even as the only factor which legitimates sexual pleasure, homosexuality lacks moral validity. Within the Roman Catholic church, interpretations of natural law based on the causal relation between sexual intercourse and procreation have produced a rejection of any use of sexual faculties which is not open to the possibility of procreation within heterosexual marriage. This argument carries much less force among Protestants because they reject the interpretation of natural law on which the argument rests. Protestants do not understand procreation as a normative purpose of sexuality, as the acceptance of artificial contraception by Protestant churches demonstrates.

Further—as to the criterion of procreation—we can question whether it is really a definitive and consistent grounds for condemnation of homosexuality. Those who raise this question point out that Christian tradition has never denied marriage to the sterile, or to women past menopause. Thus it does not demand procreation as a criterion for all sexual acts. Nor does the Presbyterian church, or many other Christian churches, forbid the use of contraceptives. For those churches, then, sexual activity can be licit for heterosexuals even when it does not intend or cannot result in procreation. Working from these bases one can go on to argue that homosexuality should not be condemned on the grounds that it is not open to procreation. A variation on this position is that procreation should be normative only for heterosexuals, those for whom procreation is possible. For those with exclusively homosexual orientation, procreation would not be normative.

The second traditional reason for prohibiting homosexuality is the assumption that gender complementarity is an essential part of creation. The assumption that men and women were made essentially different and intended for each other so that together they become one whole has been prevalent in our history. Today it is much more difficult to make this case than in the past because in recent years it has been demonstrated that the vast majority of traits and roles that once were assumed to be sex-based are in fact learned, rather than inherent. There are very few traits and no roles which seem to be inherent in greater numbers of one sex than the other, and those few traits are exclusive to neither sex. Therefore, it would seem that in terms of traits and roles wholeness is not predicated upon "complementary" relations with a person of the opposite sex. And there are other questions we can raise about the notions that the interplay of complementary traits and behaviors is necessary for wholeness and that we gain access to that complementarity only in relations with persons of the opposite gender. One simple but key question in this regard is: Aren't persons of the same sex often more different from us in personality structure and behavior than members of the other sex? Doesn't such wholeness, then, come from our relations with persons of both genders? In short, if traits and roles are not specific to one gender, then where lies the "natural" complementarity? These and other questions and counter-positions are frequently raised by those who challenge the positions on homosexuality that have been traditionally held in the church, and as further research is done into homosexuality and into the positions of theology and scripture on the matter, the debate enters new levels and is enriched.

In summary, we can say that the morality of homosexuality is not easy to assess in clear-cut and simple terms. For many, it seems reasonable to assume that homosexuals should be bound to the same moral criteria for sexual activity to which heterosexuals are bound. Many others take a stance similar to that expressed in an October 1986 Vatican letter to the U.S. bishops, "On the Pastoral Care of Homosexual Persons," which affirmed the existing ban on homosexual sexual activity, and insisted that while homosexual orientation is not sinful per se, it is a disorder because it precedes and often leads to homosexual behavior. The letter urges bishops to discourage organizations of homosexuals on the grounds that, for persons with homosexual orientation, such organizations constitute situations of temptation, called "near occasions of sin."

Clearly, at this time much of the difficulty of assessing homosexuality swirls around the distinctions between homosexual orientation and activity. Until we can separate what is essential to homosexuality from the dysfunctional aspects which attach to it because of social rejection and stigmatization, it will be difficult to judge. Such a separation can occur only where there are no social sanctions against homosexuality.

CHRISTIAN MINISTRY

The three options presented to the session at Shepherd Presbyterian seem to represent different conceptions of what Christian ministry means. Comments of members about concern for family life, and the development of sexual orientation in their children, indicate that these people see ministers as role models, persons who represent to the community the shape of authentic Christian life. It is of course true that ministers do serve as role models. Yet both sociologically and theologically, there are limits to this modeling. Ministers are not the only models children have of leaders, of respected men and women, or even of religious men and women. In addition most children will be exposed to more than one minister, and will therefore not need to choose any one person as a model. Theologically, no single person or group can ever represent the fullness of Jesus Christ. We have only a sketch of three years in the life of the historical Jesus; our imitating Jesus in new times and circumstances will produce myriad models.

Those strongly opposed to the More Light resolution protest that homosexuals are a threat to family life, and we can assume that that protest is largely based on the belief that homosexuals are dangerous models that subvert normative family structure and the orientation of children. However, we know today that modeling is not a cause of homosexuality. Children raised by homosexuals are no more likely to become homosexual than those raised by heterosexuals. The real issue thus is not modeling, but rather it has to do with our definition of the normative family. Most pleas to protect family life today refer to the endangered two-parent nuclear family where the father works and the wife keeps house. However, this type of family accounts for less than 20 percent of the families in the United States. Thus the norm is a decided minority, and we can expect that in the future the vast majority of families will continue to diverge from the traditional norm regarding families.

Should the church retain this norm that implies that most North American families are somehow defective? Where did the norm originate? The Christian church was originally structured as a family precisely to substitute for the natural family, since the majority of the early members were estranged from their families by the fact of their Christianity. The early church was founded on those who were outside the predominating model of family; it is ironic that it is today proposed that those who are marginalized from the predominating model of family should be excluded from the church in order to protect nuclear families.

This leads to a final issue regarding Christian ministry, one already raised above. It is simply this: homosexuals are marginalized; a major feature of Jesus' project was solidarity with the marginalized. Thus it is important to consider what kind of church we are modeling when we work to exclude the marginalized from membership or ministry.

DENOMINATIONAL GUIDELINES

Beyond these issues that revolve around the models and roles of ministry and the purpose of ministry itself, the function of denominational guidelines in ministry is in question. Alice Royal's "No Action" proposal seems to presume that the purpose of ministry is to unify persons in an inclusive community and avoid conflicts that could disrupt that community. She argues that Morris's election despite the General Assembly's guidance to the contrary proved that Shepherd was inclusive, and that passing the More Light resolution would only create unnecessary dissension.

Those against the More Light resolution appear to invoke a vision of ministry which is based on witness to Christian law. The guidance of the General Assembly is understood by this group to set clear limits on local congregations' ministry. In addition, many of those opposed understand scripture as a legal source, and read its references to homosexuality as final. The role of the local congregation is to abide by the judgment of scripture and the governing body. Ministry in the local congregation then takes the shape of witnessing to these judgments.

Supporters of the More Light resolution insist there is a Christian obligation to demonstrate inclusiveness of gays and lesbians because they have been despised and excluded in church and community. This group seems to understand ministry in terms of personal and communal outreach to the marginalized.

It is probable that there are other motives animating some members of these groups, motives which are questionable from an ethical perspective. Individuals who oppose the resolution may be acting out of homophobia, an unreasoning fear and hatred of homosexuality. Homophobia is common in our society, and often prevents rational approaches to this issue. On the other hand, those supporting the resolution may be denying that sexuality is a moral concern; they may understand it as private, a matter of individual preference. Neither of these perspectives is acceptable. The first is prejudice; the second fails to understand that all aspects of our lives have moral dimensions and are subject to the Gospel.

The No Action supporters may be seeking to avoid conflict at any cost, out of an understanding of unity based on conflict avoidance. But there is no love without a willingness to risk conflict. Real unity arises from resolving conflicts, not from avoiding them after they are present. We have obligations both to reach out in love to those outside the community, and to protect the common life of the community. There is often a real tension between these two obligations, a tension which does not resolve itself without conflict.

One way to think about this issue is to try to reach an "original position" regarding what rules should be binding. If we all sat down to construct the rules for a society and were ignorant of what roles we would play in that society, we might see other sides of the issue. For example, if we did not know whether we would be male or female, straight or gay, white or black, president or migrant worker, we might be forced to stretch our imaginations when seeking to structure a just society. If we suddenly discovered a homosexual orientation in ourselves, would it change our stance?

Another way to approach the issue of who should minister would be to look to crisis situations. What would happen if this community at Shepherd were hit with a devastating tragedy? What if a number of the teenage children of the speakers at the session were killed or seriously injured together in an accident or in some other type of tragedy? The next weeks and months would be filled with desperate needs for comforting the grieving, and supplying emotional, material, and spiritual help to the families who had suffered the tragedy. The community would need to grapple with its faith in the light of this suffering of the innocent. If Morris were to demonstrate his ministerial gifts, and his fellow gays their Christian neighborliness in such a time, would that affect the situation? Would the crisis shed any light on the purpose and meaning of Christian ministry?

Finally, one of the problems with the guidelines from the General Assembly is that they only bar from election and ordination self-affirmed and practicing homosexuals. Covert homosexuals can still be elected and ordained, though research shows that these are the homosexuals most likely to have adjustment problems and relational dysfunctions. To the extent that such a guideline encourages homosexuals who desire service roles in the church to remain covert, it seems both to encourage dysfunction among homosexuals and to perpetuate homophobia through ignorance about homosexuals. The guideline penalizes homosexuals for honesty.

ENCOURAGING GROWTH

In conclusion, we can say that in regard to the morality of homosexuality, both Catholic and Protestant churches are torn by divisions both among theologians and between church teaching and beliefs of vocal members. Adopting the Catholic rejection of all sexual pleasure and activity outside those heterosexual marriages open to procreation would mandate that no Christian church could ordain anyone who identified himself or herself as an active homosexual. The decision would then be to reject the More Light resolution.

However, for those who accept either artificial contraception or sexual activity outside of marriage and who believe that "complementarity" can occur outside of heterosexual relations, it is entirely possible to reach some sort of provisional acceptance of forms of homosexuality which meet moral criteria for responsible sexual relationships, given the inconclusive nature of biblical and theological reflection on homosexuality, and the lack of definitively negative social science data. Whether the best method of moving in this direction is to pass the More Light resolution, or to take No Action while planning informational programs for Shepherd, is open to debate. No Action alone, without some clear attempt to create support for inclusion of homosexuals who desire to minister, seems a too easy way out. It could be understood as the choice for unity over justice and hard-won community.

Given the debate stirred over this issue at Shepherd Presbyterian and in our society and churches in general, it is clear that the issue is going to command and demand much more reflection and dialogue in the coming years.

ADDITIONAL RESOURCES

Bayer, R. *Homosexuality and American Psychiatry.* New York: Basic Books, 1981.

Boswell, John. *Christianity, Social Tolerance, and Homosexuality.* Chicago: University of Chicago Press, 1980.

Genovesi, Vincent J. *In Pursuit of Love: Catholic Morality and Human Sexuality.* Wilmington, DE: Michael Glazier, 1987.

Green, Ronald, ed. *Religion and Sexual Health.* Norwell, MA: Kluwer Academic Publishers, 1993.

McNeill, John J. *The Church and the Homosexual.* Kansas City: Sheed and Ward, 1976.

————. *Taking a Chance on God: Liberating Theology for Gays, Lesbians, and Their Lovers, Friends, and Families.* Boston: Beacon, 1988.

Nelson, James B. *Embodiment: An Approach to Sexuality and Christian Theology.* Minneapolis, MN: Augsburg, 1978.

————. *Between Two Gardens: Reflections on Sexuality and Religious Experience.* New York: Pilgrim, 1983.

————. *The Intimate Connection: Male Sexuality, Male Spirituality.* Philadelphia: Westminster, 1988.

Shannon, Thomas A., ed. *Bioethics.* 4th ed. Mahwah, NJ: Paulist Press, 1993.

Smith, Ralph F. *Heterosexism: An Ethical Challenge.* Albany, NY: SUNY Press, 1992.

Special Committee on Human Sexuality. *Presbyterians and Human Sexuality, 1991.* Louisville: Westminster, 1991.

Spong, John Selby. *Living in Sin? A Bishop Rethinks Human Sexuality.* San Francisco: Harper and Row, 1988.

PART VIII

LIFE AND DEATH

Case

Mary Gardner's
Fourth Pregnancy

Tom and Mary Gardner had planned their trip to Spain for more years than they could remember. They felt that at last their children, now twelve, eleven, and six, were old enough for them to be away for the four weeks. The children were all in school and Mary's mother, who had always been very close to the family, had flown up to "hold down the fort," as she put it. Westminster Church, where Tom had been pastor for the past ten years, supported the leave with a potluck supper and a monetary gift which made the trip possible.

As both Mary and Tom affirmed, the first week of the vacation was glorious. Thus when Mary began to experience nausea, she was especially annoyed. Her chagrin turned to stunned confusion when she suddenly suspected she was pregnant. Several days later Mary shared her anxiety with Tom, stressing that there was no definite confirmation of her pregnancy.

Tom almost immediately raised the possibility of an abortion. He then tried to clarify his reaction, stating that through his counseling of others and personal reflection he had come to believe that in some circumstances abortion could be a responsible action. Mary felt her feelings of trust and mutuality turning to anger. She stated that she was confused, even deeply disappointed, but added that she did not feel she could ever consider an abortion. Mary then added that they should wait until she had seen a doctor before they discussed it again.

After Mary and Tom left the large hospital in Barcelona with the "positive" medical report in their possession, she cried for nearly an hour. Tom comforted her and assured her that if she decided to have the baby they would surely be able to manage and would love this child as deeply as the others. He stressed that his primary concern was for her.

During the next week Mary became increasingly preoccupied with worrying about what she ought to do. She deeply respected Tom's judgment and tried to deal with his suggestion of an abortion. She remembered her pregnancy with Sara, who was much younger than the other children, and the real difficulty she had adjusting to Sara's arrival. Now with three children she felt that the quality of individual attention she considered essential for each child was already threatened by being spread too thin. And to be blatantly practical, Tom's salary covered the family needs only with careful budgeting. Another consideration was college education for three children, the first only a few years away. Furthermore, Mary had always wanted to support a child in a poor country through the church agency. She was sure this was a responsible use of family funds. Mary tried to pray about the decision, but found little help in prayer and reflection. Suddenly Mary declared to Tom that she would have an abortion while they were still in Spain, and it would all be over, with no one at home ever knowing.

Tom refused to consider this as an option, saying that they would be home in another week with a doctor they knew and trusted and that she might feel differently in her own home environment.

When the Gardners returned home, Mary immediately made an appointment with her doctor. Tom went with her to the office. Dr. Weiss also confirmed the pregnancy, then clearly outlined the pregnancy termination procedure at what he felt was the best clinic in the area. When Mary began to discuss the abortion, however, she was unable to control her crying and expressed the great doubts she really had about the decision.

She had discussed with Dr. Weiss the possibility of sterilization following Sara's birth, but at the last moment did not request it. Dr. Weiss told Mary that if she decided to have this baby, he would deliver it only on the condition that he perform a tubal ligation following the delivery. Upon Mary's insistence, he made an appointment for her at the clinic the next week and filled out the necessary papers, but told her that she could always call him if she changed her mind.

Mary had consciously avoided her close friends after returning from the trip. Her depression deepened. Although she and Tom were able to discuss the decision to some extent, they both decided they needed the help of an uninvolved party. Mary called Carl Jenkins, an experienced family counselor and good friend. He agreed to see them immediately.

In the counseling situation Mary was asked to express the uneasiness she was feeling. "Well," she said, "Tom asked me way back in Barcelona if I had the choice, would I want to be pregnant. I definitely would not. We tried to prevent that from happening as best we could. But now is the issue really what I want? How could God bless my consciously deciding to kill this new possibility of life growing in me? How could I believe that our other three children are beautiful, joyous gifts of God and that this one is just an accident?"

After a pause, she continued. "I guess another thing that is bothering me terribly is that I know my family, certain friends, and surely some members of the church could never understand my having an abortion. The idea of sharing this with our children is absolutely unthinkable. I just could never tell any of them. As a child, any time I felt I had something to hide from my family, I always knew I was doing something wrong. And now I feel really abandoned. Tom wants this to be my decision, but I don't see how I can make it. I see so many valid reasons for not having this child, but I'm unable to affirm that choice."

Carl Jenkins encouraged Tom to respond openly. "I'm pretty sensitive to the fact that Mary will sometimes look to me for answers," he replied. "If I make this decision for her, then it becomes fully my responsibility. I am very concerned about her choosing to have the abortion and then regretting it for the rest of her life. So I want to offer her love and support but not make the decision for her."

"But," prodded Carl, "isn't this your decision too? Does love and support for Mary not demand that you tell her how you feel about the abortion?"

Tom was slow to respond. "Well, if I really speak on the gut level, I want Mary to have the abortion, and that, of course, is what I blurted out when I learned about the pregnancy in Barcelona. We married right after college, and our first son was born a little less than a year later. For so many years she has been bound by her role in the home. I see a good part of this stemming from Mary's perception of herself as a responsible mother. In the past couple of years, though, as Sara has become more independent, I have been elated to watch Mary begin to find out who she really is, to start some projects for herself, and—this is admittedly selfish on my part—to have more time for me. All that had begun to happen in the years before Sara's birth, and I felt at that time Mary's return to the full-time mother role was a real sacrifice for her and in many ways was destructive to her personal growth. I love her too much to want that to happen again."

With Carl's encouragement Mary and Tom talked well into the evening about whether or not to have the child. When they rose to leave, Carl expressed his concern and love for them both and asked Mary, if she were willing, if she would call in a week to let him know what she had decided.

Commentary

Mary Gardner's Fourth Pregnancy

Mary Gardner, with her husband Tom, faces an agonizing decision: whether to terminate with medical assistance an unwanted pregnancy in its early stages. With her decision Mary enters fierce public debates over the definition of human life, the meaning of motherhood, the issue of who should control the abortion decision, and the role of sacrifice in Christian life. If this were not enough, she must also work through a crisis in her relationship with Tom.

In facing this decision Mary needs to investigate the facts about abortion in her society; the resources of scripture and Christian tradition regarding abortion, definitions of human life, and parenting roles; and the choices and roles open to her and other women in contemporary society.

FACTS ABOUT ABORTION IN THE UNITED STATES

Mary's option to elect to have a legal abortion is provided in the United States under that landmark 1973 Supreme Court decision, *Roe v. Wade*, which ruled that in the early stages of pregnancy prior to the viability of the fetus, the decision to have an abortion must be left to a woman and her doctor. Only after viability may the state prohibit abortion and then not when the woman's life is in danger. This ruling threw out the laws of most states enacted in the second half of the nineteenth century prohibiting abortion unless a physician could claim compelling medical indications. Slightly over 1.5 million legal abortions are performed in the United States each year. This number has risen from about 650,000 (200,000 legal and a best-guess 450,000 illegal) in 1970. The years immediately after the Supreme Court's *Roe v. Wade* decision saw a sharp increase in abortions, but the numbers have remained fairly constant since the early 1980s. Approximately one in three pregnancies ends in legal abortion, with over 90 percent of these being in the first trimester. Another 15 to 30 percent end in spontaneous abortion (miscarriage). For 35 percent of the women who obtain abortions, it is not their first.

Seventy-four percent of women who get abortions are unmarried. Over 26 percent are teenagers. Of the 1.1 million or so teens who get pregnant each year, 400,000, or about 36 percent, get abortions. The rate is much higher for teens from affluent families than it is for those from poor families, and among all women, the rate is higher for whites than for blacks. Another 15 percent of teens experience spontaneous abortions. Of the roughly 50 percent of teens who give birth an overwhelming number (more than 95 percent) keep their children.

Abortions are relatively safe for the woman involved. Only one woman in one hundred forty experiences complications. The maternal death rate due to abortion-related causes is 1.6 per 100,000. The figure for live births is 14 per 100,000.

Women seek abortions for many reasons. Contraceptive failure may have been a factor in this case, as Mary states that she and Tom "tried to prevent the pregnancy as best we could." Contraceptive failure is often cited by women seeking abortions.

In the United States, opinion polls indicate substantial acceptance of abortion in cases of rape, incest, danger to the mother's life and mental health, or a deformed fetus. Most polls indicate majority approval of the *Roe v. Wade* decision, although a few polls indicate a fairly even split. Disapproval of abortion is greatest when it is viewed as a form of family planning. Studies also indicate that for most women the decision to abort is an agonizing one that is often followed by feelings of guilt and sometimes regret.

SCRIPTURE AND TRADITION

At the outset of this exploration into Christian scripture and tradition on the issue, it might be good to stress here something that is obvious in the case: Mary and Tom are Protestants. Given the name of their church, it is quite likely that they are Presbyterians, or at least members of a church of the Reformed tradition. Most Reformed churches, in particular the Presbyterian Church (U.S.A.), do not dismiss abortion as an option. In what follows a number of positions are discussed, but in the end the perspective of Tom and Mary's religious community must be appreciated, for it is from within that perspective that Mary and Tom struggle with their decision.

It also might be helpful to point out at this point that as one surveys the Christian tradition, scripture, and the contemporary views and roles of women, five central issues keep rising to the fore. These are: the goodness of life, natural law, self-sacrifice, freedom, and the well-being of women. In the rest of this commentary these issues will come up again and again in varying combinations, and will be viewed from various perspectives. Students and instructors may find it helpful to keep these views in mind as a way of focusing dialogue and thought as they reflect upon the case.

Survey of the Tradition in General

Historically, abortion has not been a major issue in the Christian tradition. For centuries it was unsafe, children were considered an economic benefit, and underpopulation, not overpopulation, was the more common problem. The Bible itself has nothing directly to say about the morality of abortion. Although the Bible does not legislate about abortion, the Old Testament does indirectly provide some insight. Within the Mosaic law, fetal life was held to have value. Anyone who caused the loss of fetal life was held guilty and subject to sanctions. But the loss of fetal life was not of equal weight with the death of the already born. Responsibility for loss of fetal life was not considered murder, but a lesser crime for which payment in coin was to be made in restitution. It is perhaps most accurate to say that the Mosaic law regarded fetal life as potential human life and therefore of value. The New Testament does not directly deal with abortion or the value of fetal life.

The Christian theological tradition has been rather consistently against abortion since the early church. Some describe this as continuity within the tradition, but others make two points which undermine the value of the tradition's consistency. It may be useful at this point briefly to discuss those two points, for that discussion will help to bring the key issues in the debate into focus.

The first point is that although "abortion" has been denounced within the theological tradition of the church, until relatively recently the term was understood to describe the deliberate termination of pregnancy after the infusion of the soul (ensoulment), which was generally held to occur anywhere from six weeks to four months after conception. Thomas Aquinas, the Scholastic thinker whose philosophy and theology were made normative for the Catholic church in 1878, adapted Aristotle's teaching and held that God infused the soul into the fetus at forty days after conception for males, and eighty days after conception for females. In fact, popular folk practice for over a thousand years in Christian Europe until after the Reformation was to regard quickening (first fetal movement) as the definitive evidence of ensoulment, which was understood to be the cause of animation. Quickening usually occurs about the beginning of the fifth month. Until that time midwives regularly practiced various methods of terminating pregnancy, most of them dangerous.

Tradition carries great weight in theological and moral thought, especially when it has been consistent. This is appropriate because of the recognition that the Holy Spirit not only enlightens the present generation, but has also enlightened past Christian communities who passed this tradition on. But if all Christian communities condemned "abortion" but permitted termination of pregnancy for some time after conception, does this really constitute a consistent tradition for banning all termination of pregnancy?

A second issue raised concerning the critical views of the Christian tradition on abortion is the fact that at least some of the tradition's opposition to abortion rested upon false understandings about the nature of conception and the natures of men and women. Many of these beliefs are no longer accepted by Christians. In the past there was widespread agreement in the theological tradition that the primary purpose of marriage was procreation; that the only purpose of sexuality was procreation; that women as a sex had been created by God solely for motherhood (although they could renounce sexuality through religious vows of celibacy); and that a woman's sole contribution to the process of procreation was acceptance in her body of the self-contained seed of her husband, which it was her role to shelter and nourish. Christian churches have modified or abandoned all these beliefs.

Today Roman Catholics and almost all Protestant churches agree that procreation is but one purpose of marriage, and that the covenant love between the spouses is equally or more important. There is similar agreement that sexuality is not an evil or near-evil tolerated for the sake of children, and that sexual pleasure is itself legitimate and valuable for its role in bonding the spouses to each other in love. All Christian churches accept the findings of biological science regarding the equal genetic contribution of parents in conception. All Christian churches recognize the equality of women at least in theory, although there are tremendous divisions among and within denominations over whether women's nature is ordained for motherhood or is open to other roles which women might choose.

Those who support the ban on abortion are quick to point out that raising the above issues within a centuries-old tradition is not sufficient reason to reverse the ban. The heart of the issue is the preservation of human life. This is why much of the discussion within and outside the churches is about when in the process of gestation fetal life becomes human and should be protected by the law and about how much to emphasize the life of the fetus in relation to the life of the mother and others affected by a birth.

Finally, as regards the tradition as a whole, there is the matter of conscience. All churches, including the Catholic church, which takes a definite and rigorous stance on abortion, have long-standing teaching regarding the moral necessity of developing and following individual conscience. There are very complex relations among one's individual conscience, the teachings of one's church, and the values of the society in which one lives, but all churches agree that the conscience is a linchpin of the process of making important decisions.

This would mean that Mary should not make her decision based on the fact that the majority believe that abortion can be moral, or that those who approve abortion tend to be more educated and middle-class. Nor should she make her decision based solely on the teaching of her religious tradition or authority. She must consult all sources and judge for herself. Religious traditions can furnish arguments that Mary finds ultimately convincing. Sociological data about the opposing sides in the abortion debate can illuminate the reasons individuals are more influenced by some reasons than others. But it is never legitimate to shortcut the formation of personal conscience and blindly accept the conclusions of others.

Groundings of Catholic and Protestant Positions

In the ethical treatment of abortion in Christianity today there is great division that appears at a number of ethical levels. As was touched upon above, a primary division occurs over the definition and value given to fetal life.

The Roman Catholic church has defined all fetal life as full human life, while most Protestant churches are unwilling to define any specific point at which the fetus is fully human. Pope Pius IX in 1869 stipulated excommunication for abortion and fixed conception as the moment when the fetus, in technical terms at this stage a zygote, becomes a person, and, religiously speaking, ensoulment occurs. In so doing he closed the door on the hitherto prevailing view that distinguished between an animate and an inanimate fetus, that fixed the moment of ensoulment at quickening, and that by implication permitted abortion before quickening. Protestants in the United States, influenced like Catholics by more than a century of opposition to abortion by physicians attempting to take over the birthing process from "unscientific" and "untrained" female midwives, generally followed suit with the pope. From the 1870s to the 1960s the matter was settled and debate virtually closed.

Today the Catholic church's strong opposition to the practice of abortion as well as to allowing women the legal option of abortion is based primarily on two moral principles. The first is that according to natural law tradition, God's will is embedded in the patterns of creation and can be apprehended by the human mind. According to the Catholic interpretation of this tradition, a rational investigation of sexuality reveals that its innate purpose is twofold: procreation and mutual love. Therefore every sexual act must be open to the possibility of conception and should express love. Anything which interferes with either thwarts God's intent. This perspective has been the backbone of Roman Catholic proscription of both abortion and artificial contraception. It is for this reason that abortion is understood as a sexual sin, as well as a form of murder.

The second moral principle used by the Catholic church in its rejection of abortion is one which absolutely forbids the direct taking of innocent life. This is not a prohibition against all taking of life. Not all life is innocent. It is not forbidden for the state to take the life of the guilty in capital punishment, or for soldiers to kill other soldiers who are presumed to be trying to kill them, or for anyone to kill in defense of self or others under attack. Further, under this principle it is possible that one would not be held responsible for killing an innocent, if that killing is indirect. For example, indirect abortions can be permitted under this principle. If a pregnant woman has a cancerous uterus, a hysterectomy to remove the cancerous uterus is permitted if the delay until delivery poses a threat to her life. The purpose of the hysterectomy is to remove the diseased body part that threatens the woman's life. The loss of the life of the fetus is indirect and not intended, for the hysterectomy would have been performed had she been pregnant or not.

Most Protestants are not convinced by these Catholic arguments because they do not share Catholic biological interpretations of natural law or Catholic assumptions about full human life existing from conception. While virtually all Protestants accept the ban on direct taking of innocent life, many deny that fetal life is fully human and therefore protected by the ban. Nor have Protestants relied on natural law as a moral grounding because historically Protestant churches have understood the Fall to have corrupted human reason to such an extent that humans are without any natural capacity to comprehend God's will, and are instead dependent on God's grace for understanding.

Today natural law is receiving more Protestant attention than in the past largely because of its role in civil morality. But the biologically based model of natural law used by the Catholic church is rejected in favor of models which draw upon other human capacities as well. For example, one might find that a number of types of actions and goals—preservation of human life by avoiding overpopulation or the use of abortion when family income is already minimal or a mother's health is in danger—rest on equally compelling interpretations of natural law, in that God gave human beings the desire to preserve the species with dignity.

A further problem for Mary in this perspective is the finiteness of human rationality. God's will can be intentionally or unintentionally misread and is always discovered through the eyes of a specific culture. What in one culture or historical period seems "natural" or clear does not in others. There is no way to decide what is natural short of imposing authority. Mary is caught in this dilemma as she struggles between the perceptions that "our children are beautiful, joyous gifts of God" and "this one is just an accident."

CONTEMPORARY ATTITUDES TOWARD WOMEN AND MOTHERHOOD

Other religious arguments which favor or condemn abortion depend heavily upon the two issues discussed above—whether the fetus is fully human life and whether God's will can be determined through investigation of biological processes. The way in which these two issues are interpreted not only shapes much of the basis for the way in which abortion is viewed, but also affects our view of motherhood and the role of women in our society. As stated above, in Christianity much debate around the issue of abortion focuses upon nuances and inconsistencies in the Christian tradition's position on the nature of fetal life. Those positions and debates have been spelled out in the previous sections because they form part of the backdrop of and resources for Mary and Tom's decision. Without losing sight of those issues, this section will shift the focus more to the varying conceptions of women and motherhood that are powerful aspects of Mary's context as she strives to reach a decision about her pregnancy. A cornerstone in the debate about motherhood and women's roles is the norm of well-being, with its attendant norms of self-sacrifice and self-development, freedom, and justice and equality. The emphasis in this section is upon the perspective that stresses freedom, justice, self-development, and equality for women. The reasons for emphasizing this perspective are that it has been a key catalyst for the current debates about abortion and is a major element in the strains in Tom and Mary's relationship.

Well-being

At the heart of the clash over abortion and what constitutes the well-being of women are two quite different views of motherhood and the role of women in society. Mary Gardner is caught between these views, and her struggle runs much deeper than the decision of whether or not to abort. It involves how she understands herself as a woman, wife, and mother. There is, of course, a great variety of views on the issues of women's role and what constitutes their well-being. Without doing too much injustice to these views and for the sake of clarity and discussion, these many views will be arranged under two opposing headings, the "traditional view" and what is called a "new conception."

The traditional view stresses that a woman's well-being is fulfilled through her service to her children and husband. Such service is what truly frees. This traditional view is held by many of the most ardent opponents of legalized abortion. In part rooted in the natural law position discussed above, their view is that there are intrinsic differences between men and women, differences which lead to dissimilar roles. Men work in paid jobs and provide for women whose primary role is child bearing and rearing. Male leadership, exercised in a benevolent way, is considered normal and right. Freedom for women to work outside the home or to abort is of little practical importance and may even be a threat since it appears to upset the natural pattern and downgrade traditional roles. In sum, at one end of the spectrum on the views of what constitutes women's well-being is the position which stresses service to children and husband, and self-sacrifice. The structure of Mary and Tom's marriage seems to reflect this traditional view, which held sway until quite recently.

Opposed to the above position is a view which, in essence, holds that women's well-being is fostered through equality with men and through the freedom to make choices about a host of issues—from careers to mother-hood to the structure of relationships between men and women. Those who advocate this position hold that the context of women's lives today is radically different from the context in which the traditional view of women's roles developed. They point out that, for instance, dramatic changes are now occurring in the relation between men and women, changes partially indicated by the great increase of women in the work force. In 1970, 43 percent of all women age sixteen or over were in the work force. By 1980 that figure had increased to over 50 percent, and in 1990 to 57.5 percent. In 1947, 87 percent of all men over sixteen were in the work force; in 1990, 76 percent. This is not a mere change in numbers. This shift reflects a new self-conception of women as free and equal partners in society capable of doing what men do, and having the right to pursue nontraditional roles.

This new conception of women, the dominant one among those who advocate women having a choice about abortion, sees men and women as substantially equal. Traditional roles are seen as reflecting not the order of nature but the ideology of a male-dominated society. The combination of male domination and oppressive ideology inhibits the full development and well-being of women. Being a mother is important, and many will elect it, but it is not the only role for women. In this view women must have choices about service and sacrifice, two central Christian affirmations it would do well to explore in greater depth before moving on to the central issues of choice and equality.

Self-sacrifice

Within the Christian tradition there are various views of self-sacrifice, all largely stemming from interpretations of the words and actions of Jesus. One powerful image that is frequently raised here is that of Jesus on the cross and the implied mandate to sacrifice the self on behalf of others. In very broad terms, we can say that many who stress this interpretation of Jesus urge a woman such as Mary to choose against having an abortion and to opt for sacrifice for others—her family, husband, and the fetus she carries. But here the discussion returns to a key question raised above—Is the fetus fully human? Does it constitute one of the "others" for whom Mary is called to sacrifice?

There are also questions about the understanding of self-sacrifice. Counter to the more traditional position is one that stresses a different interpretation of Jesus' sacrifice on the cross. In this interpretation Jesus did not go to the cross for the sake of self-sacrifice, but in order to bring others a full and new life in the realm he announced. Self-sacrifice was a means, not an end, the end being entrance into the realm of God. Thus what is normative is bringing others to this realm. Still, self-sacrifice, or, in less extreme terms, service to others, is often a good means to this end, so much so that in certain circumstances it is legitimately normative. The legitimacy of self-sacrifice depends on whether there is an integrated self to sacrifice or give in service freely. The integrated self is a gift given by God through

Jesus Christ and received in mutual love and community. It cannot be commanded or exhorted from individuals who are in a state of disintegration due to oppressive forces and repressive ideologies. These individuals literally have no self to give. This is crucial. Calling for self-sacrifice from someone without an integrated self—for example a slave or an abused and passive woman—is not a call to new life but to further slavery and oppression because it does not produce but in fact impedes the mutual love and community to which the realm of God calls us.

These cross-currents over self-sacrifice are affecting Mary and the decision she faces. Mary must carefully evaluate her personal situation. She must try to understand what kind of relationship she and the child will have and whether it ultimately will be one that will support the mutual growth of each. She must, in short, try to come to conclusions about the relative values of fetal life, her life and personal choices and development, and the life within the communities of which she is a part.

Freedom of Choice and Equality for Women

As has been discussed, the decisions Mary faces are in large measure left to her conscience. Hers is the freedom to exercise conscience, although the responsible use of conscience means consulting the wisdom available from the larger community, including her husband, her religious tradition, and her society. Mary must decide whether the use of her freedom to abort in this situation is a legitimate exercise of her power to control her own body or a misuse of her power to control her body by denying life to the fetus she carries.

Freedom is part of the biblically-based understanding of justice which has evolved in Western thought. In the United States the legal system provides for individual freedom unless democratically determined laws are broken. The norm of freedom places the burden of proof on those who would restrict the control that Mary and other women have over their bodies. Opponents of legalized abortion are convinced they have satisfied this burden. They argue that just as society rightly denies freedom to a murderer, so it should deny a woman the right to abort a fetus, which in their view has full rights as a person. Proponents of legalized abortion counter by denying full legal status to fetal life in the early stages of pregnancy and point to the injustice of the state or any other body compelling Mary to bear a child. They argue that women should have the freedom to control conception in order to control their bodies and their lives. At issue is whether the power to control conception includes the right to abort a fetus, and whether this power to control fertility is essential to women's well-being.

Obviously, this notion of the right to control one's own body is a key element in the position that sees abortion as an option. Those who hold this position argue that in order for women to take control of their lives and to construct a meaningful life plan, they must have the capacity to break the link between sex and procreation. Otherwise their bodies, or whoever controls their bodies, will control them, and pregnancy will interrupt all possible plans except mothering. Statistically effective contraceptives and safe, affordable abortions make breaking the link possible for the first time in history. Tom seems to be working out of an acceptance of this view, one he hopes Mary will share.

For many who support choice, the right to choose is more than just a symbol of the new-found freedom and equality of women. For those who hold this view the freedom to choose is fundamental to all other justice-claims of women. They argue that without the right to choose contraception and ultimately abortion—the last resort in contraception—women will be discriminated against. Employers, for example, will be reluctant to train women for or employ them in significant positions because those employers will anticipate that women will be in and out of the work force. There can be no equality in the work place when women and men function under the assumption that a woman's occupation will be subordinated to each and every pregnancy.

Those who hold this view project that if the abortion choice is eliminated, women's vocational options will narrow as women will have no certain method of controlling fertility. In effect the traditional view of motherhood will be forced on women. This would be an injustice to women, an injustice compounded by the male domination of legislatures and the medical profession. Men would make the decisions and women would suffer the consequences. In the case study there is a taste of this in the arrogance of the doctor who demands sterilization.

In essence, then, those who stand for women's choice in abortion argue that for women the capacity to choose is the capacity to gain equality, new identities, and new avenues for vocation. The very well-being of women is at stake and society has a moral obligation to further this well-being.

Finally, part of the well-being of women will include openness to the growth possibilities inherent in child rearing and housekeeping. If women are to be free to choose how to pursue their lives, then obviously they must be free to choose child rearing and homemaking as focal points of their lives. It does no one good to draw the options as being between passive, dull housewives and active, responsible career women. There are many paths between the stereotypes.

Like many women, Mary seems caught between her socialization, which led her to understand herself as first wife and mother and then secondarily a person who could plan a life for herself, and the contemporary message to women—sketched in the preceding paragraphs—that they are to evaluate themselves based on their own growth and achievements and not on their fulfillment of ascribed roles. But society gives little help to women caught between the demands of both views of women and their accompanying roles. For Mary this is not merely a choice between self and child, but a forced choice between two conflicting selves that she would like to integrate, but cannot.

THE CHOICE

The Mosaic view that regarded fetal life as potentially human and therefore of value, the norm of the goodness of life, and considerations of legitimate self-sacrifice would lead Mary Gardner in the direction of preserving the fetus. The norm of freedom makes her morally responsible for the decision. She must also consider the well-being of her family, her own circumstances, her new-found freedom, and who she is as a mother and a woman in society. While the family finances are strained, they are not impossible, and the child would enter a loving family.

Although Tom sees Mary's freedom from the restrictions of motherhood as a movement toward growth, Mary may not. Her identity may be so bound to the traditional role of motherhood that an abortion, indeed the view which allows choice in abortion, may be read by Mary as "pro-self." The sense of selfishness may so violate her identity as a care giver that it seems a denial of the invitation to fulfillment in the role of mother.

Mary speaks of a child, not a fetus. Since she sees her three children as "gifts of God," abortion might mean for her the destruction of God's good creation. Mary keeps her pregnancy a secret from almost everyone in her life. Her action implies that an abortion would be something "wrong," at least for her, and leave her with an immense burden of guilt. Her depression and emotional instability suggest she already feels this burden.

If abortion may be read as too "pro-self," then in contrast the decision to go to term and reject abortion may seem to her too "pro-birth." The norm of self-giving and self-sacrifice may be perceived as an alien demand forcing her to negate herself endlessly for child bearing and rearing.

In light of this, Tom favors an abortion. But in the early going he was not of much help to Mary. His insensitive announcement of his preference while still in Spain shocked Mary and is partially responsible for the alienation they both feel. In counseling, however, Tom expresses much greater sensitivity for Mary's growth as a person, which he feels will be enhanced if she does not have another child. Still, he offers her only the abortion option to achieve personal growth. The case does not reveal everything about Tom and Mary's discussion of the matter, but based on the information in the case it is clear that Tom does not appear ready to sacrifice and take on more child care if Mary decides to have the child. This apparent unwillingness to sacrifice suggests he wants what is best for Mary, but only if there is no cost for him.

For her part, Mary expresses concern for the quality of life of her three children already born, as well as for needy children in her global community. The suffering of children worldwide makes its claim even on the Gardners' meager resources.

Beyond these considerations there are apparently strong internal pressures for Mary to be a loving wife who pleases her husband. Tom is rightly concerned that these pressures could lead Mary to a decision based on what he wants and eventually increase the alienation between them.

Rather than facing alone an impossible choice between the potential life within her and her own and her family's needs, Mary may be freed by considering her interdependence with other persons. She might ask how her decision would enhance not only her well-being and that of her immediate family, but the well-being of those in the wider community. Mary's freedom may come in how she and Tom make the decision. She has an opportunity to help others understand the dilemma of an unwanted pregnancy and simultaneously to draw on the considerable resources of a community in making decisions and mediating care.

Opening to the community has its costs, however, and while participation in community is essential to wholeness, so is a place apart. Somehow Tom and Mary will have to balance these needs and come to a decision which mends their relationship and, above all else, makes available God's love and new life.

Whatever the decision, Mary's present depression and the seeming choice between guilt over a decision to abort and resentful surrender to having another child must be faced. Presumably both Tom and Mary "know" the healing power of forgiveness which comes through faith in Jesus Christ. The task will be to unite head and heart so that this power can do its work.

ADDITIONAL RESOURCES

Burtchaell, James Tunstead, ed. *Abortion Parley.* Kansas City: Andrews and McNeel, 1980.

Frochock, Fred M. *Abortion.* Westport, CT: Greenwood Press, 1983.

Gilligan, Carol. *In a Different Voice: Psychological Theory and Women's Development.* Cambridge, MA: Harvard University Press, 1982.

Harrison, Beverly Wildung. *Our Right To Choose.* Boston: Beacon Press, 1983.

Jung, Patricia Beattie, and Thomas A. Shannon, eds. *Abortion and Catholicism: The American Debate.* New York: Crossroad, 1988.

Luker, Kristin. *Abortion and the Politics of Motherhood.* Berkeley, CA: University of California Press, 1984.

Rubin, Eva R. *Abortion, Politics, and the Courts: Roe v. Wade and Its Aftermath.* Westport, CT: Greenwood Press, 1982.

Case

A Good Death for Gleason?

Even a year later, C. J. wondered if they had made the right decision. The death of his father, Gleason, had not been an easy one. C. J. reluctantly rehearsed in his mind the options the family had considered. Should they have pressed the physician harder on the appropriateness and availability of the lifesaving operation that was never offered to his father or the family? Had the physician's refusal to consider a lethal injection to end his father's life before the inevitable last few weeks of horrible deterioration and suffering really been humane? If the family had been more courageous, would they have found someone to help Gleason out of his misery? Would more effective pain control have made a critical difference? Overshadowing everything in C. J.'s mind was a lingering uneasiness over the way the family had decided to discontinue aggressive treatment without explicitly involving his father in the decision.

C. J. resented having to rehash these wrenching choices, especially at the request of his pastor. Where had his pastor been when the family needed guidance to make the right decision in the first place? Reverend Julius Wilson had come to the hospital but kept his distance whenever critical choices had to be made. They seemed to make him uncomfortable. Reverend Wilson was generally regarded as a wonderful pastor, a judgment C. J. would have heartily affirmed over a year ago. But now C. J. was not so sure what to think.

The pastor's question when they had passed on the street that morning had really caught C. J. by surprise. Reverend Wilson had noted that tomorrow was the Fourth of July, exactly a year after the fateful meeting with C. J.'s family. He wondered how C. J. felt in hindsight about the decisions that had been made at that meeting. He asked C. J. to stop by his office to talk after the church worship service the next day. C. J. was not sure if he wanted to do that. What would he say?

His father's death had been quite an ordeal. But then, so had his father's life. Born to poor African-American parents in the rural south, Gleason had headed north before completing high school. Working two low-paying jobs in the inner-city of Chicago had not been easy for Gleason, but C. J. never recalled his father complaining. Gleason was proud that he had been able to raise three children and that his wife, Cassie, never had to work full-time outside the home. Theirs was a blessed family in a neighborhood where two-parent families, not to mention employed fathers, were far from the norm. Blessed indeed, that is, until the illness.

Gleason had just turned sixty-five, amid kidding by friends and family alike that he was an old man now, when he began to feel the pains in his chest. He did not talk about them with the family, but C. J. could see that something was not right with his father. As the eldest of three children, C. J. felt a special sense of responsibility for his aging parents. He was reluctant, however, to press his father too aggressively when Gleason denied feeling poorly. It was not until later that C. J. learned from the doctor how much pain his father had endured before collapsing at work and being rushed to the hospital.

Gleason had revived quickly, and some medication had been prescribed for a heart problem that Gleason had a hard time understanding. C. J. doubted in hindsight that his father had taken the medication. The disease got rapidly worse. Gleason's lungs as well as his heart were soon seriously compromised. Upon hospitalization, Gleason was found to have a form of pneumonia that proved resistant to treatment. Each time he was progressively weaker after the respirator was removed, and each treatment was less effective than the previous one in combating the pneumonia. Gradually the disease did such damage that Gleason obviously was experiencing frequent chest pain. Even now, C. J. could clearly recall the sight of his father's deteriorating body.

In light of Gleason's worsening condition and the family's evident concern, Gleason's doctor, Angela Perkins, called a meeting to discuss continued treatment. C. J. could picture the circular table as if it were yesterday. He sat wedged between Dr. Perkins and his mother, Cassie, with his brother, Jesse, and his sister, Roberta, on his mother's other side, and Reverend Wilson leaning back in his chair between C. J.'s sister and the doctor. The decision belonged to someone else, C. J. thought, and he felt awkward being thrust into the middle of the discussion.

Who was he to decide whether his father was to live or die? Did they think he was God or something? If somebody had to play that role, the pastor clearly was the man for the job. Or why did the doctor not just tell them what to do? After all, was that not her job? C. J. felt totally unprepared to say anything. Certainly his education in the public school system had not equipped him for this day. Nor had over four decades at Ebenezer

Baptist Church. Or perhaps that was going too far. He did have a curious sense of support as he inwardly cried out to God without knowing the words to use. "Leaning on the everlasting arms," they would have called it at Ebenezer. But that did not answer the questions at hand.

Dr. Perkins explained to the group her inability to arrest the progress of the heart and lung deterioration. When asked by Jesse if a heart or heart-lung transplant he had heard about on TV had been considered at any point in the course of the treatment, the doctor indicated that Gleason was not a good transplantation candidate "for a variety of medical, economic, and social reasons." What did the doctor mean by that? C. J. had wondered after the meeting. Everyone had been so fixated on what the doctor was going to recommend, he realized, that they had not wanted to interrupt her explanation. Now in hindsight the question seemed much clearer and more imposing: Had there, after all, been a way available to save his father's life? And what had she meant by "social reasons?" His father's race? Age? Value to society? Spared from addressing that issue by the family's passivity, the doctor instead went on to help the family members envision the suffering that both they and Gleason would experience during Gleason's final weeks. Reverend Wilson confirmed that what she was saying was accurate.

At this point two questions arose. Should Gleason be resuscitated if his heart stopped? Should he be placed on a respirator again if his lungs deteriorated further? Explaining that these actions would extend Gleason's life a week or two at most, Dr. Perkins recommended "passive involvement," that is, no treatment except to provide comfort care, should the need arise for such emergency actions.

Cassie turned to Reverend Wilson to ask what she should do. While the pastor seemed to share the burden of her sorrow, he told her it was her decision to make, She then turned to her children. C. J. and Jesse suggested that the doctor knew best what to do. C. J. was shocked, though, by what his sister had to say. Roberta was so concerned by the suffering that lay ahead and by the mounting medical bills that she inquired about the possibility of physician-assisted suicide or even so-called "active euthanasia," which she understood to mean painlessly inducing her father's death right away for his and the family's sake. While Dr. Perkins acknowledged that either could easily be accomplished, using an overdose of the right pills or intravenous potassium chloride, she refused to consider these options. So Cassie, obviously upset, told Dr. Perkins to follow the course of passive involvement she had suggested.

At the same meeting, C. J. recalled, the doctor, family, and pastor had also considered whether to discuss the preferred course of passive involvement with Gleason himself. Gleason had consistently maintained his determination to overcome his illness. Cassie in particular felt that Gleason would maintain this attitude to the end for the family's as well as his own sake, but she added that Gleason would in fact appreciate the doctor deciding not to prolong the dying process. Everyone present agreed. So it was decided not to discuss the matter with Gleason. The doctor proceeded to order that no emergency measures be taken to maintain Gleason's life and that only standard comfort care be provided.

The decision had made things easier for the family at first. No one wanted to face Gleason's impending death. Still C. J. began to sense a distance between the family and his father during the days that followed. Had his father really known he was dying without being told? Would his dying days have been better if he and the family could have spoken together freely of his coming death and the end-of-life treatment decisions that needed to be made? Looking back a year later, C. J. felt less comfortable than he had at the time with the family's decision not to discuss the predicament with his father.

Shortly after this family meeting with the doctor and pastor, Gleason's condition began to deteriorate rapidly. Three days following the meeting, his heart stopped beating. No attempt was made to revive him. During Gleason's final days, C. J. and the rest of the family were increasingly disturbed by the sight of him wasting away. Although he was receiving pain medication, the doctor's refusal to give him more than the "customary" dosage in times of particularly great pain frustrated Gleason and his family. While no steps were taken to speed up Gleason's death, even C. J. had begun to wonder at the last if something should have been done to bring a quicker end to his father's suffering.

As he thought about talking with Reverend Wilson the next day, C. J. realized that he had more questions and uncertainty now than he had over a year ago. He felt reluctant to admit such wavering over as important a matter as how his own father's death had been handled. He was worried about admitting to Reverend Wilson that he might have concurred in a wrong decision. But what about Reverend Wilson himself? Had he not concurred by his lack of suggesting any alternatives? Was it possible that a year ago Reverend Wilson had not thought these issues through any more than C. J. had? Had the pastor done any further thinking since then? Surely the Bible from which Reverend Wilson so regularly preached must have plenty to say about matters of life and death. C. J. began to wonder if a talk with Reverend Wilson tomorrow might not be so bad an idea after all.

Commentary

A Good Death for Gleason?

C. J.'s reflection on the process around the death of his father, Gleason, during the previous year includes a number of different questions. There are questions concerning whether the treatment option chosen was adequate; whether Gleason should have been included in the decision making about his treatment; what the doctor meant when she said that Gleason was not a good candidate for heart-lung transplantation for a variety of medical, economic, and social reasons; why Gleason was not sufficiently medicated against pain, and why Reverend Wilson kept such a low profile during the ordeal but now wanted to talk about the decisions made a year ago. While it might initially seem that the central issue is whether or not the family was right in deciding for only standard comfort care rather than more aggressive measures to prolong life, the even more difficult issue is not what the family decided, but the exclusion of Gleason from the decision making.

RESPECT FOR LIFE

The biblical tradition tells us that life is a gift from God to be valued and respected. The Old Testament depicts the value of life not in terms of enduring biological functions, but in terms of participation within a human community. Accordingly, individuals who constituted a threat to the community were executed (murderers) or exiled (lepers) under the Mosaic law. In Genesis, the punishment for the murder of Abel was exile for Cain. He was forced to wander the face of the earth, a punishment considered in Israel to be increased, not diminished, by God's vow that no one would kill him to end his exile. Individual physical life is not absolutely valuable; for the Old Testament, the welfare of the human community comes first. Even so, the Old Testament gives no warrant for taking or shortening innocent life in the interest of community well-being.

The New Testament contains no warrants for taking life at all, but only for sacrificing one's life in the interests of others. The miracles that Jesus performed as signs of the coming realm of God functioned to restore community. The significance of the healing miracles was not merely the alleviation of physical ills but the restoration of the sick to the community.

The lepers and the woman with the discharge were unclean and therefore excluded from community. Those possessed by demons, the paralytics—the chronically ill in general—were also excluded from participation in the life of the community until healed by Jesus.

Scripture does not tell us at what cost life should be maintained. Virtually all Christian theological traditions forbid Roberta's suggestion of a lethal injection for Gleason. Roberta was concerned about the extension of suffering for the family as well as for Gleason and about the mounting medical bills. Many theologians would suggest that to directly kill a person in order to prevent high hospital bills or to save others from suffering an extended mourning process clearly violates not only the letter of "Thou shalt not kill," but also the spirit. Roberta's suggestion for active involvement is not separated from the option for passive involvement by the consequences, for in both options Gleason dies. Nor is the real difference in the act itself, either an act of commission or an act of omission. While there may be some moral difference between denying a seriously ill person a readily available antibiotic that would cure her and choking her to death, most people would agree that both are serious sins against the life and dignity of the neighbor.

There seems to be a major difference, however, between injecting a dying person with poison and not putting him on a respirator which could prolong his death for only a week or two. The primary difference is one of directness and indirectness. If the doctor had agreed to Roberta's suggestion, the direct cause of Gleason's death would have been poison. With passive involvement, Gleason dies of diseased heart and lungs—just as he would have with a decision for more aggressive treatment.

Respect for life prohibits humans from using other human lives as means to ends. We cannot decide to directly end lives because they are in some ways a drain on the community, though amid scarce resources we may have to decide who gets adequate resources and who does not. While most religious traditions allow killing in self-defense, the threat must be an immediate threat to one's life in order to justify taking another's life. Gleason is no threat to anyone's life.

GOD AND DEATH

The authority to claim innocent lives directly has been understood in the Christian tradition as delegated by God to natural processes in creation. While it is common to hear Christians refer to death as God's prerogative, as if God decides on the moment and kind of death for each of us, Christian theological tradition is somewhat more nuanced and complex on this issue. In the Book of Job, God taunts Job for questioning God about Job's misfortunes:

Where were you when I laid the foundation of the earth? Tell me, if you have understanding. Who determined its measurements—surely you know! . . . Who shut in the sea with doors, when it burst forth from the womb; when I made clouds its garment and thick darkness its swaddling band, and prescribed bounds for it, and set bars and doors, and said, "Thus far shall you come, and no farther, and here shall your proud waves be stayed?" (Job 38:4-11)

God emphasizes here the distinction between creator and created. But it is one thing to assert that God has the *power* to control life and death. It is another to insist that God consciously and deliberately decides the moment and kind of death for each of us. To say this makes God the puppeteer controlling the strings of the drunken driver, the terrorist bomber, the sadistic kidnapper. A God who chooses to kill millions of innocents in events like the Holocaust is not the divine Father of whom Jesus said:

And I tell you, ask, and it shall be given to you; seek and you will find; knock and it shall be opened to you. For everyone who asks receives, and he who seeks finds, and to him who knocks it will be opened. What father among you if his son asks for a fish, gives him a serpent instead; or if he asks for an egg, will give him a scorpion. If you then, who are evil, know how to give good gifts to your children, how much more will the Heavenly Father give the Holy Spirit to those who ask Him! (Luke 11: 9-13)

God explained to Job that within the process of divine creation the world was set in motion. God is responsible for the pattern in creation. But creation, both human and non-human, is gifted with freedom and dynamism which reflect God's own nature. That freedom and dynamism in creation determine specific events in the world. God gives the example of the ostrich, who lays its egg out in the open where it may be crushed (Job 39:13-18). When it is crushed, that is not God's decision, though it was God's gift of freedom to the ostrich that allowed the egg to be crushed.

God's presence in our world does not take the form of a puppeteer who controls the strings of events and occurrences. God's presence in our lives takes the form of the Holy Spirit, who supports and comforts, strengthens and energizes us to resist evil and tragedy. In the passage from Luke above, Jesus says God answers us by giving us the Spirit, not by reversing or saving specific persons from the natural tragedies of human existence.

Gleason's fatal condition is neither God's decision for Gleason nor an occasion for demanding a miraculous cure. The decision not to aggressively pursue prolongation of life for Gleason is morally acceptable, since there was no hope of prolonging life more than two weeks and he was in great pain. Such decisions are becoming more and more common, especially since increasing numbers of people, notably the elderly, leave explicit advance directions (living wills) not to put them on respirators, revive them after heart attacks, or use other "heroic" measures of sustaining life unless there is hope of recovery.

Pope Pius XII first used the distinction between ordinary and extraordinary means of preserving life in such situations, stipulating that there is an obligation to supply ordinary means of preserving life, but no obligation to supply extraordinary means. This distinction, which became well accepted even outside Catholicism, assumes that there are some things all patients have a right to, regardless of their chances for recovery. Ordinary care has been assumed to include food, water, oxygen, and adequate pain medication. It has not been considered to include any experimental treatments or drugs, any mechanical assistance, or any treatments which require undue sacrifice of the patient, the family, or society.

The rapid advance of technology in medical care has, however, undermined many of the original judgments as to what constitutes ordinary care. Surgery of any kind was originally considered extraordinary, as were antibiotics and all use of technology, including intravenous feeding, respirators, and pacemakers. Today there is great debate in many societies as to whether artificially administered nutrition and hydration are ordinary or extraordinary for patients in a Permanent Vegetative State (PVS). In Gleason's case, the only relevant question about his care is why his pain medication was consistently insufficient. It is accepted that though high levels of pain medication for dying patients do often hasten death, freedom from pain is part of ordinary care whenever it is possible.

One of the relevant questions concerning the decision for standard comfort care is why Gleason remained in the hospital. This is not only a relevant question due to the scarce economic resources of the family, though that is certainly of concern. This question is also a social question. Gleason is sixty-five, and therefore covered under Medicare. Medicare coverage, of course, is limited, and a prolonged hospital stay can still destroy the patient's savings. But because the major bill is paid not by the family but by society, the issue of why Gleason remained in the hospital is a social issue. Once the decision was made to abandon curative treatment in favor of comfort care, Gleason had no need for a hospital. Hospitals are expensive, high-tech centers for medical intervention. The purpose of hospitals is cure, not comfort. In fact, hospitals are not restful places at all, as anyone trying to recover in a hospital knows.

Gleason should have either been sent home with proper medication for pain, or, if the control of pain required more medical oversight, to a hospice for the dying. Not only was he occupying a high-cost hospital bed he did not need, but keeping him in the hospital mitigated against Gleason's own best interests.

WHO SHOULD RECEIVE SCARCE RESOURCES?

While C. J. is right to note that someone should have asked the doctor to explain her statement that Gleason was not a good candidate for a heart-lung transplant, more information as to that medical option would dispel any suspicion that Gleason might have been unfairly discriminated against on the basis of race or economic status. In fact, the two most relevant reasons for rejecting Gleason as a candidate for a transplant were almost certainly his age and his medical status, both of which seem reasonable criteria. There is a tremendous shortage of organs for transplant in the U.S. Heart-lung transplants are very experimental and fairly rare, much more so than the more well-developed processes for transplanting kidneys and corneas. Persons over sixty-five are normally not eligible for organ donor programs. Their only hope of transplants comes from donations from close kin. While this is a rare but viable option in kidney transplants because persons do have a spare kidney, the fact that humans have only one heart means that for Gleason to have a heart-lung transplant someone in his family would have to suffer a death that did not damage his or her heart and lungs.

The basic reason for the exclusion of those over sixty-five from organ donor programs is agreement that scarce donated organs should go to persons who can obtain the most life from them. Persons who are already sixty-five or more are less likely to derive as much life from a transplant as younger persons, and older persons are more likely to have other damaged organs which will cut short their lives. This is almost certainly the case in Gleason's situation. The odds of a sixty-five-year-old man only two weeks from death being able to withstand the trauma of surgical transplantation of a heart and lung are very low.

EXCLUSION FOR HIS OWN GOOD?

The decision of the family and the doctor, along with Reverend Wilson, to limit Gleason's care to that which would make him comfortable rather than that which would prolong his life was made without Gleason. Nor was Gleason informed of the decision after it was made. It may well be that the reason Gleason was kept in the hospital, rather than sent home or to a hospice, is that no one was willing to tell Gleason there was no longer hope of cure. A transfer would inevitably raise the issue.

The case points to the growing distance between Gleason and his family during the days that followed the decision. They knew that he was dying and that nothing would be attempted to hold off that death. They were forced to begin the mourning process as they grieved the death they saw looming. They inevitably reviewed their relationship with Gleason, blending the present reality of his emaciated and pain-racked body with remembered images of the stronger, younger husband and father who unfailingly supported them through hard times. They were preparing for his death. But Gleason was not free to prepare for his death in the same way, because he was not told to give up hope of recovery. He was not told that his fight against his illness was doomed and would no longer be medically supported.

There are a number of reasons why the failure to tell Gleason of his situation is morally problematic. The first, of course, is that it was his life and his body. He was a conscious patient who, as far as we are told, was in full command of his senses. Who had the right to make decisions about his medical care for him? It is amazing that no one insisted that someone tell Gleason that the fight was hopeless and obtain his consent to change the treatment plan. It is understandable that no one would want to be the carrier of such news. But the requirements of law as well as ethics require that the consent of competent patients must be obtained for any treatment. Next of kin can only take on responsibility for a patient's medical care when the patient has voluntarily abdicated it or is incompetent of exercising it. All persons have a right to control their own bodies. To this end, doctors are obliged to obtain fully informed consent from the patient before examining, testing, or treating the body of a patient. It is clear in this instance that the doctor and hospital significantly changed Gleason's medical treatment without obtaining his fully informed consent. This is a serious breach of professional ethics. The fact that the doctor and hospital were in little danger of being sued by a dying man whose estate would be handled by the very relatives who collaborated in usurping his control over his medical care should not have affected, but probably did affect, the outcome here.

At the same time, Cassie and her children also owed Gleason respect for his right to control his own body. In this case we can see very clearly that denying Gleason the ability to control his body—the medical treatment of his body—denied him the ability to control his life. Most importantly, he was denied the freedom and impetus to prepare for his own death. Cassie seemed to think that she was sparing Gleason the pain of facing the inevitability of his death. She may well have been right to believe that discovering his helplessness would be extremely difficult for Gleason, perhaps even more so than for many other persons who have more experience with and less anxiety around lack of control in their lives. But one must ask if anyone in the family considered that while Gleason no longer had a choice of whether to get well or die, he did have a choice as to how he would die.

The process of preparing for one's death has different foci for all of us. For some people it may focus on coming to grips with God and the role of God in one's life. For others it may center on coming to accept with peace the concept of personal death. For some it will entail taking leave of one's loved ones, or completing some major project, or cleaning up other loose ends in one's life. For some the immediate prospect of death causes a radical reorientation which has been incubating unseen, only to trigger such events as deathbed confessions and reconciliation of long-standing estrangements.

The traditional concept of "good death" is largely unpopular in much of Western society, which is horrified by the prospect of consciously facing one's own death. Most people want quick, clean sudden deaths, without any conscious knowledge of dying. Death is an enemy, as Dylan Thomas expressed so well for so many: "Do not go gentle into that good night; Old age should rage and burn against the close of day; Rage, rage against the dying of the light." There is a certain reasonableness to the desire to resist death and the knowledge of death. We have natural desires to maximize pleasure and minimize pain in our lives.

But there may also be a benefit to having time to prepare for death, time to move through the stages of dying, past denial and anger to acceptance and even peace. Had Gleason been included in the decision-making session about his treatment options, he and his family might have spent his last days communicating to each other their feelings about his life and impending death. They could have been an important source of consolation to each other in their grief, instead of feeling estranged by the secret between them. While Cassie might well have been right that resisting death was the option characteristic of Gleason, still the choice of whether to continue resistance or to pursue a peaceful death should have been Gleason's. Perhaps he might have regarded successfully pursuing a peaceful death as his greatest accomplishment in life and a glowing example to leave to his children. Perhaps he would see courageously resisting death to the last breath as his best legacy. Since he was not allowed to make the choice, in some way Gleason's death is more tragic than it needed to be.

PASTORAL COUNSELING CONCERNS

Reverend Wilson's request that C. J. reflect on the events around his father's death and discuss it with him may be a very good thing. C. J. and his family may have to deal with similar issues as Cassie continues to age. One would hope that C. J.'s children, nieces, and nephews would learn from their parents' involvement and be better prepared for, and perhaps somewhat more comfortable about, dealing with issues around death than their parents were. The issues raised in Gleason's death were not unique, but they have become the common experience of most families.

But Reverend Wilson may also have a personal agenda in his request to discuss Gleason's death with C. J. He may feel uncomfortable with his own role in the situation. According to the case, Reverend Wilson did not intervene during the family's meeting with the doctor, a fact which C. J. somewhat resented at the time. C. J. was uncomfortable making a decision about his father's treatment and resented the fact that the professionals— the doctor or the minister—did not make the decision. After all, the doctor was the expert in medicine, and the minister was the expert about morality. The question of treatment was a question of both medicine and morality, one which C. J. did not feel competent to decide.

Both Dr. Perkins and Reverend Wilson were right to refuse to make the decision. The doctor rightly refused to consider actively inducing Gleason's death. We should presume that Reverend Wilson would have spoken against such a step had the doctor not immediately refused. But the remaining treatment options were both well within the limits set by the Christian moral tradition. The choice between them was not Reverend Wilson's to make. The role of religious authorities is not to become the conscience for their members, but to help the members themselves develop well-formed consciences. Reflecting on moral decisions from hindsight is an important aspect of conscience development.

It is more difficult to explain why Reverend Wilson did not point out to the family and doctor the need to include Gleason in the decision making. Perhaps he was intimidated by Cassie's assumption that she knew what Gleason would want. But one is forced to wonder how Reverend Wilson dealt with Gleason during those last days. How does one provide effective pastoral care for the dying without informing the dying person of his or her impending death? It may well be that it was Reverend Wilson's dissatisfaction with the quality of pastoral care he was able to give to Gleason in those last days that alerted him to the need to rethink the decision made by the family.

ADDITIONAL RESOURCES

Callahan, Daniel. *What Kind of Life? The Limits of Medical Progress.* New York: Simon and Schuster, 1990.

Kilner, John. *Life on the Line.* Grand Rapids, MI: Eerdmann's Publishing Co., 1992.

_____. *Who Lives? Who Dies? Ethical Criteria in Patient Selection.* New Haven, CT: Yale University Press, 1990, 1992.

Shannon, Thomas, ed. *Bioethics.* 3rd ed. Mahwah, NJ: Paulist, 1987.

Sherwin, Susan. *No Longer Patient: Feminist Ethics and Health Care.* Philadelphia: Temple University Press, 1992.

Steinfels, Peter and Robert M. Veatch, eds. *Death Inside Out.* New York: Harper and Row, 1974.

Zucker, Arthur, Donald Borchert, and David Stewart, eds. *Medical Ethics: A Reader.* Englewood Cliffs, NJ: Prentice-Hall, 1992.

Appendix

Teaching Ethics
by the Case Method

The authors' use of the case method to teach Christian ethics is conscious and deliberate. The educational philosophy behind the authors' use of the method is Paulo Freire's notion of "education as liberation" from his now classic *Pedagogy of the Oppressed*. In that volume Freire distinguishes between liberating education and the "banking" approach to education. "Liberating education," he says, "consists in acts of cognition, not transference of information." In contrast the banking approach views education as a matter of possession—the teacher "deposits" information in a student who, as an "empty vessel, receives, memorizes, and repeats." A "withdrawal" is made at exam time with the hope that some "interest" has accrued.

Besides involving acts of cognition, liberating education also involves genuine dialogue between student and teacher with the realization that they are partners educating one another. The goal in this "problem-posing" approach is the development of "critical consciousness" and "creative power" leading to the transformation of one's world rather than passive adaptation to it. The authors of this book hope that the cases contained in it will engage students and teachers in a dialogue that will free them to apply new insights and learnings to their own unique experiences.

The contrast between liberating and banking approaches can be drawn too sharply, of course. By stressing education as liberation the authors do not imply that facts, theories, and knowledge of situations and contexts are unimportant. These are critical to informed ethical decisions. They are just not the essence, which should always be the individual in a community sustained by a critical consciousness and the creative work of the Holy Spirit.

The difference between making necessary background information available to students for purposes of empowerment and the banking approach is not always easy to discern. Ideally, with liberating education there are no pat answers. Dialogic forms of education stressing experience are preferred whenever possible. Questions are asked first and problems posed. Then the provision of information responds to a need and opens up alternatives. Students are encouraged to develop and share resources with other members of the learning community. Both critical and constructive tasks are taken seriously. Decision and action are important outcomes.

But problem-posing education is not just a matter of form. The spirit is different. Teachers and students are both seen as learners with something to offer. The community of learners is central, and the dynamism of community endeavor provides the spirit which pushes and pulls individuals to their best insights and makes them active participants rather than passive recipients.

Although the case approach is not without limitations, the authors have found that it has great potential for both liberating education and the teaching of Christian ethics. The approach is dialogic by its very nature. As participants in the discussion of a problem, students teach others in the process of learning themselves. Cases are written so as to transfer the point of decision to the student. The commentaries and even some of the cases provide background and alternatives for the development of a critical consciousness, a key stage on the path of liberation. The potential for creative teachers to enliven the classroom experience is virtually unlimited.

As for the teaching of Christian ethics, the case method as used in this volume opens a number of doors. First, it introduces students to contemporary ethical issues. This is the reason the cases have been arranged under specific problem areas and why the commentaries focus primarily on the central issues. The authors would contend that thorough knowledge of issues is one of the first steps in a liberating education.

Second, cases are a way of entry into Christian tradition. At some point both teachers and students need to ask how the Bible, theology, and the church inform issues. The case on euthanasia, for example, raises questions about the nature of God and the purposes of human life. The case on homosexuality challenges accepted perspectives on sin. The cases on violence lead to an investigation of the church's historical stances. Thus at the same time students are addressing issues and making decisions, they are in a position to learn the content of the tradition and how to apply it.

Knowledge of the tradition is liberating if it helps students detect selective and self-serving attempts to manipulate authority for the purpose of supporting conclusions arrived at on other grounds. Tradition provides an alternative perspective to understand and challenge cultural myopia. It provides the wisdom of experience, lends authority, offers general guidance, sets limits, and designates where the burden of proof lies—all helpful in finding ways through the maze of experience and conflicting opinion and on to good moral choices.

Third, repeated use of the method encourages students to economize in the way they approach ethical problems. That is to say, cases teach ethical method. The more cases are used and the more explicit method is made, the more indelible a pattern for making choices becomes. However little students retain of the content of a given issue or the theology which informs it, the authors are convinced they should leave a course in ethics knowing how to address ethical problems and liberated from the confusion of too many options and conflicting guidelines.

The authors also believe that an essential component of any pattern of learning is drawing on the insights of others, which the case approach encourages. Discovery of the limitations of individuals acting alone and of the liberation in learning to trust others in community is an important benefit of the dialogic approach. The case setting calls on participants to listen to one another, to challenge their own and others' perceptions, and to build on one another's insights and experiences.

Fourth and last, the case approach is an experience-based form of education. As one veteran case teacher put it, "Cases are experience at a fraction of the cost." The cases in this volume represent the experience of others which students can make their own without going through all the turmoil. The cases encourage students to express and apply their own experience. Finally, the cases push students to "practice" resolving complex dilemmas such as parenting, personal responsibility, individual and community rights, and thus to add to their own experience.

CASES FOR GROUP DISCUSSION

As stated in the Introduction, there are numerous types of cases used in contemporary education. These range from a hypothetical problem, to a one-page "critical incident" or "verbatim" which reports a specific actual incident, to a four-hundred-page case history describing an event or situation. The type of case employed in this volume is modeled after those used by the Harvard Law and Business Schools and the Association for Case Teaching: that is, each case consists of selected information from an actual situation and raises specific issues or problems that require a response or decision on the part of one or more persons in the case. The problem should be substantive enough and so balanced in its approach that reasonable people would disagree about the most effective or appropriate response. As a pedagogical tool the case calls for a response not only from the case characters but from those studying the case.

Although cases can be extremely useful for inducing reflection by an individual reader, they are specifically designed for group discussion. They might be used in classrooms, retreat settings, community gatherings, or with any group seeking to gain new perspectives.

As this is a distinctive educational approach, the authors feel it is important to offer suggestions for guiding a case discussion. To begin with, while it is possible to hand out copies of shorter cases, for example, "Mary Gardner's Fourth Pregnancy" or "Rigor and Responsibility," and ask participants to read them immediately prior to discussion, the quality of discussion is heightened by careful advance reading. The case leader might suggest that participants: (1) read through a case at least twice; (2) identify the principal case characters; (3) develop a "time line" to indicate significant dates or events; (4) list the issues which appear to surface; and (5) think through a number of creative alternatives to the dilemma posed. Small groups meeting to prepare ideas about a case prior to a larger group discussion can also be extremely beneficial to the total learning experience. This type of detailed and structured analysis of a case is equally valuable for the individual reader. A structured process for entering each case provides a base that may be challenged, expanded, or affirmed by the commentary which follows each case.

The primary functions of a case leader are catalyst, probe, and referee. A good case leader highlights insights and assists in summarizing the learnings from the discussion. As a facilitator, the case leader is responsible for clear goals and objectives for each discussion session and for guiding the quality and rhythm of the discussion. Many who have worked with cases suggest that the most crucial factor for a rewarding case experience is the leader's style. Openness, affirmation, and sensitivity to the group create the climate in which genuine dialogue can occur. Second in importance is that the case leader thoroughly master the case facts and develop a discussion plan or teaching note.

It is important to keep in mind that there is no single way to approach a case. The Introduction to this volume highlights in general terms what the authors find significant in the cases, and the commentaries offer the authors' analysis of more specific issues. Neither the Introduction nor the commentaries should constrain teachers or students from taking different entry points or addressing different topics or issues.

Whatever approach is taken should draw participants into dialogue, uncover what is needed to make an informed ethical decision, and push students to a critical consciousness and finally to a decision which will help them when they encounter similar situations in their own lives.

There are no "right" answers to the dilemmas presented in this volume. This means that the problems posed are open to a number of creative alternatives. This approach stands in contrast to a closed, problem-solving approach in which the right answer or solution known only by the teacher can be found in the back of the book. In a banking approach students are receptive objects of the teacher's wisdom and insight. In contrast, the case approach calls for participants to become active subjects in the learning process, to consider various responses, and to analyze the norms which inform their decisions.

Experienced case leaders report that recording the essence of participants' contributions on newsprint or a chalkboard gives order and direction to the discussion. A skilled instructor is able to help participants show the relation among contributions. The leader should be willing to probe respondents for additional clarification of points.

Honest conflict of opinion is often characteristic of these dialogues and can be quite constructive in a case discussion. The case leader may need to assume the role of referee and urge participants to listen to one another and to interpret the reasoning behind their conclusions. It is often helpful to put debating participants in direct dialogue by asking, for example, "Laura, given your earlier position, how would you respond to Mark's view?" The leader's role as mediator is also significant, especially as a discussion nears conclusion. It is helpful to encourage a group to build on one another's suggestions. One constructive process for closing a case discussion is to ask participants to share their insights from the discussion.

Two additional techniques are often employed by case leaders. A discussion may be focused and intensified by calling participants to vote on a controversial issue. For example, in a discussion of the case "More Light" one might ask, "If you were a member of the church governing board, would you vote for or against the motion to become a 'More Light' church?" The dynamics of case teaching reveal that once persons have taken a stand, they frequently assume greater ownership of the decision and are eager to defend or interpret their choice. Voting provides an impetus for participants to offer the implicit reasons and assumptions that stand behind a given decision. It can also be a test of the group's response, especially if one or two outspoken participants have taken a strong stand on one particular side of an issue. If a vote is taken, it is important to give participants an opportunity to interpret the reasons behind their decision.

Another way to heighten existential involvement in a case is to ask participants to assume the roles of persons in the case for a brief specified period of the discussion. When individuals are requested to assume roles before a group, experienced case teachers have found that rather than making assignments prior to class or asking for volunteers, it is better to invite participants who give evidence during the case discussion that they can identify with the characters and understand the issues. It is often most helpful for individuals in a role play to move into chairs visible to the entire group. The personal integrity of those who assume individual roles can be guarded by giving them an opportunity to "de-role." This is done by asking them, for example, how they felt during the conversation and by asking them to return to their original seats. Then the group can be called on to share learnings from the experience.

Notwithstanding the preceding suggestions for case teaching, the authors wish to acknowledge that a good case discussion is not ultimately dependent on a trained professional teacher or a learned group of participants. A gifted leader is one who listens well, encourages participants to do the same, and genuinely trusts the wisdom, insights, and personal experiences of the group. To benefit significantly from the cases a reader needs to be willing to wrestle honestly with the issues in the cases and to evaluate with an open mind the insights of the commentaries.

Most case teachers prepare in advance a "teaching note" with suggestions for the general direction of the discussion as well as clear, transitional questions to move from one topic to the next. The following note is intended as an illustration of how the first case in this volume, "Rigor and Responsibility," might be taught in a short session.

A. Read the case if not preassigned. (ten minutes)
B. Have the class sketch a biography of each character. (ten to fifteen minutes)
C. Identify the basic question: How is a family to live? Alternatively, should an affluent family follow the rigorous "holy poverty" of Jesus or another option which might be called "responsible consumption," stressing right use and good stewardship. (one to two minutes)
D. Identify alternative issues. (five minutes) (This category could be eliminated if the basic question is the focus. Or, one of the following issues could become the main issue.)
    1. Stewarding an inheritance.
    2. Living in an impoverished and malnourished world.
    3. Discovering the biblical and theological witness on justice, wealth, poverty, possessions, and consumption.
    4. Overworking in modern society.
    5. Making a family decision.
    6. Dealing with guilt.
    7. Acting as an individual in a world dominated by mass culture.
    8. Distributing income and wealth.
    9. Raising children.
E. Ask each student to identify with one of the following: (ten minutes)
    1. Nancy or Clea.
    2. Nathan.
    3. Al Messer.
    4. The children.
F. Adjourn to four separate groups. (twenty minutes)
    1. Discuss what is and what should be the normative position of the character selected. Point to:
        a. Biblical and theological views of justice, wealth, poverty, and consumption.
        b. The two normative positions identified in the title of the case.
        c. The norms of justice and sustainable sufficiency.
                    OR
    2. Discuss the family relationships and how they should be worked through to arrive at a decision. Point to:
        a. The involvement of the Trapp family in a number of issues, the extent of its giving, and the crisis of the family in the United States.

b. Cultural attitudes in the local community.
c. Poverty and malnutrition in the world community.
d. Traditional patriarchal family patterns.
OR
3. Discuss the method question. How is a Christian family to decide?
  a. Point to the normative approach and the situational approach.
  b. Apply each to the case and note the differences.
OR
4. Discuss the character question. What are the characteristics of a person who responds well to the main problem. Point to:
  a. Basic character orientation, loyalties, and worldviews.
  b. How this situation can build character.
G. Conduct a role play, selecting one from each group. Add David as an option. (ten to fifteen minutes)
  1. Role players discuss what the Trapps should do and how it relates to the main issue and to the alternative issues selected in "D" above.
H. Debrief and generate discussion. (ten minutes)
  1. De-role.
  2. Ask students to identify learnings.
  3. Open to a general class discussion of the main issue.

If more than a short period of time is available, the case leader has the opportunity to provide background in lectures, readings, films, small study groups, etc. The more background, the more the small group discussions can be open-ended.

CASES AND COURSE DESIGN

How might cases be used in a course in Christian ethics? For starters the authors recommend using cases in conjunction with other methods. Cases can be overworked and the freshness they bring lost.

In terms of overall design the teacher might select one of the cases with high student interest and open with it the first day of class. Cases are good discussion starters, and early use can introduce students to the method, to the use of critical consciousness, and to the goal of liberating education.

Following this, several general sessions on ethics would be appropriate including something on the nature and task of ethics, the use of the tradition, and the nature of situations, contexts, relationships, method, and decision making. Use of a case or two to illustrate specific aspects of the ethical discipline would also be appropriate.

The remainder of the course could be devoted to the specific issues categorized in this volume. Using all of the cases in a single semester might be ill-advised. Selectivity on the basis of student interest and teacher expertise would be more suitable.

The authors also recommend that students write "briefs," which are three- to four-page analyses of a case. This process accomplishes several things. First, it brings writing into a course. Second, particularly if graded, briefs heighten interest by increasing the stakes. Discussion is more intense because preparation is more thorough. Third, briefs offer less vocal students another avenue of expression. Fourth, briefs are a vehicle for method, since method is implicit in any act of organization. Methodological awareness is more pronounced if the teacher either requires a certain approach, or better, if the teacher insists that students be cognizant of the approach they are taking. Finally, the brief may serve as the first stage of a multiple draft term paper.

If briefs are used, students must be selective in what they cover. Three or four pages simply are not sufficient to analyze fully any case in this volume. In the briefs the students should to some extent present the facts in the case, perhaps by inserting short introductory summaries of the situation and a summation of pertinent facts or theories. Somewhere in the brief the "problem" should be clearly stated. The larger part of the brief should be devoted to the ethics of the issue, that is, to the derivation of norms, to the relating of norms to situations, and to the relationships involved in the case. Briefs may be expository and present the various sides, or they may be persuasive and argue one side in depth. While the commentaries in this volume avoid arguing for a particular side of an issue, the teacher may want students to make a decision and defend it.

For the workshop setting lack of time makes selectivity a cardinal virtue. The typical one-hour adult class is long enough for a good discussion of a single case, especially if it has been read prior to the session. Needless to say, the teacher should have a very clear idea of what he or she wants to accomplish and try to keep the class on task. An alert teacher, picking up on points in the discussion, can even insert background material through minilectures or asking students to elaborate. Small groups and role plays are especially helpful in stimulating discussion and breaking complex cases down into manageable units.

When more time is available, the two cases in each chapter are both available. One way to use both cases would be to lead off with one, then provide as much background as time permits, then finish the unit with the other. Alternatively, the teacher could utilize cases from different chapters to address the connecting themes, such as liberation and racism, listed in the Introduction.

LIMITATIONS OF THE CASE APPROACH

The case approach is not without limitations. First, case material must go through the personal filter of a writer. The situation is seen through the eyes of a single character with all the limitations of perspective. Seldom is enough information provided to satisfy participants. Crucial signals can be misread or misunderstood.

A second drawback is that the success of this form of education and presentation of material is dependent on the participation of readers and those discussing the cases. This can be quite disconcerting, even threatening, for those who are accustomed to a process in which they are handed a complete analysis from the lectern. For most learners tutored in an educational system which fosters, even if unintentionally, uncritical acceptance of the teacher's wisdom and authority, passive reception of information is the comfortable norm. This is, however, also the pattern of uncritical acceptance of the world as it is and helps lead to the loss of a vision of the world as it could be. Case leaders need to develop a mode of open rather than closed questions to induce genuine dialogue.

Third, case discussion can consume much more time and emotional energy than the direct communication of information. Intelligence is imperfectly correlated with the propensity to speak. Some participants are bent on dominating the discussion rather than learning from others. Tangents can carry the discussion into deadends. These limitations call for "referee" skills from the case leader.

Fourth, the forest can be lost for the trees, the macro for the micro, and the social for the individual by focusing on the particulars of a given situation to the exclusion of the context. For example, to reduce "Mary Gardner's Fourth Pregnancy" to a discussion of her moral decision is to lose sight of the critical social question about who should control the decision. The cases and in particular the commentaries have been written to help avoid this problem, but it is well to keep it in mind.

Finally, relative to other methods the case approach is limited in its capacity to convey large blocks of factual information. This drawback does not mean teachers need to revert automatically to the banking style of education. There are alternatives to "depositing" information, and even the lecture style can be approached with a different spirit. Many case teachers, for example, use "minilectures" in case discussion to introduce relevant material when it is needed.

The case approach is no panacea and must be seen as only one of many effective educational instruments. The authors have attempted to respond to the limitations of the approach. They have not removed them. They trust, however, that the cases in this volume and the approach can lead to constructive, liberating engagement with what they think are critical contemporary issues. Their trust is based on many years of experience with the approach. They are convinced that the approach is not only a valuable and liberating pedagogical instrument, but also a way to build community in the classroom.

List of Authors and Contributors

AUTHORS

Alice Frazer Evans is director of writing and research, Plowshares Institute, Simsbury, Connecticut. She was educated at Agnes Scott College, the University of Wisconsin, and the University of Edinburgh. She is the co-author of numerous books, including *Casebook for Christian Living, Pedagogies for the Non-Poor,* and *The Globalization of Theological Education.*

Robert A. Evans is the executive director of Plowshares Institute, Simsbury, Connecticut. He studied at Yale University, at universities in Edinburgh, Berlin, and Basel, and received his doctorate from Union Theological Seminary, New York. He is the author and editor of several books, including *The Future of Philosophical Theology, Human Rights: A Dialogue between the First and Third Worlds,* and *The Globalization of Theological Education.*

Christine E. Gudorf is associate professor in the Department of Religious Studies at Florida International University, the state university in Miami. Her Ph.D. in Christian Ethics is from Columbia University in joint program with Union Theological Seminary. Her most recent books include *Victimization: Examining Christian Complicity* and *Sexuality As God's Grace and Gift: Reconstructing Christian Sexual Ethics.*

Robert L. Stivers is professor of ethics at Pacific Lutheran University, in Tacoma, Washington. He did his undergraduate work at Yale University and holds a Ph.D. in Religion and Society from Columbia University in joint program with Union Theological Seminary. His publications include *The Sustainable Society* and *Hunger, Technology, and Limits to Growth.*

CONTRIBUTORS

Mary Agria is a researcher in rural issues with the Center for Theology and Land, University of Dubuque and Wartburg Seminaries. She received her BA and MA degrees from the University of Wisconsin and has worked for many years in the area of community development and labor force issues, particularly in rural areas.

William P. Bristol is a physician in private practice and the former dean of Mercer University Medical School, Macon, Georgia.

Nat B. Frazer is associate director, Savannah River Ecology Laboratory, University of Georgia. He has also taught biology at Mercer University, Macon, Georgia. Educated at Sagamon State University, University of the South, and the University of Georgia, he has published extensively in journals of medical education, marine science, and herpetology.

Frank Gudorf is an attorney who has practiced corporate law in New York and Cincinnati. Currently he is working in the area of low income housing law in Miami.

Shannon Jung is director of the Center for Theology and Land, University of Dubuque and Wartburg Seminaries. His areas of research interest are the environment, economics, and land. His most recent book is *We Are Home: A Spirituality of the Environment.*

John F. Kilner is a scholar noted for his writing and teaching on medical ethics. He was a senior associate until recently with the Park Ridge Center in Chicago. Before that he taught at Asbury Theological Seminary in Kentucky. He holds a Ph.D. from Harvard University. His books include *Life on the Line: Ethics, Aging, Ending Patients' Lives and Allocating Vital Resources* and *Who Lives? Who Dies? Ethical Criteria in Patient Selection.*

J. Shannon Webster is the executive presbyter of the Sierra Blanca Presbytery, Roswell, New Mexico, and past president of the New Mexico Conference of Churches. He was educated at San Juan College, the University of New Mexico, and McCormick Theological Seminary.